# Agentic AI • The Bible

Build and Master AI Agents to Transform Business, Work, and Life. Includes Video Lessons, Cheat Sheets, and Exclusive Resources

**Vincent Alton**

# Contents

**INTRODUCTION** ...................................................................................................................6

**PART I: FOUNDATIONS OF AGENTIC AI** ...................................................................9

Chapter 1: Introduction to Agentic AI..................................................................10

   Section 1: Defining Agentic AI and Its Core Characteristics................................10

   Section 2: Architectural Foundations of LLM-Powered Agents.............................12

   Section 3: The Role of Agentic AI in Modern Systems Engineering.......................15

Chapter 2: Principles of Generative and Agent-Based AI.................................18

   Section 1: Foundations of Generative AI and Agentic Systems..........................18

   Section 2: Principles of Agentic Design for LLM-Powered Systems......................20

   Section 3: Scaling, Evaluation, and Practical Constraints................................24

Chapter 3: Modular Architectures and Design Patterns..................................28

   Section 1: Principles of Modular Design in Agentic AI Systems..........................28

   Section 2: Core Architectural Patterns for LLM-Based Agents............................31

   Section 3: Practical Integration Strategies and Scaling Considerations...............35

Chapter 4: Perception, Reasoning, Memory, and Action Loops......................39

   Section 1: Foundations of Agentic Loops in LLM-Powered Systems....................39

   Section 2: Engineering Perception, Reasoning, and Memory Loops for Robust Performance ..............41

   Section 3: Designing Action Loops and Achieving Operational Reliability at Scale ...............45

**PART II: BUILDING INTELLIGENT AGENTIC SYSTEMS**................................48

Chapter 5: Practical Guide to Implementing LLM-Powered Agents ...............49

   Section 1: System Requirements, Architectural Foundations, and Development Environment............49

   Section 2: Step-by-Step Implementation of Core Agent Modules.........................51

   Section 3: Testing, Deployment, and Operationalization of LLM Agents ..............56

Chapter 6: Advanced Behaviors: Recursive Reasoning.....................................61

   Section 1: Foundations and Mechanisms of Recursive Reasoning........................61

   Section 2: Techniques and Frameworks for Self-Reflection in Agentic Systems.......63

   Section 3: Integration, Evaluation, and Operational Considerations for Advanced Behaviors...........67

Chapter 7: External Tool Use and Complex Task Planning ..............................71

   Section 1: Architectures and Interfaces for External Tool Integration ................71

   Section 2: Strategies for Complex Task Decomposition and Planning ..................74

   Section 3: Coordinating Multi-Tool Workflows and Long-Horizon Tasks ...............77

Chapter 8: Safety, Reliability, and Testability in Agents..................................81

   Section 1: Engineering Principles for Safety in LLM-Powered Agents..................81

   Section 2: Designing for Reliability and Fault Tolerance in LLM-Powered Agents .............83

Section 3: Monitoring, Evaluation, and Continuous Improvement...........................................86

Chapter 9: Multi-Agent Coordination and Collaboration...............................................90

    Section 1: Architectural Models for Multi-Agent Systems...........................................90

    Section 2: Coordination Mechanisms and Collaboration Protocols.............................93

    Section 3: Testing, Monitoring, and Scaling Multi-Agent Systems..............................96

Chapter 10: Security and Robustness in Autonomous Systems.....................................100

    Section 1: Threat Models and Attack Surfaces in Autonomous Agents.....................100

    Section 2: Defensive Design Patterns and Robustness Mechanisms..........................103

    Section 3: Testing, Auditing, and Governance for Secure Deployment.......................106

**PART III: DOMAINS OF APPLICATION**.........................................................110

Chapter 11: Agentic AI in Healthcare.......................................................111

    Section 1: Clinical Data Integration and Workflow Alignment....................................111

    Section 2: Safety, Compliance, and Risk Mitigation in Healthcare Agents.................114

    Section 3: Evaluation, Deployment, and Lifecycle Management of Healthcare AI Agents.................117

Chapter 12: Agentic AI in Finance.........................................................122

    Section 1: Core Applications of Agentic AI in Financial Services.................................122

    Section 2: Technical Architectures and Integration with Financial Infrastructure.........125

    Section 3: Risk Management, Compliance, and Lifecycle Governance of Financial AI Agents.................128

Chapter 13: Agentic AI in Robotics........................................................132

    Section 1: Architectures for Agentic AI Integration in Robotic Systems......................132

    Section 2: Operational Workflows and Multi-Agent Coordination in Robotics.............135

    Section 3: Safety, Reliability, and Evaluation of Agentic Robotics Workflows...............139

Chapter 14: Agentic AI in Business and Operations......................................144

    Section 1: Architectural Patterns for Agentic Business Systems................................144

    Section 2: Operational Applications Across Core Business Domains..........................148

    Section 3: Governance, Reliability, and Performance Evaluation in Business Workflows.................152

**PART IV: GOVERNANCE, RISK, AND HUMAN FACTORS**..............................156

Chapter 15: Legal and Ethical Landscape of Agentic AI.................................157

    Section 1: Regulatory Frameworks and Compliance Requirements..........................157

    Section 2: Ethical Principles and Responsible Design Practices................................158

    Section 3: Risk Management, Liability, and Governance in Agentic AI........................161

Chapter 16: Risk Management and Safety Playbook....................................163

    Section 1: Identifying, Classifying, and Quantifying Risks in Agentic AI Systems..........163

    Section 2: Mitigation Strategies, Safety Protocols, and Incident Response...................164

    Testing and Validation for Safety Assurance.......................................166

Section 3: Governance, Compliance, and Continuous Safety Management .......................................................167

Chapter 17: Human-Agent Collaboration and ......................................................169

Section 1: Frameworks for Human-Agent Interaction and Oversight ......................................................169

Section 2: Mechanisms for Monitoring, Feedback, and Intervention ......................................................171

Section 3: Governance, Risk Management, and Operational Protocols .......................................................175

Chapter 18: Adoption Challenges in Enterprises ......................................................178

Section 1: Organizational and Cultural Barriers to AI Integration ......................................................178

Section 2: Technical and Infrastructure Challenges.......................................................180

Section 3: Governance, Risk Management, and Change Management in Enterprise Adoption ...........................183

**PART V: TOOLS, FRAMEWORKS, AND ECOSYSTEM**.......................................................186

Chapter 19: Landscape of Agentic AI Frameworks and Libraries ......................................................187

Section 1: Core Architectural Patterns and Design Principles ......................................................187

Section 2: Widely Adopted Frameworks and Libraries ......................................................189

Section 3: Integration, Extensibility, and Evaluation Practices ......................................................193

Chapter 20: Open-Source Projects, APIs, and Ecosystem Tools ......................................................197

Section 1: Core Open-Source Frameworks and Libraries ......................................................197

Section 2: APIs and Service Integrations for Agentic AI.......................................................200

Section 3: Ecosystem Tools for Development, Monitoring, and Deployment.......................................................202

**PART VI: DEPLOYMENT AND SCALING**.......................................................206

Chapter 21: Deployment Architectures and Infrastructure Strategies.......................................................207

Section 1: Scalable Deployment Architectures for Agentic AI.......................................................207

Section 2: Infrastructure Strategies for Reliability, Scalability, and Cost Efficiency .......................................209

Section 3: Continuous Operations, Monitoring, and Reliability Strategies .......................................................213

Chapter 22: Enterprise Integration and Workflow Orchestration.......................................................216

Section 1: Architectural Strategies for Enterprise Integration ......................................................216

Section 2: Workflow Orchestration and Task Management.......................................................218

Section 3: Operational Governance, Security, and Reliability in Orchestration .......................................................221

**PART VII: PRACTICAL PROJECTS AND HANDS-ON IMPLEMENTATION** .......................................................224

Project 1: Customer Support Agent with External Tool Integration.......................................................225

Project 2: Healthcare Workflow Assistant ......................................................227

Project 3: Financial Compliance Monitor.......................................................230

Project 4: Code Review and Refactoring Agent .......................................................233

Project 5: Robotics Task Planner.......................................................236

**CONCLUSION** .......................................................238

**Exclusive Bonuses**.......................................................239

**Video Lessons**................................................................................................................239

**Printable Cheat Sheets (PDF)**.....................................................................................239

**Exclusive Resources Page Access**..............................................................................240

# INTRODUCTION

Artificial intelligence has reached a new phase, going beyond narrow models that give one-time answers to systems that can operate all the time and with confidence. Agentic AI is a type of AI that is built around loops of perception, reasoning, memory, and action. They can handle unpredictable inputs, adjust to different situations, and give consistent results in changing surroundings because they work iteratively instead of linearly. Agentic AI is important since modern applications need more than just predictions that don't change. A diagnostic assistant needs to remember past meetings. A compliance system needs to be able to adapt to new rules while still following strict ones. A robotic planner needs to be able to change plans on the flight. These requirements are demanded for agents that are not only smart, but also organized, strong, and able to be checked.

Software engineers, system architects, AI researchers, and product leaders can use this book as a technical guide. It talks about the basic ideas behind agentic systems, gives examples of proven design patterns, and shows how to evaluate systems using methods that are already in use. The main point is that engineering should be based on facts and not guesswork.

The material is set up such that theory and practice can work together. The first few chapters talk on basic ideas and modular designs. Later parts talk about implementations that are specialized to a certain field, governance and risk issues, and deployment strategies. The last portion of the book has guided projects that let readers turn ideas into real systems. The purpose is to give readers a structured guide for creating, constructing, and expanding LLM-powered autonomous bots. By using the frameworks and projects presented here, practitioners will be able to build agentic AI systems that perform well in the real world and are accurate and reliable.

**Agentic AI • The Bible**
*Build and Master AI Agents to Transform Business, Work, and Life • Includes Video Lessons, Cheat Sheets, and Exclusive Resources*

ISBN: 979-8-90046-549-4

First Edition — 2025

**Disclaimer:** This book is intended for educational purposes only. While every effort has been made to ensure the accuracy of the information contained herein, the author and publisher assume no responsibility for errors, omissions, or contrary interpretation of the subject matter. The content should not be considered professional, legal, or financial advice.

# PART I: FOUNDATIONS OF AGENTIC AI

The ideas that make up agentic AI are the basic ones needed to make systems that can see, think, remember, and act in structured loops. This section talks about the ideas that set agentic systems apart from standard single-pass pipelines. It talks about how generative models have changed from being separate predictors to being autonomous agents that work all the time in complicated settings. Readers will learn about the basic engineering trade-offs, modular design patterns, and loop-based architectures that make systems that are reliable and can grow. By the end of this section, you will have a solid understanding of the basic language, frameworks, and mental models for agentic AI. This will set the stage for more in-depth exploration in later portions of the book.

# Chapter 1: Introduction to Agentic AI

## Section 1: Defining Agentic AI and Its Core Characteristics

Agentic artificial intelligence, or agentic AI for short, is a new way to create and use massive language models and other technologies. Agentic AI is different from traditional systems because it adds persistence, autonomy, and goal-directed behavior. The goal is not just to answer a question or guess an output, but also to provide a system the ability to see its surroundings, make choices, and perform actions that are in line with goals that may last overtime and need numerous stages.

This part explains what agentic AI is, what makes it different from other types of AI, and how it fits into the bigger picture of AI and software engineering. It also looks into why these systems are becoming more and more important for making AI-driven apps that are reliable, scalable, and adaptable.

**What Is Agentic AI?**

At its core, an agentic system is one that can:

- **Perceive**: Ingest information from an environment, whether structured data, unstructured text, or real-time signals.

- **Reason**: Process this information using logic, models, or heuristics to evaluate actions.

- **Act**: Execute tasks or interact with external systems to advance toward a goal.

- **Adapt**: Update its behavior in response to new information or unexpected outcomes.

These four capacities separate agentic AI from traditional machine learning systems that may only excel at one-off predictions or static classifications. Large language models provide the reasoning and generative backbone, while agentic frameworks supply memory, control flows, and the capacity to link reasoning with execution.

**Distinguishing Agentic AI from Traditional AI**

It is important to recognize the difference between **conventional AI workflows** and **agentic architecture**:

| Feature | Traditional AI | Agentic AI |
|---|---|---|
| Input-Output Behavior | One-time predictions (e.g., classification, regression) | Continuous loops of perception, reasoning, and action |
| Memory | Often stateless; model does not recall past interactions | Incorporates short-term and long-term memory modules |
| Goal Orientation | Optimized for a narrow metric (e.g., accuracy) | Oriented toward high-level goals requiring multiple steps |
| Environmental Interaction | Typically offline, trained and evaluated on static datasets | Dynamic, capable of interacting with tools, APIs, or physical systems |
| Adaptability | Limited to retraining or fine-tuning | Can reprioritize tasks and modify behavior at runtime |

This distinction underscores why agentic AI requires additional design patterns, monitoring systems, and governance frameworks.

**Historical Context**

The concept of intelligent agents is not new. Early artificial intelligence research in the mid-20th century introduced **expert systems** that encoded rules for decision-making. These systems could mimic aspects of reasoning but lack flexibility, adaptability, and scalability. Later, reinforcement learning agents advanced the ability to operate in simulated environments, particularly in robotics and games.

What differentiates today's agentic AI is the integration of **large language models** with these agent-based principles. LLMs provide the ability to handle unstructured information, reason in natural language, and interact with humans and machines through flexible prompts. Combined with memory systems and orchestrators, they form the foundation for agents that can operate across complex, real-world domains.

## Core Characteristics of Agentic AI

To design and evaluate agentic AI systems, it is essential to understand their defining characteristics.

1. **Autonomy**

    o   Agents can initiate actions without constant human instruction.

    o   Autonomy is bound by safety rules and operational constraints, but it is fundamental to scaling beyond prototypes.

2. **Goal Orientation**

    o   Unlike static models, agents pursue objectives that can span multiple steps.

    o   Goals may be specified by humans, derived from external triggers, or reprioritized dynamically.

3. **Reasoning Capacity**

    o   LLMs enhance reasoning with language-based inference.

    o   Reasoning may include evaluating options, sequencing tasks, and identifying resource needs.

4. **Memory and Context Retention**

    o   Memory distinguishes agentic systems from stateless models.

    o   Short-term memory supports dialogue continuity, while long-term memory enables cross-session learning and contextual awareness.

5. **Perception and Environment Awareness**

    o   Agents must process inputs from varied environments, including structured databases, unstructured documents, APIs, or sensor data.

    o   Robust perception is necessary to avoid brittle or incorrect decisions.

6. **Action Execution**

    o   Agents do not stop generating responses. They may execute tasks via APIs, integrate with workflows, or control physical devices.

    o   This connection to action introduces both opportunity and risk, requiring safeguards.

7. **Adaptability**

    o   Agents can modify their strategy in response to new conditions.

    o   Adaptability is critical in environments where goals or constraints evolve.

### Why Agentic AI Matters

For software engineers and technical executives, the most important thing about agentic AI is that it can turn research-level capabilities into working systems. Traditional AI systems sometimes have problems with being too rigid, too expensive, and having a limited range, however agentic AI can help get over these problems. It lets you automate processes in several steps that go beyond one-time forecasts, lets you engage with changing surroundings in real time, and works perfectly with APIs, databases, and enterprise workflows. It also gives you a scalable foundation for taking AI ideas from proof of concept to production. Engineers may make agents that are not only powerful but also safe, clear, and reliable in the actual world by building principles like observability, testability, and reliability.

### Common Misconceptions

Several misconceptions arise when discussing agentic AI. Clarifying them early helps set realistic expectations.

- **Misconception 1: Agents are fully autonomous artificial general intelligence.**
  In practice, agents remain narrow, domain-constrained systems designed for specific purposes.

- **Misconception 2: Any LLM with a prompt is an agent.**
  A true agent requires structured loops, memory, and the ability to act in an environment.

- **Misconception 3: Agents can eliminate the need for human oversight.**
  Human-in-the-loop supervision is essential, especially in high-stakes domains.

### Transition to Architectural Considerations

Defining agentic AI and its key characteristics provides a foundation for deeper exploration. The next section will shift from conceptual definitions to **architectural design principles**, examining how perception, reasoning, and action loops are engineered and how LLMs integrate with modular components to form reliable systems.

## Section 2: Architectural Foundations of LLM-Powered Agents

After defining what agentic AI is and what makes it different from other types of AI, the next step is to look at how these systems are set up. An agent is not just one model or algorithm; it is a coordinated set of parts that work together to let you see, think, remember, plan, and act. This architecture for agents driven by large language models (LLMs) must strike a compromise between flexibility and stability. It must make sure that a system designed for autonomy is nonetheless dependable, observable, and easy to maintain.

This part talks about the basic structure of LLM-based agents. It talks about the perception-reasoning-action cycle, introduces modular parts, and talks about how to connect with other tools and settings. It also talks about the engineering problems that come up while moving from small prototypes to systems that are suitable for production.

### The Perception–Reasoning–Action Loop

At the core of every agentic system lies a feedback loop. This loop is what differentiates an agent from a static predictive model.

1. **Perception**

   - The agent gathers input from its environment. This could be text data, structured records, or sensor signals.

   - Preprocessing pipelines ensure that inputs are cleaned, normalized, and transformed into formats that can be understood by the LLM.

2. **Reasoning**

- The LLM interprets the inputs in context, applies logic, and generates candidate actions.
- Reasoning can include multi-step planning, recursive evaluation, or chain-of-thought processes, depending on the complexity of the task.

3. **Action**
   - The agent selects and executes an action, which may involve calling an API, updating a database, or issuing a command to a physical device.
   - Actions produce new environmental states, which are then fed back into perception.

This loop continues until a defined goal is reached or until the system is interrupted by constraints, such as resource limits or human oversight.

## Modular Components of Agent Architectures

Agentic AI systems are best understood as modular architectures. Each module has a specific responsibility and can be engineered, tested, and maintained independently.

- **Input Processing Layer**
  Handles raw data ingestion, normalization, and validation.
  Prevents malformed or adversarial inputs from destabilizing the system.

- **Memory Systems**
  - *Short-term memory*: Maintains immediate context, such as the last several user interactions.
  - *Long-term memory*: Stores structured knowledge, historical states, or past interactions for retrieval.

- **Reasoning and Planning Module**
  Uses the LLM to generate hypotheses, plans, or task breakdowns.
  Can include self-reflection routines that check outputs against constraints or goals.

- **Action Execution Layer**
  Interfaces with APIs, databases, software tools, or robotic systems.
  Converts high-level LLM outputs into executable commands or workflows.

- **Feedback and Error Handling Module**
  Captures results of actions, identifies errors, and decides whether to retry, escalate, or adjust the plan.
  Enables safe operation in unpredictable environments.

By separating these modules, engineers can build systems that are not only functional but also testable, observable, and maintainable.

## Integration with External Tools and Environments

An agent needs to do more than just write text; it needs to be able to communicate directly with outside resources in order to be useful. APIs and services are a typical way for agents to connect with one other. For example, a healthcare scheduling agent might query an appointment system and automatically send reminders. Another important element is databases and knowledge repositories. They give agents structured, dependable information to base their reasoning on instead of only relying on random outputs. Integration in robotics goes beyond the digital world and into the real world, where agents send commands to sensors and actuators. This requires strict safety and reliability measures.

This is what makes production-ready systems different from simple language model demonstrations: they can turn reasoning into real actions. This is what makes integration a key part of agentic AI.

## Engineering for Reliability and Maintainability

Engineering autonomous systems requires tackling unique challenges to ensure they operate reliably and sustainably over time. Reliability is a critical factor, as the system's output must remain consistent and reproducible. This means results should not fluctuate unpredictably, and when unexpected issues occur, there must be robust error-handling strategies in place, complete with fallback mechanisms to maintain performance without total failure.

Observability is another essential element. Every action and decision made by the system should be logged so that developers and operators can trace how outcomes were produced. Alongside this, monitoring dashboards are invaluable, providing real-time insights into metrics such as latency, error rates, and task completion rates. Such transparency ensures teams can quickly identify and address emerging issues before they escalate.

Maintainability ensures that systems remain adaptable as technologies and requirements evolve. A modular architecture allows updates or replacements of individual components without destabilizing the entire system. Moreover, version control is crucial, enabling teams to track and audit changes to memory structures, planning algorithms, or decision-making logic, which helps prevent regression and supports long-term stability.

Finally, testability underpins both safety and reliability. By using simulation environments, agents can be stress-tested against diverse and extreme conditions before deployment in the real world. Benchmarking frameworks also play a vital role, offering a structured way to measure decision quality, robustness, and efficiency. Together, these practices create a strong engineering foundation for autonomous systems that are reliable, observable, maintainable, and thoroughly tested.

## Challenges in Early Prototypes

When teams start making their first LLM-powered agents, they usually run into a few problems that can make them less reliable and less effective. Early prototypes often rely on fragile cue chains that break down in unexpected situations and create strange behavior if there are no guardrails. Another common problem is that agents don't handle memory well, which makes them repeat mistakes or lose track of what happened in previous sessions. A lot of early systems also rely too much on raw LLM outputs, considering the model as a definitive source instead than using trusted databases or APIs to back up results. This makes them less reliable. Finally, scaling problems happen when single-instance prototypes that seem to work fine on their own don't work well under real-world pressure or have trouble fitting into increasingly complicated ecosystems. Engineers may make systems that are more durable and scalable by thinking about these problems throughout the design phase. This saves money by not having to solve them later.

## From Academic Demos to Production Systems

The difference between a demonstration and a production-ready system is not only scale but also discipline. Academic prototypes may highlight the potential of an LLM to complete multi-step reasoning tasks, but they rarely address performance, reliability, or governance. Production engineering requires:

- Defined service-level objectives (SLOs) for accuracy, latency, and uptime.

- Structured monitoring and logging.

- Governance frameworks for safety and compliance.

- Incremental deployment strategies, such as starting in controlled test environments before scaling to enterprise-wide use.

This shift from experimentation to operationalization is where engineering discipline becomes essential.

**Transition to Next Section**

Architectural foundations provide the blueprint for how agents are assembled and how they function at a technical level. With these principles in place, the next section examines the **role of agentic AI in modern systems engineering**, including its integration with DevOps, MLOps, and industry-specific workflows. It also explores the drivers behind adoption, the risks to manage, and the practical pathways toward scaling.

## Section 3: The Role of Agentic AI in Modern Systems Engineering

Now that we know what agentic AI is and how it works, the next step is to put these systems into the larger field of systems engineering. Businesses today don't want one-off demos; they need solutions that are reliable, scalable, and easy to manage that fit into their current workflows. Because of this, agentic AI shouldn't be seen as a new technology on its own, but as part of a larger set of engineering systems.

This part talks about how agentic AI is used in modern system design. It talks about real-world reasons to use it, how it can be used in different industries, how it fits in with DevOps and MLOps, and how important safety and governance are. The section ends with a look ahead at how agentic AI fits into present engineering practice and the path it will take in the near future.

**Drivers for Adoption**

Organizations face multiple pressures that motivate the adoption of agentic AI. These pressures can be grouped into four primary drivers:

1. **Automation of Complex Workflows**

   o Many processes in industries such as healthcare, finance, and coordination involve multi-step tasks. Traditional automation handles repetitive, rule-based processes, but struggles when decisions or contextual awareness are required. Agentic AI offers the ability to orchestrate tasks with reasoning embedded in each step.

2. **Scalability of Decision-Making**

   o Human operators cannot scale infinitely. As organizations grow, the need to replicate decision-making across thousands of interactions increases. Agentic AI provides consistent decision support at scale, assuming it is designed with reliability and safeguards.

3. **Adaptability to Dynamic Environments**

   o Static systems often fail when conditions change. Agents with memory and goal-reprioritization capabilities can adapt in real time, reducing downtime and improving resilience.

4. **Integration of Heterogeneous Data Sources**

   o Modern enterprises rely on structured data, unstructured text, and real-time streams. Agentic systems can process and unify diverse data inputs, extending the reach of automation.

These drivers explain why organizations see agentic AI not merely as a research interest, but as a practical enabler of productivity and efficiency.

**Industry Applications**

Although agentic AI systems remain in early deployment stages, several domains are already realizing value.

- **Healthcare**
Agents can assist in clinical documentation, appointment scheduling, or patient education. Safety constraints are critical, with agents limited to support roles rather than direct clinical decision-making.

- **Finance**
In financial operations, agents can reconcile transactions, monitor compliance, and assist in risk analysis. Their adaptability makes them suited for environments where data changes rapidly.

- **Robotics**
Agents integrated with robotics frameworks can manage complex sensor inputs, coordinate actuators, and adjust to dynamic environments such as warehouses or hospitals.

- **Enterprise Operations**
Large organizations benefit from agents that manage IT service requests, coordinate workflows across teams, and handle internal knowledge retrieval.

Each application requires tailoring. While the architectural foundations remain similar, domain-specific safety, compliance, and performance constraints must be embedded from the beginning.

## Alignment with Modern Engineering Disciplines

Agentic AI systems cannot be engineered in isolation. They must align with established practices in software and AI engineering.

- **DevOps Principles**
Continuous integration, deployment pipelines, and monitoring are as essential for agents as for conventional software. Automated testing environments help validate performance before release.

- **MLOps Integration**
Model lifecycle management, including training, validation, deployment, and retraining, applies to the LLMs underlying agents. Adding memory and planning modules introduces additional complexity, which must be integrated into the MLOps framework.

- **System Orchestration**
Agents often act as orchestrators of multiple services. Clear APIs, standardized protocols, and modular design are required for effective coordination.

By embedding agents into these existing disciplines, organizations reduce the risk of fragmented or unsustainable deployments.

## Safety, Governance, and Ethical Considerations

Safety and governance must be included into the design of agentic AI systems from the start because they do things in the real world. Safety mechanisms set clear limits on what agents can do and make sure that fail-safe methods get them back to safe states should things go wrong. Governance frameworks make sure that people are held accountable by keeping records of design choices, audit trails, and making sure that rules are followed. This is especially important in industries like banking and healthcare. Human oversight is also very important, and methods that keep people in the loop make sure that important choices are always being looked at. In some circumstances, this overlook may be adaptive, meaning that people only look at abnormalities or exceptions that have been flagged. Ethical concerns add another level of accountability, requiring agents to be open about their actions and use bias-reducing methods in sensitive situations to keep things fair and build trust. Engineers may lower the chance of expensive failures and boost trust in adoption by dealing with these safety, governance, and ethical issues from the start.

**Scaling Strategies and Operational Readiness**

Deploying a single agent prototype is simple. Scaling to enterprise-wide deployment requires structured strategies.

- **Incremental Deployment**
  Begin with narrow-scope agents in controlled environments. Monitor performance, gather feedback, and expand gradually.

- **Evaluation Metrics**
  Establish metrics for accuracy, robustness, latency, and cost-efficiency.

- **Load Handling**
  Architect for distributed inference, caching, and fallback systems to handle increased demand.

- **Continuous Improvement**
  Incorporate monitoring, retraining, and user feedback to ensure agents remain effective over time.

Operational readiness is not about achieving perfection, but about ensuring predictable performance under realistic conditions.

**The Role of Agentic AI in Near-Term Systems Engineering**

Today, the function of agentic AI is practical. It is not meant to replace people or change whole sectors overnight; instead, it is meant to provide dependable, flexible, and scalable automation. Its worth comes from adding to current systems, organizing workflows, and giving structured rationale when static automation doesn't work.

As engineering techniques change, agentic AI will start to look more like other well-known fields, like DevOps and MLOps, which have set standards, benchmarks, and rules for governance. People will slowly start using it, and the decision will be based on how reliable, safe, and cost-effective it is, not on rumors or hype.

This chapter has laid the groundwork for comprehending agentic AI: its definition, architecture, and significance in contemporary systems engineering. In the next chapter, we'll talk about design concepts and modular patterns. We'll give you specific tips for building agents that are both autonomous and controlled, adaptable and reliable, and safe and innovative.

## Section 1: Foundations of Generative AI and Agentic Systems

Generative and agent-based artificial intelligence are two basic ideas that, when put together, make it possible for large-scale autonomous systems to work. Before looking into design patterns and scaling issues, we need to figure out the rules that govern each paradigm, find their commonalities, and explain the engineering limits that drive real-world use. This part looks at the computer science behind generative AI, the main features of agent-based systems, and the basic building blocks that make it possible to add them to dependable, large-scale workflows.

### Core Principles of Generative AI

Generative AI systems are models designed to create new outputs that resemble the statistical patterns of their training data. The most relevant class of generative models for modern agentic applications is the large language model (LLM). These models are trained on vast corpora of text using a transformer-based architecture, which enables them to predict the next token in a sequence given a context window.

Key principles include:

1. **Probability-based sequence modeling.**
   LLMs generate text by computing conditional probabilities of tokens. The model selects a token based on likelihood distribution, often modified by sampling parameters such as temperature or top-k filtering.

2. **Contextual embedding.**
   Inputs are mapped into high-dimensional vectors, allowing the model to capture semantic relationships. Context windows constrain the maximum input size, directly influencing the system's ability to reason across long documents.

3. **Generalization from pretraining.**
   Models generalize patterns from massive datasets, enabling broad capabilities across domains. However, this generalization does not equate to factual accuracy or deterministic reasoning.

4. **Instruction tuning and alignment.**
   post-training methods such as supervised fine-tuning and reinforcement learning from human feedback (RLHF) align the model with human-intended behaviors. Alignment is essential when deploying generative systems inside structured agentic loops.

Generative models are effective at tasks that involve pattern completion, synthesis, or summarization. They are less effective when reliability, consistency, or mathematical precision is required without structured scaffolding. These properties highlight why agent-based architectures often surround generative cores to provide control, verification, and reliability.

### Definition and Scope of Agent-Based Systems

Agent-based systems are computational entities designed to perceive their environment, make decisions, and act toward defined goals. In artificial intelligence research, agents are often described as programs that map perceptions to actions within a specific environment.

An **agentic system** includes three critical components:

- **Sensing or perception.** The ability to interpret inputs, which may be raw data, structured signals, or human instructions.

- **Decision-making logic.** A mechanism that selects an action based on goals, constraints, or utility functions.

- **Action interface.** An ability to affect the environment through outputs, external tool use, or state modification.

Traditional agent systems, such as rule-based or utility-driven agents, have been applied for decades in robotics, coordination, and control systems. The unique contribution of generative AI is that it expands the decision-making and reasoning capabilities of agents, allowing them to handle unstructured language and complex problem decomposition.

## Aligning Generative and Agentic Paradigms

Integrating generative AI with agent-based design results in systems that can both create and act. The generative model provides flexible reasoning and synthesis, while the agentic wrapper supplies structure, constraints, and persistence.

Key differences and alignments include:

| Aspect | Generative AI (LLM) | Agent-Based System |
|---|---|---|
| Primary Function | Generate content based on learned patterns | Act to achieve goals in an environment |
| Control Mechanism | Sampling and probability distributions | Goal-driven policies, rules, or utility functions |
| Strengths | Language fluency, generalization, synthesis | Persistence, planning, structured decision-making |
| Weaknesses | Hallucinations, lack of memory, non-determinism | Brittleness without flexible reasoning |
| Integration Benefit | Broad reasoning combined with structured action | Reliable autonomy with natural-language reasoning |

By combining these properties, engineers can create agents that not only generate responses but also evaluate, revise, and coordinate those responses toward task completion.

## Architectural Primitives

The incorporation of generative AI into agent-based systems relies on a collection of architectural primitives that serve as the basis for scalability and dependability. Input encoding makes ensuring that all outside signals, including natural language, structured data, or multimodal inputs, are changed into formats that the model can understand. This is usually done by normalization, schema mapping, and careful prompt structuring. Large language models can only handle a finite amount of context, therefore approaches like retrieval-augmented generation, memory storage, and hierarchical prompting are employed to expand reasoning horizons without sacrificing speed. The generative reasoning core is the most important part of this architecture. It is where the LLM works as a probabilistic engine that can produce answers, plans, or reasoning traces.

Verification and control layers use tests such type of validation, consistency rules, and filtering techniques to make sure these outputs are reliable. State persistence keeps things going by leveraging short-term buffers, long-term knowledge bases, or external databases to keep track of tasks across time. Finally, an action interface transforms outputs into actions that can be executed, including API calls, workflow triggers, or adjustments to internal systems. Careful design makes sure that these steps are safe and predictable. You can think of this architecture as a layered system: inputs go through encoding and context management before they get to the reasoning core. Outputs are shaped and checked before they leave the system, and an agentic shell around the system manages both state persistence and action execution. This structure integrates generative reasoning within an agentic framework, facilitating systems to achieve robust and production-ready performance.

## Engineering Constraints and Risks

Generative agentic systems inherit the limitations of both paradigms. Awareness of these constraints is essential during design.

- **Hallucination and unreliability.** LLMs may produce plausible but false information. Without verification layers, agents risk compounding errors.

- **Non-determinism.** Stochastic sampling introduces variability. Deterministic behavior requires fixed seeds, constrained decoding, or post-generation filtering.

- **Context limitations.** Long sequences exceed context windows, leading to truncation or loss of relevant details. Retrieval and summarization are necessary mitigations.

- **Latency and throughput.** Generative models are computationally expensive. Real-time applications require batching, caching, or model distillation.

- **Safety and security.** Open-ended generation can create harmful or unauthorized actions. Guard rails, policy enforcement, and monitoring are mandatory in production contexts.

These hazards elucidate why generative models cannot function as autonomous agents independently. They need to be included into engineering systems that manage variability, make sure things are done correctly, and make sure that behavior is in line with the goals of the user or business. Generative AI lets you synthesize, reason, and create in areas that aren't structured, but agent-based design gives you the persistence, structure, and control you need to be independent. By harmonizing these mindsets, engineers may build strong systems that are both creative and dependable. The architectural principles described above are the basic building blocks for making agents that use LLM. The next part will build on this by looking at the ideas behind agentic design, such as planning, reasoning loops, and organized execution.

## Section 2: Principles of Agentic Design for LLM-Powered Systems

Generative AI can combine and make sense of unstructured data, but agentic design makes sure that this reasoning is focused, long-lasting, and useful. Large language models (LLMs) are great at producing answers, but they can't dependably carry out complicated workflows without scaffolding. Agentic engineering provides the frameworks necessary for task breakdown, strategic planning, error recovery, and integration with other systems. This part talks about the basic ideas behind agentic design in LLM-powered systems, focusing on autonomy, design patterns, reasoning loops, external integration, and safety measures.

### The Role of Autonomy in LLM-Powered Agents

Autonomy refers to the ability of a system to operate independently within defined constraints. In practice, autonomy for LLM-based agents is not equivalent to unrestricted freedom. Instead, it is the engineered capability to break down tasks, make bounded decisions, and execute actions without continuous human intervention.

Core functions that define autonomy in these systems include:

1. **Task decomposition.**
   Agents must translate broad instructions into smaller, actionable steps. For example, a request to "summarize the latest compliance regulations and update the internal policy document" involves retrieval of relevant text, synthesis, draft creation, and formatting.

2. **Planning and sequencing.**
   Beyond decomposition, agents must order tasks logically, handle dependencies, and adjust when outcomes deviate from expectations.

3. **Execution and monitoring.**
   Autonomy requires the ability to perform actions, such as calling APIs or modifying databases, while continuously monitoring whether outputs align with goals.

4. **Error handling.**
   Resilient autonomy demands mechanisms for detecting and recovering from errors. For LLMs, this may involve retry logic, self-reflection, or fallback to rule-based processes.

Well-engineered autonomy ensures that agents act predictably while leveraging the generative flexibility of the LLM core.

## Core Agent Design Patterns

Agent-based systems can be structured according to distinct design patterns. Each offers trade-offs in complexity, control, and adaptability.

1. **Reflex agents.**
   These agents act based on current input without considering history or goals. In LLM contexts, this corresponds to simple prompting and response, suitable for isolated tasks.

2. **Goal-based agents.**
   These agents maintain explicit objectives and select actions that move toward achieving them. For LLM systems, goals may include answering a query accurately, generating a valid code snippet, or completing a multi-step document analysis.

3. **Utility-based agents.**
   These extend goal-based design by quantifying preferences. For example, an LLM agent may balance accuracy against latency, selecting an action sequence that maximizes utility under resource constraints.

4. **Learning agents.**
   These agents adapt over time by incorporating feedback into their decision policies. In LLM-driven systems, this may involve reinforcement from user corrections or performance metrics.

The choice of design patterns depends on application requirements. For simple query answering, reflex-style agents suffice. For enterprise-scale orchestration, goal- and utility-based patterns provide necessary structure.

A comparison table clarifies trade-offs:

| Agent Pattern | Strengths | Limitations | Suitable Use Cases |
|---|---|---|---|
| Reflex | Simple, fast, minimal overhead | No persistence, easily brittle | Single-turn queries, chatbots |
| Goal-based | Structured, persistent objectives | Requires explicit goals and constraints | Task execution, workflow management |
| Utility-based | Optimizes trade-offs, flexible | Complex design requires utility metrics | Resource-constrained systems |
| Learning | Adapts overtime, improves performance | Requires training signals and oversight | Long-lived adaptive agents |

## Reasoning Loops and Structured Thought

One of the defining innovations in agentic design with LLMs is the use of reasoning loops. Unlike reflex responses, reasoning loops allow agents to engage in multi-step deliberation.

Common reasoning loop frameworks include:

1. **Chain-of-thought prompting.**
   Encourages the model to generate intermediate reasoning steps before final output. Improves reliability in reasoning-heavy tasks, such as mathematics or logical deduction.

2. **ReAct (Reasoning and Acting).**
   Combines reasoning with action steps. The model alternates between explaining its reasoning and executing actions, such as tool calls or retrieval operations.

3. **Self-consistency.**
   Runs multiple reasoning paths in parallel and selects the most consistent output. Useful when reducing hallucination risk in knowledge-intensive tasks.

4. **Reflection mechanisms.**
   Enables agents to critique and revise their outputs, either through secondary prompts or dedicated verification models.

A typical reasoning loop can be represented textually:

- Step 1: Interpret input and set objective.

- Step 2: Generate reasoning trace.

- Step 3: Select or execute action.

- Step 4: Verify output and reflect.

- Step 5: Iterate until goal achieved or termination criteria met.

By embedding reasoning loops, agents achieve greater robustness than direct prompt-response architectures.

## Integration with External Systems

LLMs are language-based models. To operate as functional agents, they must interact with external environments through structured interfaces.

Principles for safe and reliable integration include:

1. **Tool use.**
   Agents may access APIs, databases, or computation engines. Tool schemas must be explicitly defined so the LLM can generate valid calls.

2. **Retrieval augmentation.**
   When context exceeds the LLM's window, retrieval systems provide relevant documents or structured data. This improves grounding and reduces hallucination.

3. **Structured data exchange.**
   Outputs should be constrained to machine-readable formats such as JSON. This allows deterministic parsing and downstream execution.

4. **Sandboxing and access control.**
   To prevent unintended actions, integrations must be sandboxed, with strict permissioning and logging of all operations.

5. **Monitoring and observability.**
   Every external call should be logged with input, output, latency, and error state for auditability.

These integration principles transform LLMs from isolated reasoning engines into embedded components of enterprise workflows.

## Safety, Guardrails, and Interpretability

Safety is a basic need in the design of agentic AI systems, as unrestrained LLM-powered agents might generate hazardous, prejudiced, or unlawful activities. To lower these dangers, engineers use a number of safety measures. Guardrail frameworks set clear guidelines for what outputs are okay and what aren't, usually by utilizing regex filters, policy models, or rule-based validators. Type enforcement makes sure that outputs follow preset schemas before they are run, which stops erroneous or invalid actions from spreading across a system. For important situations like medical advice or money transfers, human-in-the-loop clearance is an extra safety measure that requires confirmation before actions are taken.

Interpretability layers make things clear by keeping track of reasoning traces and making them available for review. This lets engineers see why decisions were taken. Fallback methods make systems more robust by going back to predictable pathways, like predefined templates, when generative activity fails or gives outputs that are unclear. These safety precautions are not optional; they must be built in from the beginning, tested against bad situations, and watched over all the time to make sure they are used safely and responsibly.

## Engineering for Determinism and Auditability

LLM outputs are inherently probabilistic. Agentic design introduces mechanisms to control and audit this variability.

- **Determinism through decoding control.** Use constrained sampling methods or fixed seeds to reduce variance in outputs.

- **State management.** Maintain clear separation of ephemeral (short-term) state and persistent (long-term) memory. This prevents context leakage and supports reproducibility.

- **Logging and traceability.** Every agent action must be logged with context, inputs, outputs, and timestamps. This supports debugging and compliance.

- **Version control of prompts and policies.** Just as software code is versioned, prompts and configuration files must be stored in repositories to ensure consistent behavior across deployments.

Engineers can find the fundamental causes of failures instead of treating the system as a black box thanks to auditability.

Agentic design concepts turn generative models into independent systems that can reason, integrate, and run safely. Planning, breaking down tasks, and keeping an eye on things all help people become more independent. Design patterns, like goal-based or utility-based agents, give you structural templates. Reasoning loops make things more reliable, and integration principles let things happen outside of the system. Guardrails and audit procedures make sure that people are safe and responsible.

These ideas set the stage for expanding agent-based systems in real-world settings. The next section will go into more detail about these principles by talking about ways to scale, ways to evaluate, and operational limits for real-world implementation.

Once the foundational principles of generative and agent-based design are in place, the next challenge lies in operationalizing these systems at scale. LLM-powered agents must not only function in controlled prototypes but also withstand the demands of high concurrency, distributed execution, enterprise-grade evaluation, and cost-sensitive deployment. This section examines the principles of scaling, methodologies for evaluation, performance metrics, operational constraints, and risk management strategies.

**Principles of Scaling LLM-Powered Agents**

Scaling agentic systems involves extending performance, reliability, and throughput without compromising safety. This requires a combination of architectural, computational, and process-oriented strategies.

1. **Concurrency and orchestration.**
   Multiple agents often run simultaneously, either within a single workflow or across organizational tasks. Effective orchestration ensures resource allocation, synchronization, and conflict resolution. Workflow engines such as Apache Airflow or Kubernetes-based schedulers provide proven orchestration mechanisms.

2. **Distributed execution.**
   For large-scale deployments, agents must run across distributed systems. This requires careful design of communication protocols, data sharing, and state synchronization. Message queues (e.g., Kafka, RabbitMQ) or actor frameworks (e.g., Ray, Akka) are often employed.

3. **Multi-agent coordination.**
   Some applications require collaboration among multiple agents. Coordination patterns include hierarchical control, peer-to-peer negotiation, or centralized arbitration. Robust coordination prevents duplication of work and reduces deadlocks.

4. **Horizontal and vertical scaling.**

   o *Vertical scaling* increases the resources available to a single agent instance, such as GPUs or memory.

   o *Horizontal scaling* adds more agent instances to handle higher load. Both strategies must be balanced against infrastructure cost.

5. **Resilience under load.**
   Load testing is essential to identify bottlenecks. Strategies include autoscaling, caching of frequent results, and traffic shaping to prioritize critical tasks.

Scalable design ensures that agents can transition from controlled environments to enterprise-level deployments.

**Evaluation Methodologies for Agent-Based AI**

Evaluation is critical to determining whether LLM-powered agents meet functional, safety, and efficiency requirements. Unlike static machine learning models, agentic systems involve dynamic decision-making that must be tested holistically.

Widely recognized evaluation methodologies include:

1. **Functional correctness.**
   Verification that the agent completes tasks as specified. This can be assessed through unit tests on reasoning steps, integration tests on workflows, and regression tests on updated models.

24

2. **Robust testing.**
   Exposing agents to adversarial inputs, malformed data, or noisy environments. This ensures graceful degradation rather than catastrophic failure.

3. **Efficiency and performance.**
   Measuring latency, throughput, and resource utilization under realistic workloads. These metrics are critical for user-facing systems where responsiveness is essential.

4. **Human-in-the-loop validation.**
   In high-stakes domains, human evaluators confirm correctness, safety, and compliance. Structured annotation pipelines and approval workflows ensure that agents reinforce organizational standards.

5. **Simulation environments.**
   Complex agent behaviors can be tested in simulated environments that mimic production conditions. This approach allows large-scale experimentation before real-world deployment.

Evaluation is not a one-time process. Continuous monitoring and periodic revalidation are necessary, especially as models are updated or retrained.

## Metrics for Generative-Agentic Systems

Metrics provide the quantitative foundation for evaluation. For agentic LLM systems, several categories of metrics are relevant.

- **Task success rate.** Percentage of tasks completed accurately and fully.

- **Token efficiency.** Ratio of tokens generated useful output, measuring prompt engineering efficiency.

- **Latency.** Time between request initiation and task completion, including both model inference and external actions.

- **Error rate.** Frequency of failed actions, invalid outputs, or unhandled exceptions.

- **Safety adherence.** Rate of compliance with predefined safety and policy rules.

- **Resource utilization.** GPU hours, memory usage, and bandwidth consumption are related to throughput.

- **User satisfaction.** When applicable, human ratings of relevance, clarity, or usability.

Table example:

| Metric | Definition | Relevance |
|---|---|---|
| Task success rate | Correct completions / total tasks | Primary measure of effectiveness |
| Token efficiency | Useful tokens / total tokens generated | Cost and efficiency control |
| Latency | Time to completion per request | User-facing responsiveness |
| Error rate | Invalid or failed outputs per task | Reliability measure |
| Safety adherence | Policy-compliant actions / total actions | Risk management and compliance |
| Resource utilization | Compute and memory usage per throughput unit | Infrastructure optimization |

These metrics support both technical evaluation and management-level reporting.

## Benchmarking Practices and Frameworks

Benchmarking is necessary to make sure that comparisons between models, agents, and full systems are fair and evaluations are accurate. Standard benchmarks like MMLU, GSM8K, and HumanEval test basic generating ability.

These are useful tests, but they don't work well for testing agentic performance. Task-focused benchmarks are sometimes made to meet the needs of specific fields, such legal summarizing or medical coding. Scenario-based benchmarks go beyond static datasets by simulating multi-step activities in real-world situations. This gives a better idea of how agents act in changing settings.

It is also important to do continuous benchmarking because agents need to be re-evaluated every time the underlying models, APIs, or data sources are updated to make sure the quality stays the same. Engineers are better off using established frameworks like HELM (Holistic Evaluation of Language Models) and standardized QA pipelines to examine language models. These frameworks offer structured, validated ways to do so, and engineers should adapt these tried-and-true procedures instead of relying on improvised, unverified tests. These approaches work together to form a complete evaluation procedure that balances general ability with subject relevance and real-world dependability.

## Operational Constraints

Practical deployment of LLM-powered agents introduces constraints that must be engineered around.

1. **Computer availability.**
   Inference with large models is resource intensive. Organizations must balance performance with GPU availability and scheduling.

2. **Latency sensitivity.**
   Interactive applications, such as customer service or decision support, require sub-second responses. Techniques such as model quantization, caching, or smaller distilled models may be necessary.

3. **Context window limitations.**
   Long documents or complex histories can exceed context limits. Retrieval-augmented generation (RAG), chunking strategies, and hierarchical summarization are essential workarounds.

4. **Cost control.**
   Token-based billing can escalate rapidly. Cost management strategies include prompt optimization, response truncation, and monitoring of token usage.

5. **Compliance and security.**
   Agents must adhere to organizational policies and regulatory standards. Encryption, logging, and access controls are required for sensitive data.

Operational constraints are not secondary considerations; they directly shape architecture and design decisions.

## Risk Management and Failure Recovery

Agentic systems are at risk in a special way because little mistakes can build up throughout reasoning loops, making failures worse if they aren't fixed. Schema validation, anomaly detection, and semantic consistency tests are all ways to find problems early on and stop them from getting worse. Fallback techniques offer deterministic workflows that make sure activities can still be done reliably when generative reasoning doesn't function. Circuit breakers and rate limiters can keep issues from spreading by isolating them. These stops cascading failures across interconnected parts. Recovery techniques make systems even more resilient by letting them checkpoint and replay workflows. This lets systems start again from safe states following a problem. Observability systems that track metrics, logs, and traces make ensuring that faults are evident right away and can be fixed rapidly. Engineers make systems that are not only stronger but also reliable enough to be used in important, high-stakes situations by using these methods.

## Lifecycle of an LLM-Powered Agent

An end-to-end lifecycle perspective illustrates how scaling, evaluation, and operations fit together.

1. **Design.** Define goals, architecture, and safety requirements.

2. **Implementation.** Build agent with LLM core, context management, and external integrations.

3. **Testing.** Evaluate functional correctness, robustness, and safety under controlled conditions.

4. **Deployment.** Orchestrate distributed execution with monitoring and observability.

5. **Operation.** Continuously evaluate metrics, manage resources, and enforce guardrails.

6. **Iteration.** Update models, prompts, or policies based on monitored performance.

This lifecycle reflects proven engineering practice: iterative refinement under continuous monitoring.

Scaling LLM-powered agents require careful design of concurrency, distributed orchestration, and multi-agent coordination. Evaluation methodologies must cover functional correctness, robustness, and safety, supported by well-defined metrics and benchmarking frameworks. Operational constraints such as computing availability, latency, and compliance directly influence design. Risk management strategies mitigate cascading failures and ensure resilience.

Taken together, these principles provide the foundation for reliable, enterprise-scale deployment of agentic systems. With structured scaling, rigorous evaluation, and operational safeguards, generative-agent architectures can move from experimental prototypes to robust, production-grade systems.

## Section 1: Principles of Modular Design in Agentic AI Systems

Designing large-scale agentic systems powered by large language models (LLMs) requires a disciplined approach to architecture. Modularity is the central principle that enables engineers to build systems that can be scaled, maintained, and improved over time without unnecessary coupling or fragility. In this section, the focus is on defining modularity within the context of agentic AI, examining its benefits and trade-offs, and establishing core design considerations that guide implementation.

### Defining Modularity in Agentic AI

In generic software engineering, modularity means breaking a system down into separate, well-defined parts with clear interfaces. Each part of the system has its own job, which cuts down on dependencies and makes it easier to understand the whole system.

In agentic AI systems, modularity is more than just how the code is organized. It decides how to break down vision, thinking, memory, and action skills into smaller, easier-to-manage parts. For instance, one module might be in charge of interpreting natural language, another might be in charge of retrieving long-term memories, and a third would be in charge of executing actions with external tools. Because these tasks are split out, making changes to one aspect of the system, such upgrading the memory index, doesn't mean that the reasoning engine needs to be redesigned.

Key characteristics of modularity in this context include:

- **Encapsulation**: Each module hides its internal logic while exposing only a stable interface.
- **Composability**: Modules can be assembled in different configurations to build varied agent workflows.
- **Replaceability**: A module can be updated or replaced with minimal impact on the rest of the system.
- **Testability**: Individual modules can be evaluated in isolation, reducing the complexity of debugging

### Benefits of Modular Architectures

The decision to implement modularity in LLM-powered agents is not arbitrary. It directly addresses recurring engineering challenges that emerge as systems move from prototypes to production.

### Scalability

As agents evolve, new capabilities must be integrated. A modular system allows engineers to add new modules, such as a planning component or domain-specific reasoning engine, without destabilizing the existing architecture. Scaling across multiple environments also becomes easier when modules are isolated and can be distributed.

### Maintainability

LLMs and supporting libraries are updated frequently. In a monolithic design, integrating a new model version often requires extensive regression testing. With modular separation, only the reasoning module may need adjustment while the interfaces to perception, memory, and action remain intact.

### Fault Isolation

Errors are inevitable in complex AI workflows. By isolating modules, failures in one component can be contained. For example, if a retrieval module produces an error, the system can degrade gracefully by falling back to default reasoning paths without halting the entire agent.

### Reusability

Modular components are portable across projects. A dialogue management module created for a healthcare assistant can be reused with minimal modification in a legal assistant system, provided the interface contracts are maintained.

### Core Design Considerations

Designing modular AI systems require careful attention to the principles that guide how components interact and evolve.

### Separation of Concerns

Each module must have a single, clear responsibility. For example:

- **Perception module**: Input parsing, language understanding, multimodal data handling.

- **Reasoning module**: Planning, inference, decision-making.

- **Memory module**: Short-term context, long-term storage, retrieval strategies.

- **Action module**: External API calls, environment interaction, reporting.

Without strict separation, modules risk overlapping functionality, which introduces ambiguity and maintenance difficulties.

### Dependency Management

Dependencies between modules should be minimized. Cyclic dependencies are especially harmful, as they create tight coupling that undermines modularity. Engineers can enforce dependency rules using architectural diagrams or static analysis tools to detect unwanted coupling.

### Interface Contracts

Each module should communicate through well-defined contracts. These contracts specify input, outputs, and expected behaviors. For example, a reasoning module might expect a structured JSON response from the memory module. If the format changes, the contract ensures that dependent modules are updated consistently.

### Versioning and Upgrades

Given the rapid iteration of AI components, version control for modules is essential. Interfaces should evolve in a backward-compatible manner whenever possible. When incompatible changes are required, explicit versioning strategies must be applied.

### Mapping Modularity to Agentic System Components

The general principles of modularity can be mapped to the core elements of LLM-powered agents.

| Core Function | Typical Module Responsibilities | Example Implementation |
|---|---|---|
| Perception | Input preprocessing, entity recognition, multimodal parsing | NLP preprocessing layer |
| Reasoning | Task decomposition, plan generation, inference execution | Chain-of-thought controller |
| Memory | Short-term context handling, long-term storage, retrieval | Vector database interface |
| Action | API execution, tool invocation, environment manipulation | Web request dispatcher |
| Coordination | Orchestration across modules, error handling, monitoring | Agent controller loop |

This decomposition provides a reusable blueprint for system architects when designing new agentic applications.

**Monolithic versus Modular Implementations**

When designing an agent system, one of the most important architectural choices is whether to adopt a monolithic or modular approach. Each style comes with distinct benefits and trade-offs that shape how the system evolves over time.

A monolithic design is often the simpler path when building early prototypes. Because all components exist within a single codebase, communication overhead is minimal, and developers can quickly move from concept to working product. However, the same characteristics that make it attractive for prototyping also create limitations as the system grows. Scaling becomes difficult because the entire application must be expanded as one unit. Even small changes in a single area can ripple through the entire codebase, risking new errors or instabilities. Debugging is also more challenging, as developers often need to analyze the full scope of the system rather than focusing on isolated issues.

In contrast, modular design offers far greater flexibility and long-term sustainability. By breaking the system into separate components, scaling can occur both horizontally and vertically, and specific modules can be reused or updated independently. This structure also improves resilience, as failures in one part of the system can often be contained without bringing down the whole. Yet, these benefits come with their own challenges. Building a modular system demands a higher level of upfront planning and architectural discipline. Inter-module communication introduces some performance costs, and strict governance of interfaces is required to prevent fragmentation or misalignment between modules.

Ultimately, the choice between monolithic and modular designs depends on whether the priority lies in rapid prototyping and simplicity, or in scalability, maintainability, and resilience over the long term.

A hybrid approach is often practical, where early prototypes may start with a semi-monolithic design, then evolve toward modularization as requirements stabilize.

**Case Study: Modular Decomposition of a Clinical Workflow Assistant**

Consider a workflow assistant deployed in a clinical environment where it must interpret patient records, retrieve guidelines, and generate care recommendations. A monolithic design would embed all these capabilities in a single LLM-powered script. This approach quickly becomes brittle as new requirements emerge.

By applying modular decomposition, the architecture can be structured as follows:

1. **Perception Module**
   - Extracts structured information from patient records.
   - Normalizes terminology using a controlled vocabulary.

2. **Memory Module**
   - Maintains patient history in a vector database.
   - Provides retrieval capabilities for prior encounters.

3. **Reasoning Module**
   - Applies task decomposition to generate care recommendations.
   - Cross-references retrieved knowledge with guideline databases.

4. **Action Module**

o   Produces structured outputs such as care plans.

o   Integrates with clinical record systems via secure APIs.

5.  **Coordinator Module**

o   Orchestrates data flow among modules.

o   Handles error logging and retry.

This modular design means that when medical rules change, only the reasoning module needs to be changed; the perception, memory, and action layers stay the same. This makes the system easier to keep up with, grow, and make sure it meets regulatory standards.

The basics of modular design are important for making strong LLM-powered agents. Engineers can make systems more scalable, easier to manage, fault-tolerant, and reusable by breaking them down into well-defined parts with reliable interfaces. It is important to weigh the pros and cons of monolithic versus modular designs, but for systems that are ready for production, modularity gives the structural clarity needed for long-term development.

The following part will look at specific architectural patterns that can be used with modular agentic systems. These patterns will provide you with tangible ideas for how to put these modules together in a way that makes sense and works.

## Section 2: Core Architectural Patterns for LLM-Based Agents

Architectural patterns provide reusable solutions for organizing modular components in agentic systems. While the previous section established why modularity is important, this section focuses on how it can be achieved through established design approaches. The goal is to provide engineers and system architects with concrete frameworks that align with the requirements of LLM-powered agents.

### Role of Architectural Patterns in Agentic Systems

Architectural patterns are recognized blueprints in software engineering that show how system parts should be put together and how they should work together. Instead of telling you which technologies to use, they tell you how to organize the parts and how the system should behave. In the context of agentic AI, these patterns dictate the alignment of modules for perception, reasoning, memory, and action to yield coherent and dependable results. In AI systems, they are even more important since they make sure that design principles are used the same way on all parts, which makes the system more consistent. They also help with scalability by giving the system structures that can grow as it gets more complicated. Another big benefit is that patterns help set up strategies to handle mistakes without bringing down the whole system. Lastly, they make maintenance easier by making it easier to add new features and make changes. Engineering teams can find a balance between flexibility and reliability by carefully choosing the proper architectural patterns. This lets agentic systems change while still being trustworthy.

### The Pipeline Pattern

The pipeline pattern organizes processing as a series of sequential stages. Each stage accepts input, applies a transformation, and passes the output forward. This model is particularly suited to perception and reasoning tasks where data must undergo a series of transformations before being acted upon.

### Application to Agentic AI

In LLM-based systems, a pipeline may consist of:

1.  Input parsing and normalization.

2. Entity extraction and semantic enrichment.

3. Contextual reasoning or planning.

4. Action formulation.

5. Output formatting.

**Advantages**

- Clear separation of responsibilities.

- Easy to add or remove stages.

- Debugging localized to individual steps.

**Limitations**

- Inflexible for tasks requiring feedback loops.

- Latency increases with additional stages.

**Example**

A customer-support agent might use a pipeline where incoming queries are first normalized, then passed through an intent classifier, followed by a retrieval step, reasoning with the LLM, and finally generating a structured response.

**The Blackboard Architecture**

The blackboard pattern provides a shared knowledge structure where multiple modules contribute incrementally toward solving a problem. Each module monitors the blackboard, adds partial solutions, or refines existing entries.

**Application to Agentic AI**

In LLM agents, the blackboard can act as a shared memory structure where:

- The perception module posts extracted features.

- The reasoning module adds intermediate hypotheses.

- The memory module enriches entries with retrieved knowledge.

- The action module consumes finalized instructions.

**Advantages**

- Supports incremental and collaborative problem-solving.

- Flexible for integrating heterogeneous modules.

- It is effective when solutions emerge iteratively.

**Limitations**

- Requires careful control to prevent conflicts between modules.

- May introduce overhead in synchronization.

**Example**

A research assistant agent might use a blackboard where literature retrieval results, extracted key points, and reasoning inferences accumulate until a coherent research summary emerges.

## Event-Driven and Message-Passing Architectures

Event-driven patterns rely on asynchronous communication between modules. Instead of sequential control, modules react to events or messages, enabling decoupled and highly scalable designs.

### Application to Agentic AI

- The perception module emits an event when new input is available.
- The reasoning module subscribes to reasoning-related events.
- The memory module provides retrieval results as asynchronous messages.
- The action module executes when instructed by specific triggers.

### Advantages

- Decoupling reduces dependency between modules.
- Supports parallel processing.
- Scales effectively in distributed environments.

### Limitations

- Debugging is more complex due to non-deterministic flows.
- Requires reliable message brokers for production use.

### Example

In an enterprise workflow automation agent, perception modules detect incoming documents and emit parsing events. Downstream reasoning and memory modules consume these asynchronously, allowing multiple tasks to progress in parallel without bottlenecking on a single control loop.

### Layered Architectures

Layered design structures components into hierarchical tiers, with each layer depending only on the one directly beneath it. This ensures a predictable flow of control and well-defined boundaries.

### Application to Agentic AI

A layered LLM agent might be organized as:

- **Layer 1**: Input handling and normalization.
- **Layer 2**: Domain reasoning and inference.
- **Layer 3**: Decision-making and planning.
- **Layer 4**: Action execution and reporting.

### Advantages

- Enforces separation of concerns.

- Easier to manage upgrades at one layer.

- Provides a stable structure for long-term maintenance.

## Limitations

- Can become rigid when cross-layer interactions are needed.

- Latency may increase with too many intermediate layers.

## Example

A compliance-checking agent may use a layered design where the first layer parses contracts, the second layer interprets clauses, the third layer matches them against compliance rules, and the fourth layer generates structured reports. **Microservices-Inspired Modularization**

Borrowed from distributed systems design, the microservices approach decomposes systems into independently deployable services. For LLM agents, modules such as perception, reasoning, memory, and action can be deployed as services with their own lifecycles.

## Application to Agentic AI

Memory may run as a dedicated retrieval service.

- Reasoning may be wrapped as a service exposing a planning API.

- Action modules can operate as specialized service connectors.

## Advantages

- High degree of scalability and flexibility.

- Independent deployment cycles for each service.

- Fault isolation between services.

## Limitations

- Requires robust infrastructure for service discovery and orchestration.

- Higher operational complexity compared to monolithic deployment.

## Example

A large-scale enterprise agent could adopt microservices where memory and retrieval are deployed in a cluster, reasoning runs in a scalable inference service, and action modules operate as dedicated API connectors across departments.

### Evaluating Trade-offs Among Patterns

Selecting the correct architectural pattern depends on workload, system constraints, and operational requirements. The following table summarizes typical alignments:

| Pattern | Strengths | Weaknesses | Best Fit Use Cases |
|---|---|---|---|
| Pipeline | Simplicity, sequential clarity | Rigid, limited feedback | Linear tasks, preprocessing |
| Blackboard | Collaborative problem-solving | Synchronization overhead | Research assistants, iterative reasoning |

| Event-driven | Decoupled, scalable, parallel | Debugging complexity | Workflow automation, multi-task agents |
| Layered | Structured, maintainable | Can be rigid, adds latency | Compliance, reporting systems |
| Microservices-based | Independent scaling and deployment | Operational overhead | Enterprise-scale multi-agent systems |

This assessment indicates that no singular pattern is universally superior. It is common to see hybrid architectures, where a pipeline may be part of a layered system or event-driven modules may work together through microservices.

Architectural patterns give engineers a way to organize modular agentic AI systems in a systematic way. The pipeline pattern allows sequential transformations, the blackboard architecture allows for collaborative knowledge building, event-driven systems encourage decoupling and scalability, layered designs enforce hierarchy and separation, and microservices-inspired approaches extend modularity to distributed environments.

The pattern you choose relies on the workload, the limits of the task, and how mature the system is. In practice, most agents that are ready for production use a mix of these patterns to be both flexible and strong.

## Section 3: Practical Integration Strategies and Scaling Considerations

Once modular components and architectural patterns are defined, the next challenge is to integrate them into a coherent system that can operate reliably at scale. This section addresses integration techniques, orchestration strategies, evaluation methods, and deployment practices that ensure agentic AI systems can transition from prototypes to production environments

### Strategies for Combining Architectural Patterns

In real-world use, agentic systems don't often use only one architectural pattern. They use a mix of different methods to find a balance between performance, maintainability, and scalability. The hybrid pipeline and blackboard architecture is one good way to do things. A pipeline handles tasks that have a clear answer, like parsing and normalizing data. A blackboard structure, on the other hand, facilitates iterative reasoning, which lets several modules work together until a solution is found. Event-driven pipelines are another option. In these, pipelines run like sequential workflows but are started by events from outside the system. For example, when a new user enters data, it might create an event that starts the pipeline. Each stage of the pipeline works independently, so numerous queries can occur at the same time.

A layered microservices architecture adds even more flexibility by using perception, reasoning, and action layers as separate services. This not only lets each layer scale horizontally, but it also lets updates and lifecycle management happen independently. By combining these patterns, engineers make hybrid architectures that take use of the best parts of each technique while reducing their weaknesses. This makes systems that are both strong and flexible.

### Module Orchestration and Control Flow

Integration requires clear orchestration of module interactions. Orchestration defines the control flow, error handling, and coordination mechanisms.

### Centralized Orchestration

Centralized orchestration relies on a coordinator module to manage the sequence of operations across the system. This approach works well for smaller systems with stable, predictable workflows, where a central controller can efficiently direct each step. Its main advantage lies in simplicity, as debugging and monitoring are easier when control is consolidated in one place. However, this design also introduces a single point of failure, meaning that if the coordinator malfunctions, the entire system may be disrupted. For that reason, centralized orchestration is best suited for contained environments where reliability requirements are moderate, and workflows are well understood.

### Decentralized Orchestration

Decentralized orchestration distributes control across modules that coordinate through message passing or event-driven subscriptions. This removes the dependency on a single coordinator and eliminates central bottlenecks, allowing the system to operate more flexibly and scale more effectively. Because no single component dictates execution, the architecture is inherently more resilient to failures, as other modules can continue functioning if one encounters issues. However, this approach depends on a robust communication infrastructure to ensure reliable synchronization and prevent data loss or miscoordination. When designed well, decentralized orchestration provides both fault tolerance and adaptability, making it ideal for larger, dynamic systems.

### Workflow Engines

- Workflow engines such as Apache Airflow or temporal frameworks can formalize orchestration.

- Provide visibility into execution paths, retries, and scheduling.

### State Persistence and Lifecycle Management

Agentic systems must maintain continuity across sessions and handle lifecycle transitions.

### State Persistence

- **Short-term state**: Managed in memory or fast key-value stores.

- **Long-term state**: Managed in vector databases or relational databases.

- **Checkpointing**: Ensures that system recovery is possible after failures.

### Lifecycle Management

- Initialization: Load configuration, establish module connections.

- Execution: Monitor resource usage, enforce timeouts, manage retries.

- Termination: Release resources, flush logs, archive results.

Lifecycle management ensures reliability in production environments where uptime and stability are critical.

### Evaluation of Modular Components

Each module must be evaluated independently before being integrated. Evaluation should also extend to the full system once modules are combined.

### Component-Level Evaluation

Component-level evaluation is all about figuring out how well each basic function in an agentic system works. The most important thing for perception is how well entity recognition and parsing work, which makes sure that inputs are understood correctly. The quality of task decomposition and decision-making is used to judge reasoning. This shows how well the system breaks down goals and chooses the best methods. Memory is checked for both retrieval accuracy and latency to make sure that the right information is found promptly and without mistakes. Finally, action is evaluated based on the reliability of tool execution and API calls, which makes sure that the system can always turn decisions into proper and trustworthy results. These evaluations work together to give a detailed picture of the system's strengths and flaws, which helps with making specific adjustments.

## Integration-Level Evaluation

Integration-level evaluation looks at how well the full agentic system works together as a single unit instead of as separate parts. The main measure is the end-to-end task success rate, which shows how well the system can regularly meet its goals in the real world. Latency across the entire pipeline is also very important because delays in one stage can cause problems in other stages and make the whole system less responsive. Another important aspect is error propagation, which looks at how faults in one module influence processes that come after it and if the system can fix or contain them. Engineers can learn about the system's robustness, efficiency, and dependability while it is running in production by looking at these data.

### Benchmarking Frameworks

- Use of standardized benchmarks (e.g., retrieval accuracy datasets, domain-specific QA corpora).
- Logging metrics in structured formats for reproducibility.

A modular evaluation approach ensures that failures can be attributed to specific modules rather than requiring global debugging

## Scaling Across Compute Environments

Scaling modular AI agents require careful planning across hardware and deployment platforms.

### Local Deployments

- Suitable for prototyping and small-scale testing.
- Simple to set up but limited by hardware constraints.

### Cluster Deployments

- Modules distributed across nodes in a cluster.
- Orchestrated using frameworks such as Kubernetes.
- Allows horizontal scaling of memory retrieval services or reasoning components.

### Cloud-Native Deployments

- Full elasticity of resources.
- Integration with managed services such as databases, message brokers, and observability stacks.
- Supports multi-region deployment for resilience.

Scaling decisions should align with workload demands and cost constraints.

## Monitoring, Logging, and Observability

For modular agentic systems to work reliably in production, monitoring, logging, and observability are very important. Structured logs that include timestamps, module identities, and correlation IDs are all kept in central systems for simple search and analysis. This is what good logging looks like. Metrics collection lets you see how healthy a system is by measuring things like latency, throughput, and error rates at the module level, as well as how much CPU, GPU, and memory it is using. Tracing gives you even more information by letting you track requests as they pass through different modules. This lets you find latency problems or bottlenecks. Alerting systems fill in the gaps by employing threshold-based triggers on important indicators and escalation protocols to make sure that operational teams respond fast to problems. If modular systems don't follow these observability best practices, they could become hard to see and debug, which would make them less reliable and slow down recovery when faults happen.

**Case Walkthrough: Scaling a Clinical Workflow Agent**

To illustrate practical integration and scaling, consider the modular clinical workflow assistant introduced earlier.

1. **Initial Prototype**

    o   Implemented as a semi-monolithic pipeline for parsing patient data, reasoning, and generating care recommendations.

    o   Deployed locally for controlled testing.

2. **Transition to Modular Deployment**

    o   Separated modules for perception, memory, reasoning, and action.

    o   Introducing a coordinator for orchestration.

    o   Implemented structured logging for each module.

3. **Scaling in Cluster Environment**

    o   Memory retrieval service deployed on a distributed vector database.

    o   Reasoning module scaled horizontally with load balancing.

    o   Event-driven triggers used to handle asynchronous document ingestion.

4. **Cloud-Native Production Deployment**

    o   Full observability stack integrated (metrics, logs, traces).

    o   Auto-scaling policies applied to memory and reasoning modules.

    o   Monitoring dashboards used for operational oversight.

This progression shows how modular decomposition makes it possible to scale up from a prototype to an enterprise deployment while keeping the system easy to maintain and fault-tolerant.

To make modular LLM-powered agents work together and grow, you need to use rigorous tactics. Using architectural patterns in a hybrid way gives you more freedom. Orchestration and lifecycle management make sure that everything works together. Modular evaluation makes it easier to judge someone's performance. Scaling across local, cluster, and cloud-native contexts makes sure that things stay stable. Lastly, observability practices protect the reliability of production.

By using these methods together, engineers may make AI systems that are not just theoretically flexible but also strong, scalable, and long-lasting in practice.

## Section 1: Foundations of Agentic Loops in LLM-Powered Systems

Agentic artificial intelligence systems are not built to be single-pass pipelines that connect input to output. They are instead built around loops of perception, reasoning, memory, and action that repeat over and over again to make them strong, adaptable, and scalable. This looping design is based on how control systems engineers and distributed computer systems work, where feedback and repeated corrections are necessary for reliable functioning. In this part, we provide the groundwork for these loops, explain their individual and collective roles, and show how they are important parts of large-scale autonomous architectures that use large language models (LLMs).

**The Rationale for Loop-Based Architectures**

Traditional machine learning systems often follow a linear path: data is ingested, processed, and a prediction or decision is produced. While effective in bounded tasks, this approach fails to accommodate real-world variability, where inputs may be incomplete, ambiguous, or dynamic. LLM-powered agents must instead perceive, interpret, and act in environments where uncertainty is the norm. Loops address this by enabling:

- **Iteration:** The ability to refine output through multiple passes.

- **Feedback incorporation:** Adjusting decisions based on outcomes or new inputs.

- **Error correction:** Detecting and mitigating mistakes through retries or escalations.

- **Adaptation:** Aligning to dynamic contexts such as changing user goals or external system states.

By structuring an agent around these loops, engineers can move from a brittle inference pipeline to a resilient system capable of sustained operation in production.

**Defining the Four Loops**

Each loop represents a functional pillar of the agentic lifecycle.

1. **Perception Loop:**
   The perception loop ingests raw inputs, which may be text, structured data, or multimodal signals such as audio or images. Its purpose is to parse, normalize, and validate this data so that downstream reasoning is informed by reliable representations.

2. **Reasoning Loop:**
   Once inputs are structured, the reasoning loop generates plans, decisions, or predictions. Reasoning is often iterative, where the model evaluates partial plans, considers constraints, and updates its outputs based on intermediate feedback.

3. **Memory Loop:**
   Agents require both short-term and long-term recall. The memory loop manages the retrieval of past context, storage of new states, and synchronization of relevant history. Memory ensures continuity across interactions and improves decision quality by grounding reasoning in prior knowledge.

4. **Action Loop:**
   The final loop executes outputs in the environment. Actions may include calling APIs, updating databases, sending responses, or coordinating external services. The loop incorporates mechanisms to validate, retry, or safely abort actions when anomalies occur.

Together, these loops create a cycle: inputs are perceived, processed through reasoning, contextualized by memory, and executed as actions, which then generate new inputs for subsequent cycles.

## Loops in Relation to Core Engineering Concerns

When evaluating agentic systems, four engineering concerns occur: accuracy, latency, robustness, and maintainability. The loops align directly with these concerns:

- **Accuracy:** The perception and reasoning loops determine correctness of interpretation and decision-making.

- **Latency:** Each loop adds overhead; optimizing their sequencing and concurrency is essential for real-time or near-real-time applications.

- **Robustness:** Memory and action loops enable recovery from failures and stability under noisy or adversarial conditions.

- **Maintainability:** A modular loop design supports upgrades, monitoring, and debugging without destabilizing the system.

By mapping loops to these concerns, engineers can evaluate trade-offs systematically. For instance, increasing reasoning iterations may improve accuracy but at the cost of higher latency.

## Architectural Positioning of Loops

In practical system design, loops are not isolated. They are orchestrated within a broader agent framework that manages dependencies, scheduling, and communication. Architecture typically adopts one of three forms:

1. **Sequential Loop Orchestration:** Loops are executed in fixed order: perception → reasoning → memory → action. This structure is straightforward and reliable but may underperform when inputs or contexts evolve mid-cycle.

2. **Parallel or Asynchronous Orchestration:** Loops operate in parallel threads or processes. For example, perception may continue parsing new inputs while reasoning evaluates existing ones. This improves throughput but requires careful synchronization.

3. **Adaptive Orchestration:** Control policies dynamically adjust which loops are executed based on context. For instance, if inputs are already validated, the perception loop may be bypassed. Adaptive designs increase efficiency but demand more complex orchestration logic.

Choosing among these depends on use case constraints, such as whether the agent operates in high-frequency trading, clinical support, or enterprise automation.

## Integration with Orchestration Frameworks

Modern agentic systems often integrate with orchestration frameworks that provide capabilities such as workflow scheduling, resource allocation, and error handling. These frameworks allow loops to be expressed as modular components with well-defined interfaces. For example:

- **Perception modules** expose schema validation and entity extraction APIs.

- **Reasoning modules** expose plan-generation and constraint-satisfaction APIs.

- **Memory modules** expose retrieval and persistence APIs.

- **Action modules** expose execution and monitoring APIs.

This modularization ensures that upgrades to one loop, such as adopting a more efficient vector database for memory, do not destabilize the others.

**Design Trade-Offs**

Engineering loop-based architecture requires trade-offs that balance system quality attributes. Key considerations include:

- **Complexity vs. Maintainability:** More sophisticated loops (e.g., adaptive reasoning with probabilistic planning) may improve accuracy but can become harder to maintain, especially in distributed environments.

- **Throughput vs. Latency:** Additional iterations increase decision quality but reduce responsiveness. Batching strategies or early exits may help mitigate this.

- **Reliability vs. Resource Utilization:** Persistent memory with strong consistency guarantees may require significant storage and synchronization costs. Engineers must evaluate whether eventual consistency suffices.

- **Transparency vs. Performance:** Logging and auditing enhance observability but may add latency or storage overhead.

You need to weigh these trade-offs against the needs of the deployment domain. For instance, clinical decision support needs to be very accurate and dependable, whereas a customer support chatbot might put more emphasis on speed and scalability.

This part has laid the groundwork for understanding how perception, thinking, memory, and action loops work. Loop-based architecture allows for incremental refinement, feedback assimilation, and durability in real-world contexts, which is not possible with linear pipelines. Each loop has its own set of tasks, and when they all work together, they help with important engineering issues like accuracy, latency, robustness, and maintainability. The way they are orchestrated-sequentially, in parallel, or adaptively-affects how well the system works. To find the right balance between competing priorities, deliberate design trade-offs are needed.

In Section 2, we will build on this by going into more detail on engineering strategies for using practical design patterns, data structures, and evaluation metrics to implement perception, reasoning, and memory cycles.

## Section 2: Engineering Perception, Reasoning, and Memory Loops for Robust Performance

Engineering perception, reasoning, and memory loops require careful design choices to ensure robustness, accuracy, and efficiency in large-scale LLM-powered systems. While these loops are conceptually distinct, in practice they are tightly interconnected, and failures in one often cascade to others. This section focuses on the engineering methods, data structures, and evaluation metrics required to design each loop with production-grade reliability.

**Perception Loops: Input Processing and Validation**

The perception loop is responsible for converting raw, often noisy, inputs into structured and validated representations. Without this step, downstream reasoning becomes unstable or error prone.

**Core Functions of Perception Loops**

- **Schema validation:** Ensures that inputs conform to expected formats, such as JSON structures or API call specifications.

- **Entity recognition and extraction:** Identifies relevant entities, attributes, and relationships.

- **Noise filtering:** Removes extraneous or adversarial content.

- **Normalization:** Converts heterogeneous formats into unified representations.

**Engineering Considerations**

- **Parsing Pipelines:** Modular parsers should handle text, structured data, or multimodal signals. Error detection should include fallback mechanisms, such as attempting schema repair or escalating invalid inputs for human review.

- **Error Handling:** Perception loops must gracefully manage malformed inputs. For instance, ambiguous date formats should be disambiguated with locale-specific rules, rather than passed directly to reasoning loops.

- **Latency Constraints:** Since perception is at the front of the pipeline, delays propagate downstream. Engineers should apply lightweight preprocessing where possible and defer heavier transformations until later in the cycle.

**Evaluation Metrics**

- **Accuracy of entity extraction** (e.g., F1 score).

- **Schema compliance rate.**

- **Latency per input.**

- **Error recovery success rate.**

**Reasoning Loops: Planning and Decision-Making**

Reasoning loops transform validated inputs into plans, predictions, or decisions. Unlike perception, reasoning requires iterative exploration, evaluation, and refinement.

**Core Functions of Reasoning Loops**

- **Plan generation:** Producing structured actions or workflows based on goals and constraints.

- **Constraint handling:** Incorporating safety, compliance, or resource limitations.

- **Iterative refinement:** Re-assessing partial outputs and adjusting plans.

- **Decision stability:** Ensuring output remains consistent under minor variations in inputs.

**Engineering Considerations**

- **Deterministic vs. Probabilistic Planning:**

  - Deterministic approaches enforce strict rules and repeatable outputs, suitable for high-stakes domains such as finance or healthcare.

  - Probabilistic approaches allow exploration under uncertainty, suitable for dynamic environments like coordination or conversational systems.

- **Reasoning Horizon:** Engineers must balance depth of planning with efficiency. Long-horizon reasoning may improve accuracy but increase latency. Techniques such as hierarchical planning can mitigate this by decomposing goals into subgoals.

- **Feedback Loops:** Incorporating self-checking mechanisms, where the model critiques its own outputs against predefined criteria, can improve reliability.

## Evaluation Metrics

- **Plan quality:** Agreement with expert baselines or ground truth.
- **Consistency:** Degree of stability across repeated runs with similar inputs.
- **Efficiency:** Average iterations required before decision finalization.
- **Constraint adherence rate.**

## Techniques to Improve Reliability

- **Structured prompting:** Enforcing outputs in structured formats to reduce ambiguity.
- **Verification steps:** Validating reasoning outputs against formal constraints before execution.
- **Simulation testing:** Running reasoning loops in sandbox environments to identify failure modes before production deployment.

## Memory Loops: Retrieval, Persistence, and Update Reliability

Memory loops ensure continuity of state across multiple cycles and interactions. Without reliable memory, agents behave stateless, leading to inefficiency and inconsistency.

## Core Functions of Memory Loops

- **Retrieval:** Accessing relevant prior information to inform current reasoning.
- **Persistence:** Storing new states, decisions, or contextual embeddings.
- **Update reliability:** Ensuring stored information remains accurate and consistent over time.

## Engineering Considerations

- **Memory Structures:**
  - **Vector databases:** Support semantic similarity retrieval for unstructured data.
  - **Key–value stores:** Provide fast access for structured state data.
  - **Hybrid architecture:** Combine both for flexibility.
- **Context Management:** Memory must prioritize relevance. Strategies include sliding windows, recency-weighted retrieval, or attention-based ranking.
- **Scalability:** Large-scale memory systems must handle millions of entries while maintaining sub-second retrieval times. Sharding and indexing strategies are critical for performance.
- **Persistence Reliability:** Data durability must be maintained, with replication and checkpointing to protect against corruption or node failure.

## Evaluation Metrics

- Retrieval precision and recall.
- Update latency.
- Persistence reliability rate (successful writes and reads).

- Memory utilization efficiency.

**Failure Mitigation Strategies**

- **Fallback to defaults:** If retrieval fails, agents should revert to safe defaults.

- **Versioning:** Maintain version control of memory states to allow rollback.

- **Consistency models:** Decide between strong consistency (more reliable, less scalable) and eventual consistency (more scalable, potentially less precise).

**Interdependence of Perception, Reasoning, and Memory**

While each loop can be engineered separately, their reliability depends on integration. For example:

- A perception error (e.g., misinterpreting a date) can cascade into incorrect reasoning.

- Inadequate memory retrieval may cause redundant or contradictory reasoning.

- Excessive reasoning latency may render perception stale if the environment changes.

To mitigate such risks, systems should include:

- **Cross-loop validation:** Outputs of one loop are checked by another (e.g., memory confirming perception parsing).

- **Health monitoring:** Metrics from all loops must be logged, aggregated, and monitored in real time.

- **Failure isolation:** Errors in one loop should trigger containment protocols, preventing widespread cascading failure.

**Practical Considerations for Production Deployment**

To make perception, reasoning, and memory loops production-ready, engineers must address:

- **Logging and Monitoring:** Detailed logs should track loop-level inputs, outputs, errors, and latencies. Metrics must feed into centralized monitoring dashboards.

- **Resource Allocation:** Reasoning loops often consume disproportionate resources; load balancing and throttling are necessary.

- **Compliance Requirements:** Data retention and auditability affect how memory loops are engineered, especially in regulated industries.

- **Testing Protocols:** Regression tests should validate that loop upgrades do not introduce degradation in accuracy, latency, or robustness.

This triangular arrangement shows that loops are not just a chain, but a network with many parts that depend on each other.

The technical heart of agentic systems is made up of loops for perception, reasoning, and memory. Perception guarantees dependable input normalization, thinking generates plans and conclusions within ambiguity, and memory offers continuity and durability. Every loop needs its own engineering methods, measurements, and safety measures. Because they depend on each other, they need procedures for integrated validation, monitoring, and failure isolation. By carefully considering these factors, engineers may create LLM-powered systems that are strong, precise, and dependable even when they have to work under tight deadlines.

In Section 3, we'll talk about action loops and operational reliability. We'll focus on how agents make decisions safely, recover from failures, and combine all the loops into production deployments that can grow.

## Section 3: Designing Action Loops and Achieving Operational Reliability at Scale

The action loop is where an agent transitions from internal decision-making to external execution. It is the interface between the model's outputs and the environment in which it operates, whether that environment is a software system, a physical device, or a network of services. This section examines how to engineer reliable action loops, safeguard their operation, and integrate them into production-scale agentic architectures.

### The Role of the Action Loop

While perception, reasoning, and memory enable understanding and planning, they remain inert without execution. The action loop closes the cycle by:

- **Translating decisions into operations:** Converting structured plans or outputs into API calls, database updates, or actuator commands.

- **Verifying execution:** Confirming that intended effects occur in the environment.

- **Handling failures:** Detecting anomalies and retrying, escalating, or compensating, as necessary.

- **Providing feedback:** Returning execution outcomes to inform subsequent cycles.

In this sense, the action loop is not merely a delivery mechanism but an active participant in system stability.

### Core Design Principles

#### 1. Deterministic Execution Paths
Action pathways should be deterministic whenever possible. A decision translated into an API call or SQL query should consistently produce the same result given identical conditions. Non-determinism introduces uncertainty and complicates debugging.

#### 2. Validation Before Execution
Outputs must be validated against schema and safety constraints before being committed. For example, a financial transaction request must pass limits on value, recipient, and authorization level.

#### 3. Layered Safeguards
Critical actions should be surrounded by safeguards, such as:

- Pre-execution checks.

- Dry-run simulations.

- Approval thresholds for sensitive operations.

### Feedback-Driven Correction

Action loops must interpret response codes, logs, or sensor data to confirm outcomes. Unexpected results should trigger retries, fallbacks, or escalations.

### Failure Modes in Action Loops

Action loops are exposed to diverse failure scenarios, including:

- **Transient failures:** Network timeouts, temporary unavailability of services.

- **Permanent failures:** Invalid API keys, deprecated endpoints, or removed resources.

- **Semantic failures:** Correctly executed operations that produce unintended results, often due to incorrect assumptions in reasoning.

- **Adversarial inputs:** Malicious attempts to trick the agent into executing unsafe operations.

## Mitigation Strategies

- **Automated retries** with exponential backoff for transient issues.

- **Circuit breakers** to prevent cascading failures when dependencies are offline.

- **Compensation mechanisms** to reverse unintended operations (e.g., rollback a database transaction).

- **Escalation protocols** that alert human operators when automated strategies fail.

## Safety and Security Considerations

Action loops pose higher risks than other loops because they alter the external environment. Safeguards must therefore extend beyond error handling to include systemic security controls.

- **Authentication and Authorization:** Every outbound call should be securely stored credentials, scoped with least privilege.

- **Input Validation:** Outbound parameters must be sanitized to prevent injection attacks or malformed requests.

- **Audit Logging:** All actions should be logged with time, context, and execution results for compliance and forensic analysis.

- **Rate Limiting:** Prevent overuse of downstream systems and mitigate denial-of-service risks caused by runaway loops.

- **Sandboxing:** High-risk operations should be executed in isolated environments before deployment to production systems.

## Operational Reliability in Action Loops

Reliability engineering practices from distributed systems are directly applicable. Key methods include:

**Redundancy:** Multiple pathways for action execution reduce single points of failure. For example, fallback APIs or mirrored services.

**Monitoring and Alerting:** Metrics such as execution success rate, retry frequency, and latency should feed into monitoring systems. Threshold-based alerts help detect anomalies early.

**Graceful Degradation:** If full execution is not possible, the agent should still deliver partial functionality. For example, returning cached results when live data retrieval fails.

**Resilience Testing:** Regular failure injection (similar to chaos testing) validates whether action loops degrade gracefully under stress.

## Integrating Action Loops into Agentic Architectures

Action loops must interoperate with perception, reasoning, and memory in tightly controlled ways:

- **With Perception:** Validated output from perception help ensure that actions are well-formed.

- **With Reasoning:** Plans generated by reasoning must map unambiguously to action primitives.

- **With Memory:** Execution logs and results should be stored for later analysis and to inform future cycles.

An effective integration strategy is to treat actions as **first-class objects** in architecture, with defined schemas, metadata, and traceability. This promotes observability and reduces hidden coupling.

**Deployment at Scale**

Scaling action loops from prototypes to production requires additional considerations:

**Concurrency:** Agents may attempt parallel actions. Execution managers must enforce ordering where dependencies exist and allow safe parallelism otherwise.

**Resource Quotas:** Prevent excessive consumption of downstream resources by enforcing quotas on API calls, storage, or computer usage.

**Global Coordination:** In multi-agent systems, coordination protocols are needed to prevent conflicting actions. For example, two agents should not simultaneously attempt to allocate the same physical resource.

**Continuous Deployment:** Updates to action logic must undergo regression testing with simulated scenarios before rollout. Canary releases and staged rollouts minimize risk.

**End-to-End Monitoring and Feedback Loops**

Operational reliability depends on comprehensive monitoring. For action loops, monitoring must extend beyond execution metrics to include:

- **Outcome verification:** Did the environment actually change as expected?

- **Latency distribution:** Are actions completing within required times?

- **Error taxonomies:** Are failures transient, permanent, or semantic?

- **Loop health scores:** Composite indicators that summarize success rates across all loops.

Feedback should go up to logic and perception so that mistakes affect future choices. For instance, if an API keeps timing out, reasoning should tell you to put that path lower on your list of priorities.

In agentic architecture, the action loop makes decisions happen and ends the cycle. For reliable action design, there must be predictable pathways, layered safeguards, and complete feedback. Engineers need to plan for and deal with transitory, permanent, semantic, and adversarial failure modes. Security, safety, and compliance are very important to stopping people from using things wrong or getting unwanted results. When used on a large scale, resilience mechanisms like redundancy, gentle degradation, and monitoring keep systems stable. To keep things consistent and reliable from start to finish, action loops must also be closely linked to perception, thinking, and memory.

The four loops work together to make strong agentic AI systems. Their iterative operation allows them to be far more accurate, flexible, and resilient than standard single-pass pipelines. When designed correctly, these loops turn enormous language models into useful agents that can be used in the real world and work reliably.

# PART II: BUILDING INTELLIGENT AGENTIC SYSTEMS

Now that the basic ideas are set, this portion moves on to the real work of making intelligent agentic systems. It looks at how perception, reasoning, memory, and action loops work in real life and how they might be made better to accommodate more advanced behaviors like self-reflection, recursive reasoning, and planning complex tasks. Readers will learn how to integrate outside tools, how to make sure they are secure and reliable, and how to set up systems for judging performance. This section's chapters connect conceptual design with hands-on engineering by showing you how to turn huge language models into autonomous agents that are ready for production.

Implementing an LLM-powered agent requires more than connecting a model to an interface. Engineers must begin with clear system requirements, translate them into robust architectural foundations, and configure a development environment that ensures reliability and reproducibility. This section outlines the critical preparatory steps that determine the success of downstream implementation.

## Capturing System Requirements

The foundation of any agentic system is a rigorous requirements analysis. Without clearly defined requirements, teams risk creating fragile prototypes that fail to meet production demands. This process ensures alignment between design choices and operational needs from the very beginning.

## Functional Scope

Defining the functional scope establishes what the agent is expected to do and, just as importantly, what it will not do. This may include tasks such as document classification, workflow automation, or handling multi-turn dialogues. It also involves specifying the interaction channels, whether through text-based chat, batch file ingestion, or API endpoints. Setting boundaries prevents uncontrolled scope expansion and keeps the system focused on its intended purpose.

## Performance Targets

Clear performance targets are necessary to measure system success. Latency expectations define acceptable response times, often within two to three seconds for interactive use. Throughput requirements outline how many tasks per second or concurrent sessions the system must support. Reliability targets establish acceptable failure rates and recovery times, ensuring the system remains dependable under real-world conditions.

## Compliance and Governance

Governance and compliance rules keep both users and businesses safe. You need to find and manage sensitive data types like medical or financial records in the right way. You need to connect your system design and operations to the rules you have to follow, such HIPAA, GDPR, or PCI DSS. It's also important to be able to audit things, so there should be full records of what agents do to make sure everything is clear and to prove compliance when necessary. A structured requirements matrix helps make these things official and serves as a guide throughout the development process.

## Architectural Foundation

LLM-powered agents should be built on modular and well-documented architecture. The perception, reasoning, memory, and action loops provide a logical decomposition. Beyond this decomposition, several architectural considerations ensure stability and maintainability.

## Modular Loops

- **Perception**: Normalizes inputs and structures them.

- **Reasoning**: Performs planning and decision-making.

- **Memory**: Stores and retrieves relevant context.

- **Action**: Executes outputs through APIs or tools.

## Service-Oriented Boundaries

Each loop can be implemented as a distinct service with a defined API. This improves fault isolation, enables scaling of specific bottlenecks, and supports independent updates.

**Data Flow Contracts**

- Use schemas such as JSON Schema or Protocol Buffers to define exact input and output structures.

- Apply version control to schema definitions to support backward compatibility.

**Integration Patterns**

- **Pipeline Integration** for sequential tasks.

- **Event-Driven Integration** for asynchronous or distributed operations.

- **Hybrid Integration** when both deterministic ordering and asynchronous scaling are required.

**Core Dependencies**

The choice of supporting systems directly impacts scalability and reliability.

**Language Model Interfaces**

- **LLM APIs**: Typically accessed through REST or gRPC endpoints.

- **Prompt Templates**: Standardized prompts stored as version-controlled assets.

**Data and Knowledge Stores**

- **Vector Databases**: For embedding-based retrieval.

- **Relational Databases**: For structured records and audit logs.

- **Key-Value Stores**: For fast access to session data.

**Orchestration Frameworks**

- Workflow orchestration tools such as Airflow or Prefect for batch processing.

- Task queues such as Celery or Kafka for event-driven execution.

**Monitoring and Logging Tools**

- Centralized logging using ELK (Elasticsearch, Logstash, Kibana) or Splunk.

- Metrics collection with Prometheus and visualization in Grafana.

- Distributed tracing using OpenTelemetry.

**Development Environment Setup**

The environment for developing LLM-powered agents must support reproducibility, collaboration, and controlled experimentation.

**Environment Reproducibility**

- Use containerization (Docker) with pinned dependencies.

- Store infrastructure configurations with Infrastructure as Code (e.g., Terraform, Ansible).

**Configuration Management**

- Centralize environment variables and secrets using vaults such as HashiCorp Vault.

- Version-control all configuration files.

**Testing Frameworks**

- Unit tests for validating module contracts.

- Integration tests with mock LLM responses.

- End-to-end tests using representative datasets.

**Experiment Management**

- Track model prompts, parameters, and outputs using experiment tracking systems such as MLflow.

- Record performance metrics for reproducibility of evaluations.

**Clinical-Style Example: Document Processing Agent**

Consider a document-processing agent deployed in a healthcare environment.

- **Requirements**: Classify intake forms, extract structured data, and summarize notes. Latency must remain below 2.5 seconds. Compliance must meet HIPAA standards.

- **Architecture**: Modular loops deployed as microservices with a shared vector database and orchestrator. Logs and metrics are integrated into a Grafana dashboard.

- **Dependencies**: REST-based LLM API, Postgres for structured storage, and a vector database for context retrieval.

- **Development Environment**: Dockerized services with Terraform-managed infrastructure, version-controlled schemas, and MLflow experiment tracking.

- **Governance**: Access control policies restrict retrieval of sensitive patient identifiers, and all actions are logged for compliance audits.

This example illustrates how requirements translate directly into architecture, dependencies, and environment configurations.

Before implementing LLM-powered agents, engineers must complete three foundational steps:

1. Capture precise requirements covering scope, performance, and compliance.

2. Establish modular architectural foundations with clear contracts and integration patterns.

3. Configure a reproducible development environment with secure governance and observability.

## Section 2: Step-by-Step Implementation of Core Agent Modules

Implementing an LLM-powered agent requires methodical construction of each functional loop. This section provides a detailed guide for building the perception, reasoning, memory, and action modules. Each module must be developed with strict attention to modularity, robustness, and interoperability to support scaling and long-term maintainability

**Perception Module: Input Normalization and Structuring**

The perception module is responsible for transforming raw inputs into structured representations that the reasoning engine can use.

**Core Responsibilities**

- **Validation**: Ensure inputs conform to schema requirements.

- **Normalization**: Standardize inputs across formats, encodings, and data types.

- **Segmentation**: Break inputs into relevant units such as paragraphs, records, or tokens.

- **Annotation**: Enrich data with metadata such as timestamps, source identifiers, and user IDs.

**Implementation Steps**

1. **Define Input Schema**:

   o For text, establish constraints such as UTF-8 encoding and maximum token length.

   o For multimodal inputs, define structured payloads (e.g., JSON with fields for text, image, and metadata).

2. **Build Preprocessing Pipelines**:

   o Text cleaning (punctuation normalization, whitespace trimming).

   o Language detection for multilingual inputs.

   o Tokenization is aligned with the LLM tokenizer.

3. **Apply Error Handling**:

   o Reject malformed inputs with structured error messages.

   o Log all rejected inputs for auditing.

**Example Pipeline (Clinical Document Intake)**

1. Receive scanned PDF.

2. Convert to text using OCR.

3. Normalize text encoding to UTF-8.

4. Segment into sections (patient details, history, observations).

5. Validate against schema before passing to reasoning module.

**Reasoning Module: Decision-Making and Planning**

The reasoning module is the central control unit of the agent. It converts structured inputs into planned actions or outputs.

**Core Responsibilities**

- **Task Understanding**: Map input to task type.

- **Decomposition**: Break complex tasks into ordered subtasks.

- **Decision-Making**: Select the best sequence of actions.

- **Error Recovery**: Detect inconsistencies and attempt corrective actions.

## Implementation Approaches

Different approaches can be taken when implementing intelligent agent systems, each offering unique strengths depending on the task at hand. One method is prompt engineering with templates, where standardized formats are stored for common reasoning tasks. These templates can be adapted to new situations through variable substitution, allowing the system to quickly align with incoming data while maintaining consistency in structure and reasoning style.

Another useful strategy is chain-of-thought structuring, which encourages the agent to produce reasoning in a clear, step-by-step manner. This structured thinking not only improves transparency but also makes it easier to post-process the reasoning trail and extract the final decision. By making the intermediate steps explicit, the system gains both interpretability and a higher likelihood of generating sound outputs.

The planner-executor pattern offers a more deliberate and organized approach. In this setup, a planner component produces a structured plan, outlining the sequence of steps needed to achieve a goal. The executor then carries out those steps, often by invoking the appropriate functions or APIs. This division of labor ensures that the system can balance abstract reasoning with precise execution, improving its ability to handle complex tasks.

Finally, fallback strategies are critical for ensuring robustness. When the primary method fails or produces unsatisfactory results, the system can attempt the task again using alternative prompts or strategies. For critical tasks where uncertainty cannot be tolerated, it can escalate to deterministic fallback logic, ensuring reliability even under adverse conditions. Together, these approaches provide a flexible toolkit for building adaptive, resilient, and intelligent agent systems.

## Example Workflow (Logistics Request)

- Input: Delivery request with missing address details.

- Reasoning process:

    1. Detect incomplete information.

    2. Formulate plan: request clarification → validate details → confirm task.

    3. Pass plan to action module for execution.

## Memory Module: Context Persistence and Retrieval

The memory module provides continuity across interactions and supports retrieval of relevant knowledge.

## Core Responsibilities

- **Short-Term Memory**: Maintain conversational state or task context within a session.

- **Long-Term Memory**: Store knowledge across sessions, such as historical records.

- **Retrieval**: Provide relevant context to the reasoning module.

- **Update Mechanisms**: Write back new knowledge and remove obsolete data.

## Storage Options

- **Vector Databases**: Store embeddings for semantic search.

- **Relational Databases**: Maintain structured records, logs, and metadata.

- **Key-Value Stores**: Support low-latency access to session state.

## Retrieval-Augmented Generation (RAG) Pattern

1. Encode query into embedding.

2. Retrieve top-k similar vectors.

3. Supply retrieved text snippets to LLM prompt as context.

4. Produce augmented reasoning output.

## Example Workflow (Customer Support Agent)

- Input: "What is the status of my last order?"

- Memory process:

    1. Identify customer ID from context.

    2. Query order history from relational database.

    3. Retrieving last order details.

    4. Supply details to reasoning module to form final response.

## Action Module: Tool Use and Execution

The action module interfaces with external systems to complete tasks based on reasoning outputs.

## Core Responsibilities

- **Command Interpretation**: Parse structured reasoning output into executable actions.

- **Tool Invocation**: Call APIs, databases, or external programs.

- **Response Handling**: Capture results and feedback into reasoning or memory.

- **Safety Checks**: Prevent unsafe or unauthorized actions.

## Implementation Steps

1. **Define Tool Registry**:

    o Each tool is defined by name, input schema, output schema, and authentication.

    o Example: send email (to string, subject: string, body: string).

2. **Implement Execution Layer**:

    o Validate inputs against schema.

    o Send requests with proper authentication.

    o Handle errors with retry policies.

3. **Result Feedback**:

- o Return structured success or failure messages.
- o Store results in memory if relevant for future tasks.

## Example Workflow (Healthcare Agent)

- Reasoning output: schedule appointment (patient_id=123, time="2025-09-15 10:00").
- Action process:
    1. Validate patient ID against database.
    2. Call scheduling API.
    3. Confirm success.
    4. Log action to audit system.

## Cross-Module Coordination

Although modules are designed independently, their interactions must be carefully orchestrated.

## Orchestration Options

- **Central Orchestrator**: One service manages all loops in strict sequence.
- **Event Bus**: Modules communicate via events with loosely coupled coordination.
- **Hybrid**: Orchestrator for critical paths, event-driven messaging for background updates.

## Control Flow Example

1. Perception normalizes input.
2. Reasoning generates plan.
3. Memory provides context for missing details.
4. Action executes plan.
5. Output returned to user.

## Error Handling and Recovery

LLM-powered agents must handle uncertainty and partial failures.

## Techniques

- **Validation Layers**: Reject invalid inputs before reaching LLM.
- **Retry Policies**: Apply exponential backoff when external APIs fail.
- **Fallback Logic**: Switch to deterministic logic when reasoning fails.
- **Error Logging**: Record errors with full trace for debugging.

## Example Error Handling Flow

1. Input arrives with missing required field.

2. Perception flags error and prompts user for correction.

3. Reasoning retrieves with corrected input.

4. Action completes successfully.

**Clinical-Style Example: Patient Scheduling Agent**

**Requirements**: Receive appointment requests, check patient eligibility, and confirm scheduling.

**Implementation**:

- **Perception**: Validate input form, normalize patient identifiers.

- **Reasoning**: Plan sequence of steps (verify eligibility → find available slot → confirm booking).

- **Memory**: Retrieve patient history and prior appointments.

- **Action**: Execute scheduling API call and send confirmation.

**Flow**: Input form → normalized JSON → reasoning plan → memory query → scheduling API → confirmation message → audit log.

Implementing LLM-powered agents requires modular construction across four critical loops:

1. Perception ensures inputs are validated, normalized, and structured.

2. Reasoning decomposes tasks, generates plans, and manages decision-making.

3. Memory provides contextual continuity and knowledge retrieval.

4. Action executes plans through controlled tool use and integration.

With strict modular boundaries, error handling, and orchestration strategies, these modules form a reliable foundation for scalable and compliant agent systems.

## Section 3: Testing, Deployment, and Operationalization of LLM Agents

Constructing modular perception, reasoning, memory, and action loops is only the foundation of an LLM-powered agent. To achieve reliability in production environments, these modules must be integrated, tested, deployed, and maintained using disciplined engineering practices. This section provides a practical guide to operationalizing agents at scale.

**Testing Strategies for LLM-Powered Agents**

Testing agentic systems is more complex than testing deterministic software due to probabilistic outputs and emergent behaviors. A layered approach ensures that each module and integration pathway performs reliably.

**Unit Testing of Individual Modules**

- **Perception Module**: Validate input schemas, encoding normalization, and preprocessing pipelines.

- **Reasoning Module**: Test prompt templates, task classification, and plan decomposition.

- **Memory Module**: Verify read and write operations, retrieval quality, and embedding generation.

- **Action Module**: Confirm API invocations, input validation, and error handling.

**Integration Testing**

Integration tests ensure modules interact as expected:

1. Feed structured input through perception.
2. Confirm reasoning generates appropriate plan.
3. Verify memory provides correct contextual retrieval.
4. Ensure action module executes plan correctly.

## Stress and Fault-Injection Testing

- **Stress Testing**: Simulate high request volumes to observe latency and throughput under load.
- **Fault Injection**: Deliberately causes API failures, malformed inputs, or memory timeouts to evaluate resilience.

## Evaluation Metrics

- **Accuracy**: Task completion rate and correctness of outputs.
- **Latency**: Time from input receipt to action completion.
- **Cost Efficiency**: Token usage and infrastructure overhead.
- **Reliability**: Mean time between failures (MTBF).

A tabular framework for test types and metrics provides engineers with clear coverage mapping.

## Benchmarking Agent Performance

Benchmarking ensures that the agent meets operational thresholds. Unlike deterministic systems, benchmarking LLM agents require scenario-based testing.

## Example Benchmarks

- **Perception**: Text parsing accuracy across 1,000 varied input samples.
- **Reasoning**: Plan correctness rate on standardized test cases.
- **Memory**: Retrieval precision at k=5 on knowledge base queries.
- **Action**: Execution success rate for API calls with 99.9% uptime target.

Benchmark datasets can be domain-specific, such as medical records, financial transactions, or coordination orders. Consistency in benchmarking provides evidence for compliance and customer assurance.

## Deployment Models

Deployment of LLM-powered agents depends on organizational infrastructure and compliance requirements.

## Local Deployment

- **Use Case**: Development, prototyping, and testing.
- **Advantages**: Lower cost, developer control.
- **Limitations**: Limited scalability, manual updates.

## Containerized Deployment

- **Use Case**: Standardized deployment across environments.
- **Advantages**: Reproducibility, dependency isolation.
- **Tools**: Docker, Kubernetes.

## Cloud-Native Deployment

- **Use Case**: Enterprise-scale operations.
- **Advantages**: Elastic scaling, managed infrastructure, high availability.
- **Considerations**: Vendor lock-in, data residency compliance.

## Observability and Monitoring

Observability ensures that engineers can track agent behavior in production.

### Logging

- Log structured events at each module boundary.
- Include correlation IDs to trace requests through perception, reasoning, memory, and action loops.

### Metrics

- **Module-Level Metrics**:
    - Perception: input acceptance rate.
    - Reasoning: plan success rate.
    - Memory: retrieval latency.
    - Action: API success percentage.
- **System-Level Metrics**: Overall task completion rate, request latency distribution.

### Distributed Tracing

Trace entire workflows across services to diagnose latency bottlenecks and cascading failures.

### Alerts

Configure threshold-based alerts for latency spikes, API failure rates, or abnormal token usage.

## Scaling Strategies

Scaling agents require balancing computing efficiency with reliability.

### Horizontal Replication

- Run multiple replicas of the agent service behind a load balancer.
- Each replica processes independent requests.

### Elastic Scaling

- Automatically scale replicas go up or down based on demand.

- Requires integration with orchestration tools like Kubernetes or serverless frameworks.

**Workload Partitioning**

- Assign specialized agent instances to different task categories.

- Example: separate agents for data extraction, reasoning, and action execution.

**Memory Scaling**

- Shard vector databases to support larger knowledge bases.

- Apply caching layers for frequently accessed data.

**Maintenance and Iterative Improvement**

Once deployed, agents require continuous improvement.

**Version Control**

- Store prompts, templates, and orchestration workflows in source control.

- Tag releases for reproducibility.

**Continuous Integration and Continuous Deployment (CI/CD)**

- Automated pipelines for running test suites.

- Deploy to staging and production environments with rollback support.

**Feedback Loops**

- Collect user feedback and error logs.

- Use feedback to refine reasoning templates and memory retrieval logic.

**Lifecycle Management**

- Regularly update dependencies and APIs.

- Decommission obsolete modules safely.

**Case Walkthrough: Enterprise Workflow Automation Agent**

Consider an enterprise deploying an LLM-powered workflow automation agent in a financial services context.

**Step 1: Testing**

- Build test suite of 5,000 transaction requests.

- Benchmark accuracy (98%), latency (1.2 seconds median), and API success (99.95%).

**Step 2: Deployment**

- Stage in containerized environment with Kubernetes.

- Migrate to cloud-native cluster with autoscaling enabled.

**Step 3: Monitoring**

- Log all perception errors, reasoning failures, and action retries.
- Enable distributed tracing for inter-service workflows.

**Step 4: Scaling**

- Deploy 20 replicas for peak demand.
- Partition workloads by transaction type: payments, reporting, compliance checks.

**Step 5: Maintenance**

- Weekly prompt updates reviewed via CI/CD.
- Monthly security audits of API integrations.

Operationalizing LLM-powered agents requires disciplined processes across testing, deployment, observability, scaling, and maintenance.

1. Rigorous testing ensures reliability across modules.
2. Benchmarking provides measurable evidence of performance.
3. Deployment models range from local prototyping to cloud-native scaling.
4. Observability practices enable real-time monitoring and troubleshooting.
5. Scaling strategies support enterprise-grade workloads.
6. Maintenance practices sustain long-term performance and compliance.

When implemented systematically, these practices convert modular prototypes into robust production agents capable of serving critical real-world applications.

## Section 1: Foundations and Mechanisms of Recursive Reasoning

One of the most important advanced behaviors in agentic AI systems is recursive thinking. The essence of recursive reasoning enables an agent to iteratively apply a reasoning process, either to its own outputs or to segmented issue states, until a suitable solution is reached. This method is similar to what is done in domains like cognitive architectures, logic programming, and search-based problem solving. In the realm of large language model (LLM)-driven agents, recursive reasoning facilitates enhanced analysis, iterative refinement, and methodical investigation of alternate solutions.

This part talks about the ideas, tools, and building blocks that make recursive reasoning possible in agentic AI.

### Definition and Scope

In traditional computing, recursion refers to a function calling itself with modified parameters until a termination condition is reached. In agentic AI, recursive reasoning takes a similar structural role but applies to decision-making and problem decomposition rather than purely mathematical operations.

### Characteristics of Recursive Reasoning in Agents

- Iterative Process: Reasoning steps are repeated until a goal condition is satisfied.

- Decomposition: Large problems are broken into smaller sub-problems.

- Feedback Incorporation: Each cycle incorporates output from previous cycles.

- Termination Criteria: Defined stopping points prevent infinite loops.

For example, when analyzing a complex document, an agent may first identify major sections, then recursively analyze each section into paragraphs, then further refine the interpretation at the sentence level.

### Historical Parallels

Recursive reasoning in AI systems has clear antecedents in earlier computational frameworks:

- Cognitive Architectures: Systems such as Soar and ACT-R implemented recursive problem solving through production rules and subgoal creation.

- Search Algorithms: Depth-first and breadth-first search use recursive structures to explore decision trees.

- Expert Systems: Early rule-based systems often applied recursive evaluation of inference chains to resolve complex diagnoses.

These precedents demonstrate that recursion is a well-established principle for handling complexity, now adapted for the probabilistic reasoning style of LLMs.

### Core Implementations

Several implementation approaches have proven effective for enabling recursive reasoning in LLM-based agents.

### Iterative Prompting

The agent re-prompts itself with the output of a prior reasoning step.

- Input: Original question.

- Output: Partial reasoning trace.

- Next Step: Feed reasoning trace back into the model with instructions to refine or expand.

- Termination: Predefined number of iterations or convergence to consistent output.

## Tree Search Methods

The agent expands multiple candidate reasoning paths in parallel.

- Breadth-First Search: Explore reasoning alternatives at each level before progressing.

- Depth-First Search: Explore one reasoning path deeply before backtracking.

- Best-First Search: Use scoring metrics to prioritize more promising paths.

## Planner-Executor Loops

Reasoning is divided into a recursive planner and executor.

- Planner: Generates a sequence of steps, with nested sub-steps.

- Executor: Implements each step and reports results back to planner.

- Recursion occurs when the planner decomposes a step into new sub-steps.

## Architectural Requirements

Supporting recursive reasoning in a modular agent architecture requires a set of core capabilities that ensure both stability and efficiency. One of the most important is state management, which allows the system to maintain structured records of reasoning traces as it moves through multiple iterations. This not only preserves continuity but also guarantees consistency when earlier outputs are revised or expanded during recursion.

Equally critical is the presence of control logic. Without boundaries, recursive reasoning risks falling into infinite loops or unnecessary complexity. Defining recursion depth limits and clear stopping conditions-whether that is the successful completion of a plan or the exhaustion of a maximum number of iterations-helps the system remain both efficient and predictable.

Evaluation hooks add another layer of refinement by enabling the system to validate progress at each step. Through scoring mechanisms or targeted checks, the agent can quickly identify when a line of reasoning is unproductive and discard it before wasting additional resources. This selective pruning ensures that only the most promising paths are pursued further.

Finally, resource monitoring safeguards against inefficiency and runaway costs. By tracking token consumption, iteration time, and overall computational expense, the system can make informed decisions about whether to continue or halt the process. If thresholds for time, tokens, or costs are exceeded, recursion can be terminated before it undermines the system's practicality. Together, these architectural requirements create a balanced foundation that allows recursive reasoning to be both powerful and manageable.

## Trade-Off Analysis

Recursive reasoning provides powerful benefits but introduces measurable costs.

## Benefits

- Deeper Analysis: Enables multi-step problem solving that exceeds single-pass reasoning.

- Improved Accuracy: Iterative refinement can reduce errors.

- Flexibility: Supports decomposition of tasks of varying complexity.

**Limitations**

- Latency: Multiple cycles increase response time.

- Resource Consumption: Higher token usage and computer load.

- Complexity: Requires robust control mechanisms to prevent runaway loops.

- Debugging Challenges: Recursion introduces multiple potential failure points.

**Example Trade-Off Table**

| Factor | Positive Impact | Negative Impact |
|---|---|---|
| Accuracy | Increased correctness | Diminishing returns after depth |
| Latency | Better quality with more steps | Longer processing times |
| Cost | Potential higher reliability | Increased computer expenditure |
| Maintainability | Modular recursion improves clarity | More complex orchestration logic |

**Clinical-Style Illustration: Recursive Reasoning in Differential Diagnosis**

A diagnostic support agent may use recursive reasoning to assist clinicians in narrowing down conditions.

Workflow:

1. Initial Input: Patient presents with fever and cough.

2. First Reasoning Pass: Agent generates a list of common conditions (influenza, pneumonia, bronchitis).

3. Recursive Decomposition: For each condition, agent evaluates additional distinguishing symptoms.

4. Feedback Integration: Incorporate laboratory results.

5. Termination: Converge on diagnosis with supporting evidence.

In this case, recursion helps the agent narrow down from many options to specific differential outcomes, just to how clinical workflows test and rule out hypotheses over and over.

Recursive reasoning gives LLM-powered agents organized ways to solve problems, break them down, and improve them over and over again. The method is based on well-known ideas from cognitive architectures and search algorithms, but they have been changed to work with probabilistic LLM reasoning. Recursion makes things more accurate and flexible, but it also adds latency, cost, and complexity that must be addressed by careful architecture design.

Now that we've laid the groundwork, the next section will look at self-reflection techniques, which work well with recursion since they let agents review and improve their work.

## Section 2: Techniques and Frameworks for Self-Reflection in Agentic Systems

Self-reflection is an advanced activity that goes along with recursive reasoning. Recursion lets you break down and build on problems over and over again, whereas self-reflection lets an agent look at, criticize, and improve his own work. In practice, self-reflection adds a meta-cognitive layer to the system, which looks at both the validity of its results and the reasoning techniques that led to them.

This part talks about the practical ways, architectural needs, and set frameworks for adding self-reflection to LLM-powered agents.

### Definition and Scope

Self-reflection in agentic AI is the structured process of analyzing prior outputs with the explicit goal of detecting weaknesses, inconsistencies, or opportunities for improvement. Unlike recursion, which is focused on solving sub-problems, self-reflection centers on evaluating solution quality.

### Characteristics of Self-Reflection

- Meta-Evaluation: The agent critiques its own reasoning traces and outputs.

- Error Detection: Identification of logical inconsistencies, factual inaccuracies, or misaligned steps.

- Corrective Refinement: Proposes revisions or alternate reasoning paths.

- Feedback Loop: The evaluation process feeds into subsequent reasoning cycles.

### Core Mechanisms

Self-reflection in LLM-powered agents can be implemented through several widely recognized techniques.

### Output Critique and Revision

- Step 1: Agent generates an initial output.

- Step 2: A dedicated reflection pass critiques the output using predefined evaluation criteria.

- Step 3: Revised output is generated based on critique findings.

This mirrors academic peer review, where an initial draft undergoes systematic review before publication.

### Self-Consistency Checking

The agent generates multiple reasoning paths and then compares them to identify consistent conclusions.

- Agreement across paths increases confidence.

- Divergence triggers reflection on which path aligns better with available evidence.

### Rule-Based Validation

Integration of external validation rules into the reflection loop.

- Syntax rules for programming tasks.

- Domain-specific clinical guidelines for medical reasoning.

- Mathematical verification for quantitative outputs.

### Confidence Estimation

Assigning confidence scores to outputs and invoking self-reflection when confidence is below threshold.

- Probabilistic calibration techniques.

- Heuristic metrics such as reasoning depth or evidence coverage.

## Architectural Requirements

Implementing self-reflection in agent systems requires carefully designed architectural components that enable the agent to critique and refine its own reasoning. At the center of this process is a dedicated reflection module, a specialized reasoning unit that takes on the role of evaluation. This module can be instantiated either through a secondary call to a language model or through a targeted evaluation function designed for systematic critique. By separating reflection from primary reasoning, the system gains a structured way to review its outputs before finalizing them.

To guide this reflection, an evaluation criteria repository is essential. This repository houses explicit rules, checklists, or domain-specific metrics that define what successful reasoning should look like. Whether it involves adhering to coding style conventions or following medical safety protocols, these criteria ensure that reflection is grounded in objective standards rather than arbitrary judgments.

Another critical element is memory integration, which allows the agent to store and recall its reflection history. By recording past errors and common failure patterns, the system can avoid repeating the same mistakes, ultimately becoming more efficient and reliable over time. This historical awareness strengthens the corrective power of reflection and accelerates improvement across repeated tasks.

Finally, control logic plays a crucial role in governing when and how reflection should occur. It determines the conditions that trigger reflective evaluation, manages the recursion between reasoning and reflection, and prevents endless cycles of self-review that would stall progress. Established frameworks in the field already demonstrate how such mechanisms can be structured, showing the value of embedding disciplined self-reflection into LLM-based systems for improved accuracy, safety, and adaptability.

## Reflexion Framework

- Introduces a dedicated self-reflection loop where the agent critiques past actions and adjusts strategies.

- Demonstrated effectiveness in reinforcement learning tasks by improving sample efficiency and stability.

## Chain-of-Thought with Reflection

- Extends standard chain-of-thought prompting with an additional evaluation step.

- Example: After reasoning through a problem, the model checks for logical consistency before finalizing the answer.

## Debate-Based Reflection

- Multiple agents generate competing answers.

- A reflective module or external adjudicator compares and synthesizes results.

- Useful in high-stakes domains where cross-validation improves reliability.

## Self-Improving Prompts

- Agents refine their own instructions by reflecting on task performance.

- This approach reduces dependency on manual prompt engineering. Practical Techniques

## Structured Self-Review Checklists

- Logic Verification: Are steps internally consistent?

- Evidence Alignment: Are claims supported by inputs or references?

- Completeness: Are all sub-questions addressed?

- Clarity: Is the explanation unambiguous?

## Automated Error Detection

- Use static analysis tools for code.

- Apply domain-specific validators for structured data.

- Integrate quality assurance pipelines for outputs.

## Confidence Thresholding Workflow

| Step | Action | Example |
|------|--------|---------|
| 1 | Generate initial output | Draft diagnosis |
| 2 | Estimate confidence | Low confidence score |
| 3 | Trigger reflection | Apply domain checklist |
| 4 | Revise output | Adjust diagnosis with supporting labs |
| 5 | Finalize result | Output revised, validated answer |

## Clinical-Style Illustration: Self-Reflection in Treatment Planning

Consider an agent assisting in clinical treatment planning:

1. Initial Plan Generation: Based on symptoms, lab results, and guidelines, the agent recommends a treatment plan.

2. Reflection Pass: The agent reviews the plan using a checklist: contraindications, dosage alignment, and consistency with evidence-based standards.

3. Error Detection: Detects a dosage inconsistency with patient weight.

4. Refinement: Revises the dosage recommendation.

5. Finalization: Outputs corrected plan for physician review.

This demonstrates self-reflection as a safeguard mechanism, improving reliability and patient safety.

## Trade-Off Analysis

Benefits

- Error Reduction: Self-reflection reduces factual and logical errors.

- Improved Reliability: Produces more consistent and verifiable outputs.

- Adaptability: Supports dynamic correction across varied domains.

Limitations

- Latency Increase: Reflection adds additional computation cycles.

- Complexity in Design: Requires dedicated evaluation modules.

- Diminishing Returns: Excessive reflection may overfit or slow performance without proportional benefits.

**Example Comparison Table**

| Factor | With Reflection | Without Reflection |
|---|---|---|
| Accuracy | Higher due to error correction | Lower due to uncorrected mistakes |
| Latency | Longer due to extra cycle | Shorter response time |
| Reliability | More consistent results | More variability |
| Cost | Higher due to additional tokens | Lower but riskier outputs |

**Integration with Recursive Reasoning**

Self-reflection and recursive reasoning operate in complementary ways:

- Recursive reasoning decomposes complex tasks.

- Self-reflection ensures each decomposed solution is valid and consistent.

They work together to provide a dual mechanism in which tasks are solved again and over again and checked all the time, making agentic systems stronger overall.

Self-reflection gives LLM-powered agents a disciplined way to look at and improve their own work. It uses well-known methods like criticism and revision, checking for consistency, and rule-based validation. It needs special reflection modules, evaluation criteria repositories, and memory and control logic integration in terms of architecture. Self-reflection is an important feature in advanced agent design since it makes things more accurate and reliable, even though it costs more and takes longer to compute.

The last part will show how to use recursion and reflection together in a single process, focusing on how to build strong, large-scale systems.

## Section 3: Integration, Evaluation, and Operational Considerations for Advanced Behaviors

Recursive reasoning and self-reflection represent advanced behaviors that significantly improve the robustness and reliability of LLM-powered agents. Implementing these capabilities independently can yield value, but the highest levels of performance are achieved when both are integrated within carefully designed system architectures. This section details strategies for combining recursion and reflection, evaluation methodologies for assessing their effectiveness, and operational considerations for scaling them into production environments.

### Combining Recursive Reasoning and Self-Reflection

Recursive reasoning and self-reflection complement each other functionally. Recursive reasoning decomposes complex problems into structured sub-steps, while self-reflection verifies that those steps and their outputs maintain correctness, consistency, and alignment with goals.

### Sequential Integration

A common pattern is to apply recursion first, followed by reflection:

1. Recursive Expansion: Task is decomposed into sub-steps.

2. Sub-Step Execution: Each branch or task is completed.

3. Self-Reflection Pass: Outputs are validated and refined against quality criteria.

This ensures that while recursion generates potential solutions, reflection improves their quality.

**Interleaved Integration**

An alternative pattern is to interleave reflection within recursive cycles:

1. Decompose a task into a sub-step.

2. Solve sub-step.

3. Immediately reflect on that solution.

4. Only then proceed to the next sub-step.

This approach catches errors earlier in the reasoning process, reducing propagation of mistakes across later stages.

**Hybrid Integration**

Hybrid strategies allow for flexible switching between sequential and interleaved reflection depending on task type or confidence thresholds. For example:

- Use interleaved reflection for high-stakes sub-tasks such as compliance validation.

- Use sequential reflection for low-stakes tasks where efficiency is more critical.

**Evaluation Methodologies**

Measuring the effectiveness of recursion and reflection requires structured evaluation techniques. Established metrics and benchmarking protocols should be used to avoid overestimating benefits.

**Benchmark Datasets**

- Reasoning Benchmarks: Datasets such as GSM8K for arithmetic reasoning and StrategyQA for multi-step logical reasoning.

- Domain-Specific Corpora: Medical guidelines, financial compliance records, or programming tasks depending on the deployment environment.

**Metrics**

- Error Reduction Rate: Percentage decrease in factual or logical errors due to reflection.

- Task Completion Accuracy: Improved success rate when recursion is added.

- Consistency Score: Degree of agreement across recursive reasoning paths.

- Latency Overhead: Additional time introduced by recursion and reflection.

- Cost Efficiency: Token usage or computational cost relative to accuracy gains.

**Evaluation Frameworks**

- Ablation Testing: Compare performance with recursion only, reflection only, and both integrated.

- Controlled Error Injection: Intentionally introduce errors to evaluate reflection's ability to detect and correct them.

- Human-in-the-Loop Validation: For high-stakes domains, involve subject matter experts to assess corrected outputs.

**Deployment Strategies**

Integrating recursion and reflection into production environments requires careful system-level design.

**Controlling Recursion Depth**

Uncontrolled recursion can lead to excessive latency and costs.

- Set maximum recursion depth parameters.
- Introduce early stopping rules when solutions converge.

**Setting Reflection Triggers**

Reflection should not be applied indiscriminately.

- Use confidence thresholds to trigger reflection only on low-confidence outputs.
- Define domain-specific triggers, such as compliance-critical tasks.

**Managing Computational Costs**

- Implement caching for repeated sub-queries.
- Use lightweight validation models for reflection rather than full-scale LLMs.
- Apply batching strategies to handle multiple reflection tasks in parallel.

**Monitoring and Observability**

To ensure reliability of recursive and reflective processes, monitoring must be built into operational workflows.

**Key Observability Metrics**

- Recursion Utilization: Number of recursive expansions per task.
- Reflection Frequency: Proportion of outputs undergoing reflection.
- Error Detection Rate: Percentage of reflection cycles resulting in corrections.
- System Latency: Additional time per cycle introduced by advanced behaviors.

**Monitoring Infrastructure**

- Logging Pipelines: Capture recursion depth, reflection critiques, and revisions.
- Dashboards: Visualize error trends, latency profiles, and reflection triggers.
- Alerts: Triggered when recursion depth exceeds thresholds or reflection error detection rate drops.

**Scaling Considerations**

Scaling recursive and reflective behaviors across large agent systems introduces further engineering challenges.

**Distributed Recursion**

When tasks involve multiple agents or nodes:

- Decompose recursions across distributed workers.

- Aggregate intermediate outputs through a central coordinator.

## Parallel Reflection

Reflection can be parallelized by:

- Running multiple reflections passes on independent sub-tasks simultaneously.
- Aggregating results via ensemble or voting mechanisms.

## Resource Allocation

Reflection and recursion demand significant computational resources, making careful allocation essential for efficient operation. Workflows that rely heavily on reflection often benefit from dedicated GPUs or hardware accelerators to handle the added processing load. To balance performance with efficiency, resource allocation should also be prioritized according to the criticality of the task. High-stakes processes, such as those involving compliance or safety, warrant greater computational investment than less sensitive operations.

An enterprise-scale workflow automation agent for processing insurance claims illustrates how these principles can be applied in practice. Such an agent may employ recursive reasoning to break down a complex claim into distinct sub-tasks, including eligibility checks, documentation review, fraud detection, and the final approval stage. Each of these sub-tasks can then be solved independently by specialized modules, ensuring precision at every step.

Throughout the process, interleaved reflection allows the system to validate results in real time. For instance, the eligibility assessment is not only calculated but also cross-verified against relevant policy databases, reducing the risk of oversight. Once all sub-tasks are completed, a comprehensive final reflection pass is performed to ensure compliance, detect inconsistencies, and identify potential anomalies before the decision is finalized.

The workflow concludes with an output finalization phase, where the system produces a verified claim decision. Alongside this, detailed audit logs are generated to capture the entire reasoning process as well as each reflective step. These records provide transparency and accountability, meeting regulatory standards while reinforcing trust in the system's reliability.

## Best Practices Summary

| Best Practice | Purpose | Implementation Detail |
|---|---|---|
| Limit recursion depth | Prevents runaway cycles | Set maximum step thresholds |
| Trigger selective reflection | Reduces latency and cost | Confidence- or domain-based triggers |
| Use hybrid integration | Balance efficiency and safety | Apply interleaved for critical tasks, sequential for others |
| Monitor key metrics | Ensure operational stability | Track recursion depth, reflection frequency, and latency |
| Optimize resources | Controlling computer costs | Use lightweight evaluators, caching, and batching |

Recursive reasoning and self-reflection work together as a twin mechanism to make LLM-powered agents far more reliable, accurate, and easy to audit. To avoid high costs or long waiting times, their integration needs careful design, appraisal, and operational protection. When used correctly, these sophisticated behaviors let agentic systems handle complicated workflows with organized reasoning and built-in error correction. This makes them reliable for large-scale deployments.

## Section 1: Architectures and Interfaces for External Tool Integration

Using external tools is one of the things that sets a simple LLM-driven conversational agent apart from an engineered autonomous system. Engineers can increase the number of things agents can do while keeping them accurate, efficient, and reliable by linking language models to structured external capabilities like databases, APIs, or computational engines. But this needs thorough planning of the architecture and strong control of the interface. This part talks about the rules, design patterns, and operational needs for making it possible for agentic systems to work with outside tools.

### The Role of External Tools

LLMs excel at pattern recognition, text generation, and unstructured reasoning, but they are not optimized for deterministic computation, persistent storage, or domain-specific retrieval. External tools fill these gaps.

### Primary roles of external tools in agent workflows:

- **Computation**: Handling precise numeric or symbolic calculations beyond LLM reliability.

- **Knowledge Retrieval**: Querying structured databases or searching indexes for up-to-date or domain-specific information.

- **Action Execution**: Performing actions in external systems such as booking, file manipulation, or workflow orchestration.

- **Verification**: Validating outputs, for example running code snippets or cross-checking results with authoritative systems.

### Architectural Layers for Tool Integration

A well-structured architecture separates the reasoning core of the agent from the execution layer where tools are invoked. This reduces complexity and improves security.

1. **Reasoning Core**: The LLM handles problem understanding, task decomposition, and decision-making.

2. **Tool Interface Layer**: Middleware responsible for invoking external APIs or services. Includes schema definitions, authentication, and error handling.

3. **External Systems**: Databases, APIs, symbolic engines, or enterprise applications that provide capabilities unavailable to LLM.

This separation allows controlled communication, prevents direct unrestricted access, and supports monitoring of tool usage.

### Tool Interface Patterns

Different categories of tools require different interface designs.

### API-Based Tools

- **Definition**: External REST, GraphQL, or gRPC endpoints.

- **Integration**: Requires schema exposure and serialization formats (JSON, XML, Protocol Buffers).

- **Use Case**: Financial transaction processing, clinical EHR queries, coordination APIs.

## Database Query Tools

- **Definition**: Interfaces that translate natural language prompt into structured queries (SQL, SPARQL).

- **Integration**: Requires schema alignment and query validation layers to avoid injection risks.

- **Use Case**: Enterprise analytics, inventory management, compliance reporting.

## Symbolic and Computational Engines

- **Definition**: Deterministic systems for mathematics, logic, or code execution.

- **Integration**: Often sandboxed for security.

- **Use Case**: Clinical dosage calculation, engineering simulations, algorithmic analysis.

## Retrieval-Augmented Tools

- **Definition**: Vector search or document retrieval systems connected to the agent.

- **Integration**: Embedding models for indexing, retrieval APIs, and reranking logic.

- **Use Case**: Knowledge base augmentation, legal document review, clinical guideline lookup.

## Managing Tool Selection

Agents often have access to multiple tools. Choosing the correct tool for a given sub-task requires explicit mechanisms.

**Common strategies:**

- **Schema-Guided Selection**: Each tool is registered with metadata (capabilities, input-output schema). The agent matches sub-task requirements against schema.

- **Router Models**: Lightweight classifiers or secondary models that predict the correct tool based on input.

- **Rule-Based Selection**: Deterministic mapping where task type corresponds to a predefined tool.

**Example Table: Tool Selection Methods**

| Method | Strength | Limitation | Example |
|---|---|---|---|
| Schema-Guided | Flexible and extensible | Requires schema maintenance | Query routing in multi-database system |
| Router Model | Learn from context | Requires training data | Selecting between translation vs. summarization tools |
| Rule-Based | Simple and predictable | Limited adaptability | Mapping diagnostic code lookups to ICD database |

## Tool Invocation and Chaining

Once a tool is selected, invocation must follow strict patterns to ensure reliability.

**Invocation process:**

1. Construct input based on schema.

2. Call tool through interface layer.

3. Parse response into structured format.

4. Feed result back into reasoning loop.

**Tool chaining** occurs when the output of one tool becomes the input to another. This requires orchestration logic.

**Example:**

- Tool 1: Retrieve patient lab values from database.

- Tool 2: Apply clinical calculation engine to determine dosage.

- Tool 3: Generate treatment plan draft for physician review.

## Safety and Access Control

External tools carry security risks if not carefully managed.

**Key safeguards:**

- **Sandboxing**: Run computational tools in isolated environments to prevent unintended effects.

- **Authentication Control**: Use tokens, API keys, or OAuth to restrict access.

- **Rate Limiting**: Prevent excessive tool invocation that could overwhelm systems.

- **Validation Layers**: Check queries and responses against predefined schemas before execution.

## Error Handling and Recovery

Tool integration introduces points of failure that must be mitigated.

**Error categories:**

- **Connectivity Failures**: API downtime or network issues.

- **Schema Mismatches**: Incorrectly formatted inputs or outputs.

- **Execution Errors**: Failures within computational engines.

**Recovery strategies:**

- Retry policies with exponential backoff.

- Fallback to alternate tools or cached results.

- Human-in-the-loop escalation for unresolved failures.

## Clinical-Style Illustration: Patient Monitoring System

Consider a patient monitoring agent in a hospital setting.

1. **Reasoning Core**: Identifies that a patient requires a dosage adjustment based on new lab results.

2. **Tool Selection**: Chooses EHR database query tool to retrieve lab data.

3. **Tool Invocation**: Queries blood panel values.

4. **Tool Chaining**: Passes results into a clinical dosage calculator.

5. **Reflection**: Validates output with medical guidelines retrieval tool.

6. **Final Output**: Recommends dosage adjustment for physician verification.

This workflow highlights the role of structured external tools in clinical-grade decision support.

**Trade-Offs in Tool Integration**

While tool use expands agent capabilities, it also introduces complexity.

| Factor | Benefit | Risk |
|---|---|---|
| Accuracy | Offloads deterministic tasks to reliable engines | Misuse if wrong tool selected |
| Scalability | Enables high-throughput task handling | Increased operational overhead |
| Security | Access to secure systems | Higher attack surface if not sandboxed |
| Flexibility | Broadens functionality | Requires continuous schema and interface updates |

External tool integration is essential for building practical LLM-powered agents capable of real-world operation. Architecture must clearly separate reasoning and execution layers, use structured tool interfaces, and implement safeguards for safety, access control, and error recovery. Properly designed, these integrations allow agents to extend beyond language-only reasoning to perform high-value, deterministic, and domain-specific tasks at scale.

## Section 2: Strategies for Complex Task Decomposition and Planning

Large-scale autonomous agents are frequently utilized to address challenges that surpass the limits of single-pass reasoning. Structured decomposition is needed for tasks like multi-step data analysis, workflow orchestration, or making decisions that include more than one area of knowledge. With complex task planning, an agent may turn big goals into smaller, more manageable tasks, use tools in the right order, and keep track of progress until the task is done. This part talks about tried-and-true ways to break down tasks, plan frameworks, and operational techniques that help LLM-powered systems do dependable multi-step reasoning.

**The Necessity of Task Decomposition**

Language models can produce detailed responses to open-ended prompts, but without structured planning they are prone to errors in long or multi-step workflows.

**Reasons for decomposition are necessary:**

- **Cognitive Limitations of LLMs**: Models struggle with extended reasoning over many steps due to token window and memory constraints.

- **Error Propagation**: Small mistakes in earlier steps amplify in later outputs without explicit sub-task verification.

- **Operational Transparency**: Decomposed tasks can be logged, monitored, and audited, making agent behavior inspectable.

- **Parallelization**: Breaking tasks into sub-components allows execution across multiple tools or agents simultaneously.

**Planning Paradigms for LLM Agents**

Several established planning paradigms from AI and software engineering can be adapted for LLM-based agents.

**Sequential Planning**

- **Definition**: The agent generates a linear sequence of actions.

- **Strengths**: Simple, minimal overhead, effective for deterministic workflows.
- **Limitations**: Brittle in dynamic environments; failure at one step disrupts the chain.
- **Example**: A coordination agent scheduling shipments in order of dependencies.

## Hierarchical Task Networks (HTN)

- **Definition**: High-level tasks are recursively decomposed into sub-tasks.
- **Strengths**: Supports modular design, reusable planning templates.
- **Limitations**: Requires well-defined decomposition schemas.
- **Example**: Clinical workflow planning where "perform diagnosis" decomposes into "order labs," "review results," "generate treatment plan."

## Goal-Oriented Planning

- **Definition**: The agent evaluates potential actions relative to a desired final state.
- **Strengths**: Flexible and adaptive to changing contexts.
- **Limitations**: Computationally expensive if search space is large.
- **Example**: An enterprise compliance agent aiming to minimize audit risks by selecting the most efficient document validation path.

## Graph-Based Planning

- **Definition**: Tasks represented as nodes, dependencies as edges.
- **Strengths**: Effective for managing interdependent sub-tasks.
- **Limitations**: Requires graph construction and traversal algorithms.
- **Example**: Research assistant agent managing literature reviews across interlinked citation graphs.

## LLM-Specific Planning Techniques

General planning frameworks must be adapted to account for the characteristics of LLMs.

## Common adaptations:

- **Chain-of-Thought Structuring**: Prompting models to explicitly reason step-by-step before producing outputs.
- **Self-Refinement Loops**: Iteratively re-evaluating intermediate outputs before committing to next steps.
- **Instruction-Conditioned Generation**: Embedding schema or task constraints directly in prompts to guide planning.
- **External Memory Integration**: Using vector stores or databases to persist intermediate results and prevent context loss.

## Task Decomposition Strategies

Decomposition involves systematically reducing complex goals into simpler, verifiable units.

## Manual Schema Definition

- Engineers define explicit task trees for known workflows.

- Suitable for environments where domain knowledge is stable and well-defined.

- Example: Standard operating procedures in manufacturing.

## Model-Guided Decomposition

- LLM generates sub-tasks dynamically based on high-level instructions.

- Useful when tasks are variable or domain knowledge is open-ended.

- Example: Generating subtasks for exploration data analysis.

## Hybrid Decomposition

- Combines schema templates with model-driven elaboration.

- Balances predictability with adaptability.

- Example: Legal agent using predefined steps for case review but generating adaptive subtasks for argument analysis.

## Execution Control and Monitoring

Once decomposed, sub-tasks require structured execution control.

## Core requirements:

1. **Scheduling**: Determine execution order based on dependencies.

2. **Parallelization**: Identify tasks that can be run concurrently.

3. **State Tracking**: Persist intermediate states in structured storage.

4. **Failure Recovery**: Detect errors at sub-task level and attempt corrective measures.

- 

## Verification and Quality Control

Without verification, decomposed plans risk silent failure.

## Verification methods:

- **Intermediate Result Checks**: Use external validators or deterministic tools to confirm sub-task outputs.

- **Consistency Checking**: Cross-validate results across different reasoning passes or models.

- **Schema Enforcement**: Ensure sub-task results conform to expected formats.

- **Human-in-the-Loop Review**: Escalate ambiguous or critical steps to domain experts.

## Clinical-Style Illustration: Diagnostic Workflow

Consider an autonomous agent assisting in medical diagnostics.

1. **High-Level Goal**: Determine patient diagnosis.

2. **Decomposition**:
   - Order appropriate lab tests.
   - Retrieve results from EHR system.
   - Apply diagnostic criteria based on structured guidelines.
   - Generate preliminary diagnosis report.

3. **Execution**:
   - Labs are retrieved via database query tool.
   - Results processed through medical computation engine.
   - Criteria validated using knowledge retrieval system.

4. **Verification**:
   - Outputs cross-checked against guideline databases.
   - Ambiguous cases escalated to physician review.

This demonstrates systematic decomposition, execution, and validation.

**Trade-Offs in Planning Strategies**

| Strategy | Benefit | Limitation |
|---|---|---|
| Sequential | Low overhead, easy to implement | Fragile to failure at any step |
| HTN | Modular and reusable | Requires schema definition |
| Goal-Oriented | Adaptive to changes | Computationally expensive |
| Graph-Based | Handles complex dependencies | Requires graph management overhead |

Task decomposition and planning make LLM-powered agents more than just one-time responders; they turn them into organized autonomous systems. Engineers can make agents that can reliably break down, carry out, and check multi-step tasks by using traditional planning methods and making changes to fit LLM restrictions. The main needs are systematic breakdown, structured control of execution, and strong verification. When done right, these principles let agents handle real-world workflows in a way that is secure, open, and scalable.

## Section 3: Coordinating Multi-Tool Workflows and Long-Horizon Tasks

It takes a lot of planning to make LLM-powered agents that can do long-term, multi-tool tasks. Long-horizon workflows, on the other hand, require various dependencies, repeated decision-making, and coordination between different external systems. Without strong orchestration, these kinds of workflows can fail because tools don't operate well together, context is lost, or execution mistakes pile up. This part talks about the techniques, concepts, procedures, and safeguards needed to reliably manage multi-tool and long-horizon tasks in real-world agentic systems.

**Characteristics of Multi-Tool and Long-Horizon Workflows**

Multi-tool workflows extend beyond simple tool invocation. They often involve complex chaining of heterogeneous systems.

**Key characteristics include:**

- **Heterogeneity of Tools**: Databases, APIs, symbolic solvers, computational libraries, and retrieval systems often work in combination.
- **Dependency Structures**: Outputs of one tool serve as inputs to another, forming directed acyclic graphs (DAGs).
- **Extended Times**: Some tasks span hours or days, requiring persistent memory and checkpointing.
- **Uncertainty Handling**: Failures, timeouts, or partial results must be anticipated and managed.

## Coordination Models

Several architectural models can be used to manage tool coordination.

## Centralized Orchestration

- A central controller schedules all tool invocations.
- **Advantages**: High transparency, easier monitoring.
- **Disadvantages**: Single point of failure, potential bottleneck.
- **Example**: Workflow engines such as Apache Airflow.

## Decentralized Agent Collaboration

- Multiple sub-agents manage different tools and collaborate through a shared communication protocol.
- **Advantages**: Scalability, modularity.
- **Disadvantages**: Coordination complexity, potential inconsistency.
- **Example**: Multi-agent frameworks coordinating retrieval, summarization, and computation tasks.

## Hybrid Models

- Combine centralized oversight with decentralized execution.
- **Advantages**: Balances transparency with flexibility.
- **Disadvantages**: Requires well-defined escalation protocols.

## Task Graph Construction and Execution

For long-horizon workflows, explicit task graph construction is essential.

## Execution pipeline:

1. **Graph Definition**: Nodes represent tasks, edges represent dependencies.
2. **Scheduling**: Independent tasks are executed in parallel, dependent tasks in sequence.
3. **State Management**: Intermediate output stored in persistent memory.
4. **Monitoring**: Each task node logs execution metadata, success/failure status, and outputs.

## Memory and Context Management

Long-horizon workflows exceed the short-term context capacity of LLMs. Persistent memory mechanisms are necessary.

**Strategies include:**

- **External State Stores**: Databases or vector stores for intermediate results.

- **Checkpointing**: Saving workflow progress to enable resumption after interruption.

- **Context Windows**: Retrieving only relevant state subsets into the active LLM session.

- **Schema Enforcement**: Structuring intermediate results in standardized formats such as JSON to prevent ambiguity.

## Error Handling and Recovery

In multi-tool workflows, failure is expected and must be managed.

**Recovery practices:**

- **Timeout Detection**: Abort and retry tool calls exceeding time limits.

- **Fallback Paths**: Define alternative tool sequences when primary tools fail.

- **Partial Completion Handling**: Allow workflows to complete remaining independent tasks even if one branch fails.

- **Escalation Policies**: Route unresolved failures to human supervisors for review.

## Evaluation of Workflow Reliability

Evaluation requires metrics beyond single-turn accuracy.

**Recommended evaluation dimensions:**

1. **Task Success Rate**: Percentage of workflows completing correctly.

2. **Latency**: Time per workflow stage and overall end-to-end completion.

3. **Error Recovery Rate**: Proportion of failures successfully recovered.

4. **Scalability**: Performance under high parallel load.

5. **Auditability**: Completeness of logs and traceability of tool decisions.

**Illustrative table:**

| Metric | Measurement Method | Engineering Implication |
|---|---|---|
| Success Rate | Automated test cases | Indicates robustness of planning |
| Latency | Timestamped logs | Reveals bottlenecks |
| Recovery Rate | Failure injection tests | Assesses resilience |
| Scalability | Load testing | Guides resource allocation |
| Auditability | Log completeness checks | Ensures regulatory compliance |

**Clinical-Style Illustration: Multi-Tool Workflow in Diagnostics**

A diagnostic support agent may require coordination across multiple tools:

1. Retrieve patient records from EHR database.

2. Query laboratory systems for recent test results.

3. Apply statistical models for anomaly detection.

4. Cross-reference findings with medical guideline retrieval system.

5. Generate structured report for physician review.

Each stage depends on prior outputs and requires persistent state tracking. Failures, such as missing lab data, trigger fallback mechanisms, such as requesting repeat queries or escalating to human oversight.

**Operational Best Practices**

To ensure reliability in production, the following practices are recommended:

- **Structured Logging**: Capture inputs, outputs, and metadata for every tool invocation.

- **Monitoring Dashboards**: Real-time status tracking of workflow nodes.

- **Redundancy**: Maintain alternative tool providers to avoid single points of failure.

- **Security Controls**: Restrict access tools via scoped credentials and sandboxing.

- **Testing Frameworks**: Use synthetic workloads to evaluate workflows before deployment.

- **Human-in-the-Loop**: Insert manual checkpoints for critical tasks where full automation is unsafe.

To set up reliable agentic systems in production, it's important to coordinate multi-tool workflows and long-term activities. Centralized, decentralized, and hybrid orchestration approaches offer adaptable coordination mechanisms. Explicit task graph building, persistent memory management, and strong error handling make sure that workflows stay reliable even when there are a lot of dependencies. A full examination and operational measures make sure that resilience and transparency are even more secure. Using these concepts, engineers can create agents that can think through problems in real-world settings using a variety of tools over a long period of time.

To keep LLM-powered agents secure, you need to put in place planned architectural controls, operational safeguards, and continual monitoring. Agentic systems are different from standard deterministic software in that they use statistical reasoning, external tools, and long-term task execution. If these traits aren't limited, they make it more likely that people will do things they didn't mean to or that could hurt them. This part talks about safety engineering principles, proven safety measures, and design methods that lower risks when putting agents in real-world situations.

## Defining Safety in Agentic Systems

Safety in the context of autonomous agents involves preventing outcomes that violate functional, ethical, or regulatory requirements. Specifically, safety encompasses:

- **Prevention of harmful outputs**: avoiding biased, toxic, or misleading text generation.

- **Controlled tool use**: ensuring external systems are accessed only within defined permissions.

- **Resource constraints**: preventing uncontrolled consumption of computers, memory, or bandwidth.

- **Task containment**: guaranteeing that recursive reasoning or planning does not escalate indefinitely.

- **Human protection**: enabling clear intervention points where operators can override or stop execution.

Safety is not a single module but a cross-cutting property of the entire system, requiring integration at every architectural layer.

## Architectural Safeguards

### Sandboxing

Agents interacting with external systems should operate in controlled execution environments. Sandboxing isolates untrusted or error-prone behaviors. For example, agents executing code or database queries should run in containers with limited privileges, network restrictions, and explicit resource quotas.

### Role-Based Access Control (RBAC)

Agents should never have unrestricted access to tools. RBAC ensures that an agent has permissions only for the minimal set of actions needed for its assigned tasks. Access policies should be centrally managed and auditable.

### Policy Enforcement Layers

Before executing actions, agent outputs can be routed through policy enforcement modules. These layers apply validation rules; block disallowed commands and check compliance with operational requirements.

## Input and Output Validation

### Input Validation

Inputs from users or external systems must be validated before reaching the reasoning core. Techniques include:

- Schema validation to ensure structural correctness.

- Sanitization to prevent injection attacks in SQL or API calls.

- Range and type checks for numerical or categorical fields.

**Output Validation**

Output generated by the agent should undergo post-processing before release. Approaches include:

- Regular expressions are checked for forbidden terms.

- Rule-based validators that verify JSON or structured responses.

- External classifiers were trained to detect unsafe or biased content.

By treating all agent-generated outputs as untrusted until validated, developers reduce the risk of harmful or non-compliant behavior.

**Guardrails in Reasoning Loops**

Recursive reasoning and planning loops introduce risks of runaway execution or unbounded complexity.

**Guardrail mechanisms include:**

- **Recursion Depth Limits**: enforce maximum iteration counts.

- **Resource Quotas**: restrict token consumption, API calls, or wall-clock execution time.

- **Termination Conditions**: define explicit stop criteria, such as successful completion of goals or detection of repeated reasoning cycles.

Implementing guardrails ensures that agent behavior remains predictable, bounded, and measurable.

**Human-in-the-Loop Safety Models**

Human oversight remains essential in high-stakes or regulated domains. Safety can be enhanced by embedding human decision points within workflows.

**Models of human involvement:**

1. **Pre-approval**: human reviews agent-generated plans before execution.

2. **Intervention points**: system pauses at defined checkpoints, allowing humans to approve or reject actions.

3. **Override mechanisms**: operators can stop or roll back workflows in real time.

4. **Escalation policies**: unresolved failures or ambiguous decisions are automatically routed to human experts.

These models align with established safety practices in aviation, healthcare, and financial compliance.

**Example: Safety in Medical Record Summarization**

Consider an agent designed to retrieve and summarize electronic health records (EHRs). Safety measures must include:

- **Input validation**: ensuring only authorized clinicians can query the EHR.

- **Access control**: restricting the agent to read-only database operations.

- **Policy enforcement**: blocking any attempt to include personally identifiable information (PII) in outputs not authorized for disclosure.

- **Output validation**: applying medical-domain content filters to detect missing context or prohibited terminology.

- **Human oversight**: requiring clinician review before generated summaries are added to patient files.

This clinical-style example illustrates how layered safeguards prevent unsafe behaviors while enabling the agent to support critical workflows.

## Best Practices for Safety Engineering

To standardize safety across implementations, the following practices are recommended:

- Apply **least privilege principles** to all tools and data access.

- Separate **reasoning, validation, and execution** layers.

- Enforce **deterministic validation rules** before executing external actions.

- Use **structured logging** for all blocked or overridden actions to support audits.

- Regularly **test guardrails** under adversarial conditions.

- Integrate **human-in-the-loop checkpoints** for high-risk tasks.

Safety in LLM-powered agents should not be an afterthought. It needs architectural protection, strict checks on inputs and outputs, limited reasoning loops, and the ability for people to watch over things. Engineers make sure that advanced systems stay in line with regulatory standards, operational needs, and user safety expectations by putting these concepts directly into the design and operation of agents.

## Section 2: Designing for Reliability and Fault Tolerance in LLM-Powered Agents

Reliability and fault tolerance make sure that LLM-powered agents work well in a variety of situations, fail gracefully, and keep providing service. Agentic systems deal with uncertainties that come from probabilistic reasoning, relying on external APIs, and the quality of the incoming data. This is different from standard software systems. This part talks about engineering methods for making agent architectures more reliable, making sure that error-handling channels are strong, and making sure that production environments are always available.

## Defining Reliability and Fault Tolerance

- **Reliability** refers to the ability of an agent to consistently perform its intended functions across repeated trials and varying contexts.

- **Fault tolerance** is the ability to continue operating when individual components fail, degrade, or return unexpected results.

These principles are critical for agent adoption in domains where downtime, misbehavior, or data corruption can create cascading risks.

## Sources of Unreliability in Agents

Reliability challenges arise from multiple layers of the system:

1. **LLM reasoning variability**: identical inputs may yield different outputs due to probabilistic sampling.

2. **External dependency failures**: APIs, databases, or third-party services may become unavailable or return malformed responses.

3. **Resource limitations**: computing or memory exhaustion can lead to incomplete or dropped tasks.

4. **Long-horizon planning**: multi-step reasoning chains may compound minor errors into major failures.

5. **Network volatility**: distributed architectures introduce latency, dropped connections, or inconsistent states.

Understanding these sources informs the selection of fault-tolerant strategies.

## Architectural Strategies for Reliability

### Layered Reasoning Pipelines

Reliability increases when agent reasoning is separated into modular stages: interpretation, planning, execution, and validation. If one stage fails, localized recovery mechanisms can re-execute or adjust without collapsing the entire workflow.

### Redundancy and Replication

Agents can improve robustness by maintaining redundant strategies:

- **LLM redundancy**: multiple models generate responses, with voting or ranking to select the best candidate.

- **Execution redundancy**: critical external actions are verified through double execution or cross-checks.

- **Service replication**: distributed deployment across regions ensures availability during infrastructure outages.

### Checkpointing and State Management

Checkpointing records intermediate states in long workflows, enabling recovery from the last stable step rather than restarting from zero. Reliable state storage should use transactional databases or versioned logs to ensure atomicity and consistency.

### Fault Detection and Recovery

Fault-tolerant systems depend on early detection and structured recovery strategies.

### Error Detection Mechanisms

- **Input/output validation failures** (schema mismatches, missing fields).

- **Timeouts and latency check** for API responses.

- **Anomaly detection** models that flag abnormal patterns in agent reasoning or tool use.

### Recovery Mechanisms

- **Retries with exponential backoff** for transient network errors.

- **Fallback plans** when primary tools are unavailable (e.g., switching from API A to API B).

- **Graceful degradation**: serving partial but useful outputs instead of failing entirely.

- **Escalation**: unresolved failures trigger human intervention or supervisory systems.

### Monitoring and Observability

Continuous monitoring is essential to verify reliability in real-world deployments.

### Key Metrics

- Task completion rate.

- Error frequency by type (timeouts, validation errors, execution failures).

- Latency distribution across reasoning and execution phases.

- Resource utilization (tokens, memory, CPU).

## Logging and Traceability

Structured logs should capture:

- Inputs and generated outputs.

- Actions proposed and executed.

- Validation results and blocked commands.

- Recovery actions and escalation events.

Full traceability supports debugging, incident response, and regulatory audits.

## Human-in-the-Loop for Reliability

While automation maximizes efficiency, human supervision enhances reliability by resolving edge cases. Strategies include:

- **Approval workflows** for mission-critical tasks.

- **Escalation dashboards** where unresolved failures are surfaced in real time.

- **Post-incident reviews** involving operators to refine safeguards and recovery policies.

Human-in-the-loop reliability complements safety models discussed in Section 1, ensuring systems remain resilient under unexpected conditions.

## Example: Fault Tolerance in Legal Document Processing

An agent deployed for automated legal document review face's reliability risks if external citation databases go offline or if extracted text is corrupted. Fault-tolerant design would include:

- **Redundancy**: two separate legal databases queried in parallel.

- **Fallback**: if both databases fail, the agent generates summaries with references flagged as incomplete.

- **Checkpointing**: saving extracted sections as the process progresses, avoiding total restart after mid-task failures.

- **Human escalation**: attorneys notified if references cannot be validated within defined time limits.

This example illustrates how fault tolerance preserves productivity without compromising accuracy or compliance.

## Best Practices for Reliability and Fault Tolerance

- Design agents as **modular, restartable pipelines**.

- Use **redundant models and services** for critical decision points.

- Implement **graceful degradation paths** for partial results.

- Enforce **timeouts and retries** for all external dependencies.

- Continuously **monitor performance metrics** with automated alerts.

- Provide **human escalation workflows** to resolve unrecoverable states.

Reliability and fault tolerance turn LLM-powered agents from experimental prototypes into reliable systems that may be used in production. Engineers may make sure that agents stay strong even when things go wrong by redundancy, using checkpointing, finding defects early, and making structured recovery systems. Monitoring and human oversight make resilience even stronger, making agentic systems ready for long-term use in the real world.

## Section 3: Monitoring, Evaluation, and Continuous Improvement

Safety and dependability are not fixed characteristics. When deployed, LLM-powered agents work in places where user actions, data inputs, and outside dependencies are always changing. Teams need to use strict monitoring, formal evaluation methods, and structured improvement cycles to keep their performance reliable. This part gives engineers advice on how to set up observability pipelines, create assessment frameworks, and make feedback-driven processes that make sure agents stay trustworthy throughout their lives.

### The Role of Monitoring and Evaluation

Monitoring and evaluation enable engineering teams to:

- Detect emerging failures before they affect end users.

- Quantify agent performance across dimensions such as accuracy, efficiency, and compliance.

- Identify drifts in model behavior caused by changing inputs or tool dependencies.

- Guide systematic retraining, fine-tuning, or pipeline adjustments.

Without continuous oversight, agentic systems risk silent degradation, where reliability gradually erodes until failures accumulate into critical incidents.

### Observability in Agentic Systems

Observability is the ability to understand internal system states by examining outputs, logs, and metrics. Unlike traditional services, LLM-based agents require observability at both the reasoning and execution layers.

### Core Monitoring Metrics

1. **Task-level performance**: success rates, completion times, partial completions.

2. **Error taxonomy**: distribution of validation failures, tool invocation errors, and reasoning inconsistencies.

3. **Resource consumption**: token usage per task, latency, and compute cost.

4. **User interaction metrics**: frequency of corrections, overrides, or escalations.

5. **Safety incidents**: number of blocked unsafe outputs, human interventions, or compliance rule violations.

### Logging Structures

Effective logs capture:

- Prompt inputs and contextual grounding data.

- Model-generated plans and intermediate reasoning steps.

- Tool calls with parameters and returned outputs.

- Validation results, retries, and fallback decisions.

- Final outputs delivered to end users.

Logs should be structured in machine-readable formats (e.g., JSON) to support automated analysis, anomaly detection, and audit trails.

**Visualization and Alerting**

Dashboards aggregate monitoring data into operational views. Common features include:

- Latency heatmaps to detect bottlenecks.

- Error-rate trend lines across modules.

- Compliance alerts when unsafe behaviors exceed thresholds.

Alerts must be routed to on-call engineers or supervisors, using severity levels to prioritize responses.

**Evaluation Frameworks**

Evaluation complements monitoring by systematically measuring agent quality against predefined benchmarks.

**Dimensions of Evaluation**

- **Accuracy**: correctness of outputs relative to ground truth.

- **Consistency**: stability of reasoning across repeated runs.

- **Robustness**: resilience to malformed inputs or unexpected tool behavior.

- **Safety**: adherence to guardrails and absence of policy violations.

- **Efficiency**: resource and time consumption relative to task complexity.

**Evaluation Methods**

1. **Unit-level tests**: validate correctness of tool integrations and schema enforcement.

2. **Scenario tests**: simulate full tasks with realistic inputs, checking whether workflows complete successfully.

3. **Adversarial tests**: probe agents with edge cases, malformed prompts, or conflicting instructions.

4. **Regression tests**: ensure that modifications to pipelines do not reintroduce prior errors.

5. **A/B experiments**: compare performance between two agent versions in controlled environments.

Evaluation should be automated where possible but supplemented by expert human review for high-stakes domains.

**Continuous Improvement Cycles**

Reliable agent deployment requires structured loops that translate monitoring and evaluation insights into actionable changes.

**Feedback Sources**

- **Automated logs**: identify recurring error patterns.

- **User feedback**: highlight usability gaps and misunderstand intents.

- **Human-in-the-loop reviews**: uncover nuanced safety or compliance risks.

**Improvement Actions**

1. **Prompt refinements**: adjusting instruction templates or reasoning constraints.

2. **Retraining and fine-tuning**: incorporating new data that reflects updated requirements or failure modes.

3. **Pipeline adjustments**: modifying orchestration logic, fallback rules, or validation layers.

4. **Tool ecosystem updates**: replacing unreliable external services or integrating new APIs.

**Governance and Release Management**

Continuous improvement should operate under structured governance:

- Version control for prompts, configurations, and model checkpoints.

- Formal approval workflows before production deployment.

- Staged rollouts with canary testing to minimize risk.

**Case Example: Continuous Improvement in a Healthcare Assistant**

Consider a clinical documentation assistant deployed to help physicians generate structured summaries. Monitoring shows that 5 percent of outputs omit mandatory regulatory codes. Evaluation reveals that failures correlate with long patient histories. Improvement actions include:

- Refining prompts to explicitly prioritize code inclusion.

- Introducing automated validators that block missing codes.

- Updating the evaluation suite with synthetic long-history cases to ensure robustness.

- Deploying the improved version through a staged rollout, with ongoing monitoring to confirm reduced error rates.

This illustrates how continuous improvement cycles directly enhance both safety and reliability.

**Best Practices for Monitoring and Continuous Improvement**

- Define **clear metrics** before deployment.

- Log **all reasoning and tool actions** for auditability.

- Build **dashboards and alerting pipelines** for real-time visibility.

- Maintain **automated evaluation suites** covering accuracy, robustness, and safety.

- Incorporate **human review** for sensitive domains.

- Establish **version-controlled improvement workflows** with staged deployment.

Monitoring, evaluation, and ongoing improvement are the main parts of safe and dependable agent deployment. Through defined observability pipelines, formal evaluation frameworks, and controlled feedback cycles, engineering teams make sure that LLM-powered agents are reliable even when things change.  These approaches seal the loop between design, deployment, and operation, making the agent safer and more fault-tolerant over its entire lifecycle.

## Section 1: Architectural Models for Multi-Agent Systems

Designing multi-agent systems requires a clear framework for how individual agents collaborate, coordinate, and exchange information in order to accomplish objectives that go beyond what a single agent can achieve. When powered by large language models (LLMs), these systems inherit both the advantages and constraints of the underlying models, making deliberate architectural design essential for achieving scalability, reliability, and predictable task execution. This section explores the main architectural models used in multi-agent systems, the communication methods they depend on, and the approaches by which responsibilities are distributed among agents.

### Scope of Multi-Agent Systems in Agentic Design

A multi-agent system (MAS) can be understood as a network of autonomous or semi-autonomous agents that operate within a shared environment, working either cooperatively or competitively to complete tasks. For LLM-driven agents, this often includes specialized components tailored to distinct roles such as retrieval, reasoning, planning, or execution. These agents exchange information through structured communication channels like JSON messages or API calls, while shared or distributed memory provides continuity across interactions. Coordination strategies enable agents to jointly solve problems of higher complexity, such as multi-step enterprise workflows or distributed knowledge retrieval. The approach is especially valuable when tasks demand multiple perspectives, domain expertise, or simultaneous execution. For example, in a corporate setting, one agent may handle database queries, another may enforce compliance checks, and a third may deliver a summarized output to the end user.

### Core Architectural Models

Most multi-agent systems are organized according to one of three foundational architectural styles: centralized orchestration, decentralized peer-to-peer, or hybrid models. Each comes with unique trade-offs in terms of scalability, fault tolerance, and overall control, making careful evaluation critical during system design.

### Centralized Orchestration

In a centralized orchestration design, a single coordinating agent directs the overall workflow, assigns tasks, and integrates the outputs from all participants. The orchestrator maintains a global state of the system, with communication structured in a hub-and-spoke pattern where all agents interact through the central controller. This setup simplifies error detection and mitigation since the orchestrator has direct oversight of the process. The advantages of this approach include predictable system behaviour, clear accountability, and simplified monitoring, making it effective for small to mid-sized applications. However, its weaknesses lie in its reliance on a single point of control, which poses risks if the orchestrator fails. Scalability is also limited by the throughput of the central controller, and communication bottlenecks may arise as more agents are added.

### Decentralized Peer-to-Peer

In decentralized architectures, agents operate autonomously and coordinate with one another directly without a central controller.

### Characteristics:

- Each agent maintains partial or local knowledge of the system.

- Communication occurs peer-to-peer using distributed protocols.

- Agents make decisions based on local context and shared communication.

### Advantages:

- High fault tolerance with no single point of failure.

- Scales effectively for large systems with many agents.

- Supports emergent behaviors and flexible adaptation.

**Disadvantages:**

- Coordination complexity increases as the number of agents grows.

- Consensus and synchronization mechanisms may introduce overhead.

- Debugging and monitoring require more sophisticated instrumentation.

**Hybrid Architectures**

Hybrid architecture combines centralized and decentralized principles. For instance, a central orchestrator may assign high-level tasks, while peer-to-peer collaboration resolves subtasks.

**Characteristics:**

- Hierarchical or layered control structure.

- Agents may switch roles depending on context.

- Combines predictability of centralized control with flexibility of decentralized execution.

**Advantages:**

- Balance's reliability and scalability.

- Reduces risk of single points of failure.

- Allows dynamic adaptation to task complexity.

**Disadvantages:**

- Architectural complexity is higher.

- Requires careful design of role transitions and escalation mechanisms.

**Communication Protocols and Data Exchange**

Communication is the backbone of multi-agent systems. LLM-powered agents typically use structured message formats and standard interfaces to ensure interoperability.

**Common patterns include:**

1. **Message Passing:**
   o Agents exchange structured data packets, often JSON objects.
   o Messages typically include headers for metadata (sender, timestamp, priority) and payloads for task data.

2. **Shared Memory:**
   o Agents interact through a shared data store such as Redis or a vector database.

- o   Suitable for maintaining global state or knowledge bases.

3. **Publish-Subscribe:**
    - o   Agents subscribe to topics of interest and publish updates asynchronously.
    - o   Useful for event-driven architecture.

**Best Practices:**

- Define a schema for messages to prevent ambiguity.
- Implement logging at communication boundaries for traceability.
- Use standardized transport mechanisms such as gRPC or HTTP for external integrations.

## Role Assignment and Specialization

Multi-agent systems often require explicit role assignments to ensure efficiency and prevent redundant work. Roles can be assigned statically at design time or dynamically during execution.

- **Static Role Assignment:** Each agent is preconfigured for a specialized function, such as retrieval or summarization.
- **Dynamic Role Assignment:** Roles are allocated based on current workload, availability, or observed performance.

**Dynamic assignment strategies include:**

1. Load-based assignment, where idle agents are assigned new tasks.
2. Competence-based assignment, where agents with higher accuracy on certain domains receive domain-specific queries.
3. Market-based assignment, where agents bid for tasks using metrics like expected execution time or confidence scores.

## Comparative Table of Architectural Models

| Architecture Type | Scalability | Fault Tolerance | Coordination Complexity | Typical Use Cases |
|---|---|---|---|---|
| Centralized Orchestration | Moderate | Low | Low | Enterprise workflows, compliance systems |
| Decentralized Peer-to-Peer | High | High | High | Distributed monitoring, swarm intelligence |
| Hybrid | High | Moderate | Moderate | Large-scale systems requiring adaptability |

## Engineering Considerations

When selecting architecture, engineers must align design choices with system goals. Key considerations include:

- **Reliability:** Is predictable behavior critical, or can the system tolerate emergent dynamics?
- **Scalability:** How many agents must the system support?

- **Resource Constraints:** What is the computer, memory, and network requirements?

- **Testability:** How easily can failures be traced and reproduced?

- **Integration:** Does the architecture support existing enterprise infrastructure?

Architectural decisions form the foundation of any multi-agent system. Centralized models offer simplicity and control but risk bottlenecks, decentralized systems provide resilience but demand complex coordination, and hybrid designs balance trade-offs at the cost of added complexity. Role assignment and structured communication are critical across all models. Proper alignment of architecture with organizational requirements ensures that multi-agent coordination remains both reliable and scalable.

## Section 2: Coordination Mechanisms and Collaboration Protocols

Once the architectural foundation of a multi-agent system is established, the next priority is defining coordination mechanisms that allow agents to interact productively and safely. Coordination involves distributing tasks, synchronizing activities, and resolving conflicts. In LLM-powered systems, coordination must account for the probabilistic nature of language models, variability in response quality, and the potential for misaligned outputs. This section examines proven coordination techniques, collaboration patterns, and the application of established distributed systems protocols to agentic design.

### Foundations of Coordination in Multi-Agent Systems

Coordination is the mechanism that allows agents to collaborate effectively toward common goals while minimizing overlap and interference. Its core objectives include distributing tasks so that all required functions are covered, avoiding conflicts that could lead to wasted resources or contradictory outputs, synchronizing dependent activities so they happen in the right sequence, and establishing consensus when agents generate differing results. The main difficulty lies in striking the right balance-too much rigidity can limit adaptability, while too little structure can lead to ambiguity and cascading errors.

### Scheduling and Task Allocation

Assigning tasks to the right agents at the right time is central to system efficiency, and the method used often depends on the chosen architecture. In centralized scheduling, a controller oversees the process and distributes responsibilities using global knowledge of the system, which provides predictability and control. For example, a planning agent might assign subtasks to agents responsible for retrieval, validation, and summarization. Distributed scheduling, by contrast, allows agents to negotiate or self-select tasks, reducing reliance on a central authority but requiring robust coordination protocols to avoid conflicts. An example is a pool of data-processing agents pulling work from a shared queue based on their availability. Hybrid scheduling combines both approaches by having a central orchestrator set high-level boundaries while leaving the finer details of task assignment to agent negotiation, blending control with adaptability.

### Coordination Mechanisms

Different coordination mechanisms can be applied depending on workload, reliability requirements, and communication constraints.

### 1. Token-Based Coordination:

- A control token circulates among agents, granting the holder permission to perform specific tasks.

- Prevents conflicts by ensuring only one agent acts at a time on critical sections.

### 2. Locking and Resource Reservation:

- Agents reserve access to shared resources (e.g., memory stores or APIs) before execution.
- Ensures consistency but may introduce contention delays.

## 3. Market-Based Coordination:

- Agents "bid" for tasks based on competence, confidence, or resource availability.
- Effective in heterogeneous systems where agents have varying strengths.

## 4. Priority Queues:

- Tasks are placed into priority queues, with agents selecting based on urgency.
- Useful for real-time or mission-critical systems.

## Collaboration Protocols

Collaboration protocols define structured interactions between agents. Borrowing from distributed systems, these include both negotiation and consensus protocols.

## 1. Contract Net Protocol (CNP):

- A central manager announces tasks.
- Agents bid to perform tasks based on their estimated cost or performance.
- Manager awards contracts to the most suitable agent.

## 2. Consensus Protocols:

- Algorithms like Paxos or Raft can be adapted for multi-agent agreement.
- Used when agents produce different outputs that must converge into a single accepted result.
- Ensures reliability in decision-making.

## 3. Iterative Refinement:

- Agents collaborate sequentially, with each refining or verifying the previous agent's work.
- Particularly effective in LLM systems, where output can be noisy and benefit from multi-step review.

## 4. Majority Voting:

- Outputs from multiple agents are compared, and the majority decision is accepted.
- Provides robustness against occasional failures or poor-quality outputs.

## Collaboration Strategies

Agents can collaborate in several structured patterns depending on the nature of the task.

## Sequential Workflows:

- Agents operate in a defined pipeline.
- Example: Agent A retrieves data, Agent B validates, Agent C summarizes.

- Advantage: Predictability. Disadvantage: Bottlenecks at each stage.

**Parallel Execution:**

- Multiple agents perform tasks simultaneously.

- Example: Multiple search agents query different data sources in parallel.

- Advantage: Faster execution. Disadvantage: Requires merging and deduplication of results.

**Iterative Collaboration:**

- Agents repeatedly pass work among themselves for refinement.

- Example: Multiple agents review and correct draft responses until consensus is reached.

- Advantage: Quality improvement. Disadvantage: Higher computer cost.

**Hybrid Collaboration:**

- Combines sequential, parallel, and iterative strategies.

- Often necessary in real-world deployments with diverse task requirements.

**Conflict Resolution**

When agents provide conflicting outputs, systems must resolve discrepancies systematically.

**Common strategies include:**

1. **Majority Voting:** Accepting the most common answer.

2. **Confidence Scoring:** Selecting the output with the highest confidence or probability.

3. **Hierarchical Escalation:** Passing conflicts to a supervisory agent for adjudication.

4. **Aggregation:** Combining outputs where possible, for example merging different data points into a unified summary.

**Table: Conflict Resolution Techniques**

| Method | Strengths | Limitations | Typical Use Case |
|---|---|---|---|
| Majority Voting | Simple, robust against outliers | Requires multiple redundant agents | Classification tasks, fact checking |
| Confidence Scoring | Utilizes probability estimates | It depends on calibration of models | LLM answer ranking, search queries |
| Hierarchical Escalation | Provides oversight and control | Adds complexity and latency | Compliance or safety-critical tasks |
| Aggregation | Combines diverse information | May dilute precision | Summarization, data synthesis |

**Practical Engineering Considerations**

When implementing coordination and collaboration, engineers must address:

- **Scalability:** Coordination protocols should not become bottlenecks as agent count increases.

- **Fault Tolerance:** Ensure failure of one agent does not disrupt the entire system.

- **Transparency:** Log coordination decisions for traceability.

- **Safety:** Prevent agents from amplifying errors through uncontrolled interactions.

- **Efficiency:** Balance between overhead of coordination and task execution speed.

Coordination and collaboration protocols determine whether a multi-agent system operates efficiently or descends into conflict and inefficiency. Established techniques from distributed systems, including scheduling, resource control, consensus, and iterative refinement, can be adapted for LLM-powered systems. The choice of coordination mechanisms depends on system goals, scale, and reliability requirements. Clear conflict resolution strategies, combined with structured workflows, enable agents to work as cohesive units rather than isolated components.

## Section 3: Testing, Monitoring, and Scaling Multi-Agent Systems

After defining architectures and implementing coordination protocols, the next challenge is ensuring that multi-agent systems operate reliably at scale. Testing and monitoring provide visibility into system performance, while scaling strategies determine whether the system can handle increased workloads or complexity without degradation. In LLM-powered multi-agent environments, additional considerations include probabilistic outputs, integration with external tools, and variable performance across agents. This section details evaluation methodologies, monitoring approaches, fault-tolerance mechanisms, and scaling strategies, concluding with governance and safety measures for real-world deployments.

### Evaluation Metrics for Multi-Agent Collaboration

Effective evaluation requires metrics that capture both the performance of individual agents and the overall behavior of the system. Common categories include:

**1. Reliability Metrics**

- **Task Success Rate:** Percentage of tasks completed successfully without human intervention.

- **Error Recovery Rate:** Ability of the system to recover from partial failures.

- **Consistency:** Degree to which repeated runs of the same input yield similar results.

**2. Efficiency Metrics**

- **Latency:** Average time to complete tasks, including coordination overhead.

- **Introduction:** Number of tasks processed per unit time.

- **Resource Utilization:** CPU, memory, and network load per agent.

**3. Collaboration Metrics**

- **Conflict Frequency:** Rate of conflicting outputs among agents.

- **Resolution Time:** Time taken to resolve conflicts through consensus or escalation.

- **Redundancy Overhead:** Extra work performed by multiple agents on the same task.

**4. Fairness and Load Distribution**

- **Task Balance:** Whether workload is evenly distributed across agents.

- **Starvation Prevention:** Avoiding scenarios where some agents remain idle.

## Testing Approaches

Testing multi-agent systems requires a combination of traditional software testing techniques and specialized methods for distributed and probabilistic systems.

### 1. Unit Testing for Agents:

- Verify individual agent behavior in isolation.

- Example: Testing a retrieval agent with controlled queries to ensure expected output.

### 2. Integration Testing:

- Assess interactions between agents, focusing on communication protocols and message formats.

- Detects schema mismatches or inconsistent handling of edge cases.

### 3. Scenario-Based Testing:

- Define representative workflows (e.g., end-to-end business process).

- Evaluate system behavior under realistic, multi-step conditions.

### 4. Fault Injection Testing:

- Intentionally introduce failures, such as delayed responses or corrupted messages.

- Verify that the system can recover gracefully without cascading errors.

### 5. Regression Testing:

- Re-run previous test suites after updates to ensure no unintended behavior changes.

**Table: Testing Techniques and Objectives**

| Testing Type | Scope | Objective | Example in MAS Context |
|---|---|---|---|
| Unit Testing | Individual agents | Validate agent correctness | Validate query parsing logic |
| Integration Testing | Agent interactions | Ensure message consistency | Verify data exchange via JSON |
| Scenario Testing | Full workflows | Confirm task completion | Test document retrieval workflow |
| Fault Injection | System under stress | Evaluate resilience | Drop network packets between agents |
| Regression Testing | Updated system | Ensure stability after changes | Confirm unchanged task accuracy |

## Monitoring Agent Interactions

Monitoring provides operational insight into running systems, enabling engineers to detect failures, inefficiencies, or anomalies.

### Core Monitoring Components:

1. **Event Logging:** Capture structured logs of agent interactions, including timestamps, inputs, outputs, and error states.

2. **Metrics Collection:** Aggregate system metrics such as task completion times, resource usage, and conflict counts.

3. **Tracing:** Correlate interactions across agents for end-to-end visibility of workflows.

4. **Alerting:** Define thresholds for abnormal behaviors, such as prolonged response times or repeated failures.

**Best Practices:**

- Standardize logging schemas to ensure consistency.

- Include correlation IDs in messages for traceability.

- Monitor both agent-level and system-level performance.

**Fault Tolerance and Recovery**

In distributed multi-agent systems, failures are inevitable. Designing for resilience ensures that individual failures do not compromise the entire system.

**Strategies:**

1. **Redundancy:** Deploy multiple agents with overlapping capabilities.

2. **Failover Mechanisms:** When one agent fails, another takes over its responsibilities.

3. **Timeouts and Retries:** Define strict timeouts for agent responses and retry mechanisms to prevent deadlocks.

4. **Graceful Degradation:** Allow partial completion of tasks if some agents fail, instead of full system collapse.

**Example:**
If a validation agent fails to confirm retrieved data, the orchestrator may escalate the task to a redundant agent or log the result with a lower confidence rating.

**Scaling Multi-Agent Systems**

Scaling requires maintaining efficiency while increasing agent count, task complexity, or data volume.

**Horizontal Scaling:**

- Add more agents to handle increased workload.

- Requires load balancing to distribute tasks evenly.

**Vertical Scaling:**

- Increase computational resources per agent.

- Limited by physical resource constraints.

**Load Balancing Strategies:**

1. **Round-Robin Allocation:** Assign tasks sequentially across agents.

2. **Least-Loaded Allocation:** Direct tasks to agents with the lowest current workload.

3. **Domain-Specific Routing:** Send tasks to specialized agents based on task type.

**Infrastructure Considerations:**

- Use container orchestration platforms such as Kubernetes for deployment.

- Employ distributed message queues (e.g., Kafka, RabbitMQ) for scaling communication.

- Monitor system saturation points to determine when scaling is necessary.

## Governance and Safety in Multi-Agent Systems

As multi-agent systems expand in complexity, they must be built with strong governance and safety frameworks in addition to technical scalability. Governance involves ensuring accountability and control, which includes maintaining detailed logs of agent decisions for compliance, enforcing access controls to limit permissions and reduce risk, applying rate limits to prevent excessive resource use, and incorporating human oversight for critical, high-stakes decisions. Safety requires rigorous checks, such as validating external tool calls before execution, enforcing boundaries on iterative loops to prevent runaway behavior, and monitoring for anomalies or harmful outputs that could compromise trust. Moving from prototype to production demands thorough testing, continuous monitoring, and strategies for scaling. Testing confirms reliability, monitoring provides operational visibility, and scaling methods ensure the system can handle growing workloads. Together, governance and safety practices guarantee that multi-agent coordination remains reliable, auditable, and compliant while enabling these systems to tackle complex tasks with resilience.

Security in autonomous systems requires a precise understanding of where vulnerabilities exist and how attackers may exploit them. In LLM-powered agents, the risks extend beyond conventional software concerns. These systems combine natural language interfaces, external tool integrations, memory persistence, and multi-agent communication. Each component introduces unique attack surfaces, and when combined, the risk profile becomes more complex. This section provides a structured framework for analyzing threats and defines the common attack vectors relevant to real-world deployments of agentic systems.

### Foundations of Threat Modeling for Autonomous Agents

Threat modeling is the systematic process of identifying potential adversaries, attack vectors, and weaknesses. For autonomous agents, this process differs from traditional application security due to the probabilistic and language-driven nature of large language models. Instead of only static vulnerabilities, the system may be manipulated dynamically through crafted input or interactions.

Key objectives of threat modeling in this context include:

1. **Identifying adversarial capabilities.** Understanding what resources or knowledge an attacker requires.

2. **Locating exploitable system surfaces.** Analyzing where external input, tools, or data can be influenced.

3. **Estimating impact.** Measuring potential consequences such as data leakage, unauthorized execution, or decision-making failures.

4. **Prioritizing mitigations.** Allocating security controls to the most critical risks based on likelihood and impact.

A widely used framework for structuring this analysis is **STRIDE** (Spoofing, Tampering, Repudiation, Information Disclosure, Denial of Service, Elevation of Privilege). This can be adapted for agentic AI environments by mapping each STRIDE element to the unique features of LLM-driven agents.

### Attack Surfaces in LLM-Powered Agents

Unlike traditional deterministic programs, LLM-based agents expose new types of attack surfaces due to their reliance on unstructured input and generative reasoning. The main categories include:

### Prompt Interfaces

- **Risk:** Malicious actors can craft prompts that cause unintended behavior, override instructions, or extract hidden system information.

- **Example:** An injection attack asking the model to ignore safety rules and expose API keys stored in memory.

- **Impact:** Information disclosure, loss of control over reasoning flow, and execution of unauthorized actions.

### Memory and State Persistence

- **Risk:** Persistent memory systems can be poisoned with adversarial data that influences future outputs.

- **Example:** An attacker contributes false entries to a knowledge base, leading the agent to repeat incorrect information.

- **Impact:** Model biasing, misinformation propagation, and persistent compromise.

## Tool and API Integrations

Allowing agents to interact with external tools introduces security risks if proper safeguards are not in place. Weak input validation or poorly configured APIs can be exploited by attackers, for instance through query injection that tricks the agent into executing harmful shell commands. The potential consequences include unauthorized control over systems, data theft, or even fraudulent activity when financial services are involved.

## Multi-Agent Communication

In distributed environments, communication between agents presents another attack surface. A compromised or malicious agent could spread adversarial instructions or manipulate shared messages, leading to disrupted consensus in planning clusters. Such interference can corrupt system-wide decision-making, undermine reliability, or even trigger denial-of-service conditions.

## Human-in-the-Loop Channels

User feedback and interactive pathways also carry risks when exploited. Attackers may craft deceptive inputs or engage in social engineering to disguise harmful intentions as legitimate guidance. Over time, this can manipulate agent policies, override safety constraints, or cause gradual leakage of sensitive data. The result may be shifts in long-term system objectives or covert exfiltration of information.

## Common Threat Models for Autonomous Systems

The security posture of an agent depends on anticipating adversarial strategies. The following threat models are the most relevant in practice:

### Prompt Injection and Jailbreaks

- **Method:** Attackers craft input to override system instructions or exploit ambiguity in natural language directives.

- **Target:** Core reasoning process of the LLM.

- **Mitigation Focus:** Input sanitization, hierarchical prompting, and controlled execution boundaries.

### Adversarial Input Crafting

- **Method:** Subtle modifications to input designed to alter output without obvious malicious content.

- **Target:** Model decision boundaries and embedding spaces.

- **Mitigation Focus:** Adversarial training, ensemble detection, and input anomaly filtering.

### Data Poisoning

- **Method:** Insertion of manipulated or biased data into persistent memory or fine-tuning datasets.

- **Target:** Long-term system behavior and stored knowledge.

- **Mitigation Focus:** Data validation pipelines, provenance tracking, and redundancy in memory management.

### Model Extraction and Reverse Engineering

- **Method:** Repeated queries designed to replicate or approximate the behavior of the deployed model.

- **Target:** Proprietary model weights, decision-making logic, or sensitive training data.

- **Mitigation Focus:** Rate limiting, monitoring for anomalous query patterns, and watermarking outputs.

## Denial of Service (DoS) and Resource Exhaustion

- **Method:** Overloading the system with computationally expensive requests.

- **Target:** LLM inference infrastructure, orchestration layers, or tool execution environments.

- **Mitigation Focus:** Rate controls, request prioritization, and resource quotas.

## Unauthorized Privilege Escalation

- **Method:** Exploiting poorly configured permissions for tool use, memory access, or API calls.

- **Target:** Control plane of the agent, often through indirect natural language manipulation.

- **Mitigation Focus:** Strict access control policies and sandboxed tool execution.

## Structured Classification of Risks

A structured risk matrix helps practitioners evaluate both likelihood and severity of threats.

| Threat Category | Likelihood | Impact | Example Scenario | Priority Level |
|---|---|---|---|---|
| Prompt Injection | High | High | Jailbreak instructions override guardrails | Critical |
| Data Poisoning | Medium | High | False entries in memory corrupt agent knowledge | High |
| Tool/API Exploitation | Medium | High | Malicious API calls causing financial transactions | High |
| Model Extraction | Medium | Medium | Querying system to reconstruct training data | Medium |
| Denial of Service | High | Medium | Flooding with costly requests to degrade performance | Medium |
| Privilege Escalation | Low | High | Unauthorized access to shell execution | High |

This classification provides a practical basis for prioritizing defensive engineering.

## Risk Amplification in Multi-Component Systems

In real-world deployments, agents rarely operate in isolation. Risks become amplified when:

1. **Multiple agents share a memory store.** A single poisoned entry can propagate through the entire system.

2. **Agents invoke high-impact tools.** Errors or manipulations cascade from language-level reasoning to critical infrastructure.

3. **External data sources are used without validation.** Unverified information sources can act as persistent attack vectors.

When threat modeling for autonomous agents, you need to think about both regular software risks and language-driven manipulation that is specific to LLMs. The key places where attacks might happen include prompt interfaces, memory stores, tool integrations, communication amongst agents, and channels for people to talk to each other. We need to deal with threat models including rapid injection, data poisoning, adversarial inputs, model extraction, and denial of service in a systematic way. Engineers set the stage for defensive design by putting hazards into structured frameworks and identifying how they get worse in systems with many parts. This will be explained in more detail in the next section.

Identifying dangers is not enough for autonomous agents to be safe. To defend systems well, you need carefully designed patterns and mechanisms that make them more resistant to attacks and failures. These steps need to be included into several levels, from checking the input and controlling internal logic to integrating tools and coordinating the whole system. This part gives you real-world, evidence-based defense methods that have been used in both research and real-world situations.

## Principles of Defensive Design

Defensive design in LLM-powered agents is guided by three foundational principles:

1. **Defense in Depth.** Security controls must be distributed across layers of the system. No single safeguard is sufficient against the diversity of threats.

2. **Least Privilege.** Agents, tools, and users should have only the permissions necessary for their function, minimizing potential damage from compromise.

3. **Fail-Safe Defaults.** In the presence of uncertainty, the system should prioritize safety, declining actions that may result in risk without explicit confirmation.

These principles ensure that robustness is not an afterthought but a core property of the system.

## Input-Level Defenses

The first line of defense against adversarial activity lies at the point where external input enters the system.

## Prompt Sanitization

- **Technique:** Filtering or rewriting inputs before they reach the model.

- **Implementation:**

    o   Pattern matching for known jailbreak phrases.

    o   Context-aware preprocessing to separate instructions from data.

    o   Restricting unsupported commands through structured parsers.

- **Limitations:** Cannot guarantee full protection since adversarial phrasing evolves rapidly.

## Structured Interfaces

Instead of accepting raw natural language for high-risk tasks, enforce structured schemas.

- Example: Requiring JSON-based queries for database access rather than free text.

- Benefit: Reduces ambiguity, limits injection opportunities, and simplifies validation.

## Anomaly Detection at Input

- Use embedding-based similarity checks to flag unusual or suspicious inputs.

- Integration with rate-limiting to stop automated adversarial probing.

## Core Reasoning Defenses

Even after inputs are validated, protective measures must extend into the LLM's reasoning process and the orchestration layer to guard against manipulation. One approach is hierarchical prompting, which organizes instructions into separate layers: one defining task objectives, another enforcing safety constraints, and a third guiding reasoning steps. This layered structure lowers the risk that a single malicious prompt can override the entire system. Another defense is self-verification loops, where the model produces an initial response and then reviews it against predefined safety or accuracy checks.

For example, a medical assistant might generate a draft recommendation but then scan it to ensure no unsafe guidance is included before sharing it with users. Guardrail models add an additional layer of protection by using smaller, specialized classifiers to screen the outputs of the main LLM. These can detect potential data leaks, unsafe actions, or violations of system policies. Finally, response randomization introduces controlled variability into outputs, which prevents adversaries from exploiting predictable behavior and makes attempts at reverse engineering or model extraction more difficult.

## Tool and API Integration Defenses

Agents become significantly more powerful, and more vulnerable, when connected to external tools. Robust control is essential.

## Sandboxed Execution

- Execute high-risk tools (shells, code interpreters) in isolated environments with strict resource limits.

- Use containerization or virtual machines to ensure that any malicious output cannot propagate.

## Permission Management

- Assign explicit, minimal permissions for each tool.

- Example: A financial transaction API should only be accessible when confirmed by multiple checks, not by default.

## Mediator Components

- Introduce a mediator service that intercepts all tool calls.

- Performs checks for format, scope, and authorization before allowing execution.

## Execution Confirmation

- For critical operations, enforce dual approval.

    1. The agent proposes the action.

    2. A verification mechanism, which may be another model or a human operator, confirms execution.

## Memory and Knowledge Base Defenses

Persistent memory can greatly enhance the usefulness of an agent system, but it also introduces vulnerabilities that must be carefully managed through defensive strategies. One of the most important safeguards is the use of validation pipelines. Before any entry is added to memory, it should undergo integrity checks to confirm accuracy and reliability. Whenever possible, this validation should include verification against trusted external sources, ensuring that only high-quality information is preserved.

Redundancy further strengthens defenses by distributing knowledge across multiple independent memory stores. When information is retrieved, cross-validation between these stores can help detect inconsistencies and mitigate the risk of memory poisoning. This layered approach prevents a single corrupted source from compromising the entire system.

To minimize long-term risks, expiry and rotation mechanisms are also essential. Rather than permanently storing unverified entries, volatile data should be assigned time-to-live policies, ensuring that potentially adversarial content does not persist indefinitely. By regularly expiring and refreshing memory, the system reduces the likelihood of malicious data embedding itself into its knowledge base.

Finally, strict access control provides another layer of protection. Systems should clearly differentiate between short-term reasoning context and long-term persistent memory, restricting access so that only functions requiring memory can interact with it. This disciplined approach helps preserve memory integrity, reduces the attack surface, and ensures that sensitive information is only exposed where absolutely necessary.

### System-Level Robustness Mechanisms

At the orchestration level, entire classes of robustness mechanisms must be enforced.

### Rate Limiting and Quotas

- Control the number of tool invocations, API requests, or memory writes per time interval.

- Protects against denial-of-service and automated probing.

### Redundancy and Cross-Checking

- Deploy multiple agents or reasoning pathways that verify one another.

- Example: Majority voting across outputs from several agents trained with different seeds.

### Monitoring and Logging

- Centralized monitoring of input, output, and tool usage patterns.

- Detect anomalies such as repeated failed tool invocations, sudden spikes in resource consumption, or attempts to access restricted capabilities.

### Circuit Breakers

- Automatically disable risky functionality when abnormal patterns are detected.

- Example: Temporarily suspending financial transaction capability if irregular request frequency is observed.

### Defensive Design Patterns

Several architectural patterns occur in successful robust systems:

### Pattern 1: Mediator-Sandbox Pattern

- All external tool calls pass through a mediator that enforces validation.

- Execution occurs in a sandbox with strict isolation.

### Pattern 2: Dual-Agent Verification Pattern

- One agent performs the task; another independently verifies before action is taken.

- Reduces reliance on single outputs and minimizes injection success.

**Pattern 3: Guardrail Layer Pattern**

- Insert lightweight models or rule-based systems as a guardrail between input/output and external exposure.

- Provides constant filtering of unsafe or unexpected data.

**Pattern 4: Consensus and Voting Pattern**

- For high-value decisions, deploy multiple reasoning paths and aggregate results through voting.

- Mitigates risks of adversarial steering of a single model.

**Trade-offs in Robustness Mechanisms**

Every defensive measure in agentic systems comes with practical compromises. Sandboxing provides stronger isolation and security but introduces additional latency and consumes more resources. Redundancy improves system reliability yet increases computational expenses. Guardrails reduce the chance of unsafe outputs but may mistakenly block valid actions, creating unnecessary friction. Rate limiting curbs potential misuse, though it can negatively affect user experience when workloads spike. Choosing the right defenses requires carefully balancing technical safeguards with organizational priorities, weighing cost, performance, and acceptable levels of risk.

Robustness in autonomous systems is best achieved through a layered strategy. Input sanitization, structured interfaces, hierarchical prompting, guardrail models, and self-verification all contribute to strengthening reasoning integrity. Tool execution is made safer by incorporating sandboxing, mediator layers, and permission management. Memory reliability is supported through validation pipelines, redundancy, and strict access policies. At the system level, operational safeguards such as monitoring, rate limiting, and circuit breakers enhance resilience under stress. By applying proven design strategies like mediator-sandbox combinations, dual-agent verification, guardrail layering, and consensus mechanisms, engineers can significantly lower vulnerabilities.

These protections create a hardened baseline, but resilience cannot rely on design alone. Ongoing testing, regular audits, and strong governance practices are essential to ensure defenses remain effective in production. The next discussion will turn to these operational measures in more detail.

## Section 3: Testing, Auditing, and Governance for Secure Deployment

Security and robustness in autonomous systems cannot be guaranteed by design patterns alone. Sustained reliability requires rigorous testing, systematic auditing, and strong governance structures throughout the lifecycle of an LLM-powered agent. This section outlines practices for validating security controls, identifying vulnerabilities, and embedding accountability into deployment pipelines.

**Role of Testing in Autonomous Systems Security**

Testing provides empirical assurance that security and robustness mechanisms are effective under operating conditions. In autonomous agents, testing is complicated by dynamic reasoning, open-ended inputs, and tool integrations. Unlike traditional software, these systems cannot be exhaustively verified through static analysis.

Effective testing frameworks for LLM-powered agents share three attributes:

1. **Realism.** Tests must simulate realistic adversarial conditions, including prompt injection and misuse of tools.

2. **Coverage.** Both input-output behaviors and internal reasoning pathways should be tested.

3. **Repeatability.** Results must be reproducible across versions and environments to detect regressions.

**Security-Focused Testing Methods**

**Penetration Testing for Agents**

- **Definition:** Controlled attempts to compromise the system by simulating adversaries.

- **Scope:** Includes prompt injection, adversarial queries, and attempts to escalate privileges through tool calls.

- **Practice:** Combine automated fuzzing with human security teams trained in adversarial prompting.

**Red-Teaming**

- **Objective:** Identify unexpected vulnerabilities through creative adversarial exploration.

- **Implementation:** Diverse human testers interact with the agent, using varied phrasing and techniques to bypass defenses.

- **Output:** Categorized vulnerability reports feeding back into design improvements.

**Fault Injection**

- **Technique:** Intentionally introducing errors into inputs, memory stores, or tool responses.

- **Purpose:** Assess whether the system fails safely or propagates corrupted data.

- **Examples:**

  o Feeding malformed JSON into structured interfaces.

  o Returning manipulated responses from external APIs.

**Regression and Stress Testing**

- Regression tests confirm that defenses remain effective after updates.

- Stress tests evaluate robustness under high query volumes, concurrent tool requests, and adversarial traffic spikes.

**Evaluation Metrics for Secure Deployment**

To ensure consistent measurement, quantitative metrics must be defined.

| Metric | Definition | Purpose |
|---|---|---|
| Attack Success Rate | Percentage of adversarial attempts that bypass defenses | Evaluates resilience to prompt injection |
| Recovery Time | Time required to restore safe operation after an error or attack | Measures incident response effectiveness |
| False Positive Rate | Proportion of legitimate inputs incorrectly blocked | Balances robustness and usability |
| Fault Containment Rate | Percentage of injected errors confined without propagation | Indicates resilience of error isolation |
| Monitoring Coverage | Fraction of critical interactions logged and observable | Ensures auditability and detection capability |

**Auditing Practices**

Auditing plays a vital role in ensuring that system security remains transparent and accountable, not just technical. Comprehensive logging is central to this process, capturing prompts, reasoning traces, tool invocations, and final outputs. To protect sensitive information, logs must use techniques such as anonymization or encryption, while still allowing for effective post-incident reviews and regulatory compliance checks. Audit trails extend this by requiring every critical action to be linked to a verifiable sequence of approvals and validations, which is particularly essential in domains like finance, healthcare, and safety-critical operations.

Independent audits add another layer of assurance, with external security specialists periodically assessing both design and operational performance to avoid dependence solely on internal checks. Continuous auditing, supported by automated tools, strengthens oversight further by using anomaly detection pipelines to flag deviations in real time, such as unusual patterns of tool use that differ from established baselines. Together, these practices ensure systems are not only secure but also demonstrably accountable.

## Governance Structures

Governance aligns technical safeguards with organizational accountability.

### Policy Frameworks

- Define acceptable use policies for agentic systems.
- Specify boundaries for tool access, data retention, and decision-making autonomy.

### Risk Classification

- Categorize agents by risk level (low, medium, high).
- Higher-risk agents require stronger testing, auditing, and human oversight.

### Human-in-the-Loop Oversight

- Critical decisions must pass through human approval.
- Provides accountability for actions that carry ethical, financial, or legal risk.

### Regulatory Alignment

- Ensure compliance with existing standards such as ISO/IEC 27001 for information security or NIST AI Risk Management Framework.
- Document practices for audits by external regulators or certification bodies.

## Continuous Monitoring and Incident Response

Even the most rigorously tested and well-governed systems are not immune to failures or attacks, which makes continuous monitoring and incident response a crucial part of resilient architecture. Preparedness begins with careful monitoring across multiple dimensions. Performance monitoring tracks latency, error rates, and throughput to ensure the system is running smoothly. Security monitoring focuses on detecting injection attempts, unauthorized tool usage, and abnormal memory operations that may signal adversarial activity. At the same time, behavioral monitoring looks for sudden deviations in reasoning patterns or output style that could indicate a compromise or malfunction.

Automated alerting strengthens this process by ensuring anomalies do not go unnoticed. Threshold-based triggers flag unusual behaviors, and escalation pipelines ensure that human operators are notified immediately when intervention becomes necessary. This rapid feedback loop allows teams to act before issues can cause broader harm.

When problems do arise, incident response playbooks provide predefined procedures for handling them. These workflows guide operators through isolating affected components, rolling back to safe versions, and restoring stable operation. They also include clear communication protocols to keep stakeholders and regulators informed, maintaining trust and compliance even during disruptions.

The process does not end once stability is restored. Post-incident reviews are essential for long-term resilience, requiring a root cause analysis of every major event. The insights gained are then fed back into the system, informing design improvements and expanding test coverage. In this way, each incident becomes not just a challenge, but also an opportunity to strengthen the system against future risks.

### Integrating Testing, Auditing, and Governance into Deployment Pipelines

Security measures need to be in place all the time, not just sometimes. Integrating with CI/CD processes makes sure that every new release is tested.

This pipeline makes sure that no deployment skips security checks.

Testing, auditing, and governance make sure that design-time defenses work in real life. Penetration testing, red-teaming, fault injection, and regression suites check that a system can handle both intentional and unintentional errors. Logging, independent review, and compliance tracking are all parts of auditing that make sure people are held accountable. Governance structures make sure that technical protections work with the obligations of the company. This is done through constant monitoring and incident response procedures.

This combination of testing, auditing, and governance into the deployment lifecycle makes autonomous systems very secure. Even the best-designed defenses get worse over time if you don't follow these rules. With them, businesses can keep their agents safe, reliable, and trustworthy on a large scale.

# PART III: DOMAINS OF APPLICATION

This section shows how agentic AI can be used in important areas, turning ideas into real-world effects. Each chapter looks at a different area, such healthcare, finance, robotics, corporate operations, or new industries, and talks about both the chances and the limits in that area. The emphasis is on pragmatic design factors, compliance mandates, and specialized issues that influence system architecture. These chapters demonstrate how agentic AI can be grounded in certain contexts, illustrating how perception, reasoning, memory, and action loops can adjust to the requirements of various environments while ensuring accuracy, safety, and reliability.

## Section 1: Clinical Data Integration and Workflow Alignment

Designing and deploying agentic AI systems in healthcare requires more than building accurate models. The success of these systems depends on how effectively they can integrate with the diverse and fragmented data environments of modern healthcare institutions, and how closely they align with existing clinical workflows. This section provides a structured view of the technical and procedural considerations necessary to achieve safe and effective integration.

### Characteristics of Healthcare Data

Healthcare data presents a distinctive level of complexity, requiring agentic AI systems to manage multiple formats while ensuring consistency and reliability. Structured data forms the backbone of clinical records, encompassing electronic health records with patient demographics, diagnoses, prescribed medications, and laboratory findings. It also includes standardized billing and administrative codes, such as ICD-10 and CPT, as well as vital signs and physiological measurements captured from bedside monitors.

Alongside this, semi-structured data adds another layer of challenge. Medical imaging is typically stored in standardized formats like DICOM, while laboratory results are often transmitted through HL7 messages. Increasingly, healthcare systems also exchange information through FHIR bundles, enabling interoperability across applications but demanding robust parsing and alignment.

Unstructured data, however, is perhaps the most difficult to manage. Physician notes, discharge summaries, radiology interpretations, and pathology reports often appear as free text, requiring natural language processing to extract actionable insights. Patient-provided inputs, such as questionnaires or secure messages, further add to this category, bringing in valuable but highly variable information.

Finally, modern healthcare environments generate real-time data streams that must be processed without delay. Intensive care units produce continuous waveforms from monitors, while wearable devices and remote platforms track patients outside the hospital setting. Alerts from infusion pumps, ventilators, and nurse call systems also demand immediate attention. To operate effectively, agentic AI must normalize and reconcile these diverse data types, ensuring they are harmonized into a consistent format that supports reliable reasoning and decision-making.

### Standards for Healthcare Data Exchange

To interoperate safely across systems, AI agents must comply with widely adopted standards:

- **HL7 v2 and v3**: Used extensively for hospital information systems and laboratory systems. Despite variability in implementations, HL7 remains foundational for clinical messaging.

- **FHIR (Fast Healthcare Interoperability Resources)**: Provides a modern, web-based standard for structured data exchange. Its modular design makes it well-suited for API-based integration with AI agents.

- **DICOM (Digital Imaging and Communications in Medicine)**: The standard for medical imaging, critical for radiology, cardiology, and oncology workflows.

- **LOINC (Logical Observation Identifiers Names and Codes)**: Used for identifying laboratories and clinical observations.

- **SNOMED CT**: A comprehensive clinical terminology system that enables semantic interoperability.

### Integration with Clinical Workflows

Healthcare is governed by structured processes that ensure patient safety. AI agents must adapt to these workflows rather than impose entirely new paradigms.

**Key Workflow Examples**

1. **Admission, Discharge, and Transfer (ADT)**

   o Agents monitor patient movement across departments and update task priorities accordingly.

   o Example: An agent reassigns pending laboratory requests when a patient moves from the emergency department to an inpatient unit.

2. **Medication Management**

   o Agents cross-check prescriptions against allergy information, laboratory values, and current medications.

   o Integration ensures that alerts are routed through the established clinical decision support (CDS) pathways used by pharmacists and physicians.

3. **Diagnostic Imaging**

   o Agents retrieve and interpret DICOM studies.

   o Reports are passed through established radiology workflows for verification before being added to the patient record.

4. **Care Coordination**

   o Agents help synchronize information between physicians, nurses, and allied health staff.

   o Task lists and communication channels must remain consistent with hospital-approved paging, messaging, or collaboration tools.

**Challenges in Data Integration**

Despite the presence of standards, integration remains difficult. Common challenges include:

- **Heterogeneity of Systems**: EHRs from different vendors implement standards inconsistently.

- **Data Quality Issues**: Missing values, inconsistent coding, and unstructured free text reduce reliability.

- **Latency**: Real-time decision-making requires rapid ingestion and processing of data streams.

- **Semantic Gaps**: Clinical concepts may not map directly between different coding systems.

- **Access Control**: Strict authorization is needed to ensure compliance with HIPAA and GDPR.

**Technical Strategies for Integration**

1. **Middleware and Integration Engines**

   o Use healthcare integration engines such as Mirth Connect or Rhapsody to translate between HL7 and FHIR.

   o Implement mapping services that normalize laboratory codes to LOINC or clinical findings to SNOMED CT.

2. **Data Normalization Pipelines**

   o  Apply Extract, Transform, Load (ETL) processes to unify structured and unstructured data.

   o  Implement de-identification pipelines for privacy-preserving AI training.

3. **APIs and Microservices**

   o  Provide RESTful or GraphQL interfaces that expose standardized patient data.

   o  Support FHIR-based query and subscription mechanisms for real-time updates.

4. **Natural Language Processing (NLP) for Unstructured Data**

   o  Use domain-specific NLP models to extract structured features from clinical notes.

   o  Ensure outputs are coded with standard terminologies before being fed into downstream reasoning modules.

## Alignment with Clinical Roles and Responsibilities

AI agents in healthcare must be designed to align with the established roles and responsibilities of clinical staff, ensuring that their support enhances rather than disrupts existing workflows. For physicians, this means providing decision support that aids in diagnostics, ensures adherence to clinical guidelines, and delivers accurate risk scoring. Such outputs must integrate seamlessly into their clinical reasoning process, offering clarity without overwhelming them with unnecessary detail. Nurses, by contrast, benefit from tools that assist with continuous monitoring, the prioritization of tasks, and streamlined documentation. Since nurses are often the first to respond to alerts and patient changes, agents must present information in a concise, actionable manner that helps them triage effectively.

Pharmacists depend heavily on AI-driven checks for drug interactions and dosage validation. Precision and reliability are crucial here, as even minor errors can have serious clinical consequences. Agents serving this group must therefore emphasize accuracy and clarity in communicating potential risks or corrective recommendations.

For administrators, the value lies in operational efficiency and resource allocation. AI support should focus on optimizing schedules, balancing workloads, and identifying systemic inefficiencies that can be addressed to improve overall care delivery. Across all roles, agents need to tailor their communication style and respect the boundaries of professional responsibilities. By adapting outputs to the specific needs of each group, AI systems can integrate effectively into the clinical environment, supporting staff while maintaining trust and accountability.

## Example: Clinical Workflow Integration

Consider a hospital implementing an agent to monitor sepsis risk:

1. The agent ingests structured EHR data (vitals, labs, comorbidities).

2. It normalizes laboratory results to LOINC codes.

3. Free-text nursing notes are processed with NLP to extract mentions of fever or confusion.

4. The agent calculates risk scores using a validated sepsis model.

5. Alerts are routed through the existing CDS pathway so that physicians and nurses receive messages in their normal workflow.

6. The decision and supporting evidence are logged in the EHR for traceability.

This structured integration ensures that the agent's function strengthens existing workflows rather than introducing parallel, unverified processes.

**Best Practices for Workflow Alignment**

- **Embed within Existing Systems**: Agents should operate through EHRs, pharmacy systems, or radiology viewers rather than separate dashboards when possible.

- **Provide Contextual Explanations**: Outputs must be traceable to source data and linked to relevant guidelines.

- **Respect Clinical Governance**: All automated suggestions should fall under existing clinical decision-making authority.

- **Iterative Testing**: Pilot deployments in shadow mode before agents actively influence patient care.

Successful deployment of agentic AI in healthcare requires systematic data integration and workflow alignment. Data must be ingested across structured, semi-structured, unstructured, and real-time sources, normalized through recognized standards such as HL7, FHIR, and DICOM, and aligned with clinical terminologies like SNOMED CT and LOINC. Technical strategies include middleware, APIs, and NLP pipelines. Alignment with clinical roles ensures usability and trust, while integration with existing workflows guarantees safety and compliance.

## Section 2: Safety, Compliance, and Risk Mitigation in Healthcare Agents

Ensuring safety, regulatory compliance, and effective risk mitigation is fundamental in the design of agentic AI systems for healthcare. Unlike general-purpose AI deployments, clinical applications operate within tightly regulated environments where patient safety and legal accountability are paramount. This section outlines the technical and procedural measures required to maintain compliance with healthcare regulations, safeguard patients, and minimize risks in real-world deployments.

**Principles of Safety in Healthcare AI**

Safety in healthcare AI rests on three foundational principles that guide both design and deployment. The first is non-maleficence, or the commitment to do no harm. AI agents must never produce actions or recommendations that could place a patient's health at risk. To uphold this standard, systems should adopt conservative defaults, incorporate human verification steps, and implement fallback mechanisms that prevent unsafe behavior when uncertainty arises.

The second principle is transparency and traceability. Every output generated by an agent must be auditable, with comprehensive documentation of the input data, the reasoning or decision logic, and the provenance of the underlying model. Detailed logging is essential so that clinical staff can reconstruct the steps leading to a conclusion, ensuring accountability and supporting trust in the system's recommendations.

The third guiding principle is alignment with established standards of care. AI outputs must remain consistent with evidence-based clinical guidelines, whether issued by global authorities such as the World Health Organization, national agencies like the Centers for Disease Control and Prevention, or specialty-specific professional societies. By grounding recommendations in recognized best practices, agents reinforce the reliability of their guidance and strengthen their role as trusted partners in patient care.

**Technical Strategies for Safety and Compliance**

**1. Fail-Safe and Human-in-the-Loop Design**

- Clinicians must review critical decisions.

- Agents should include fallback modes that return control to standard workflows if anomalies are detected.

## 2. Access Control and Data Governance

- Implement role-based access to ensure agents only access the minimum required data.
- Maintain audit trails of every data request and decision output.

## 3. Validation and Verification Pipelines

- Conduct pre-deployment testing using retrospective datasets.
- Use prospective validation in controlled environments before full release.
- Compare outputs against gold-standard clinical guidelines.

## 4. Bias and Fairness Testing

- Evaluate performance across demographic subgroups.
- Report on subgroup performance metrics transparently to regulators and stakeholders.

## 5. Continuous Monitoring

- Deploy runtime monitoring agents that track accuracy, latency, and data drift.
- Establish thresholds that automatically trigger alerts when deviations occur.

## Risk Assessment Methodologies

Healthcare AI risk assessments can draw on established methodologies:

- **Failure Modes and Effects Analysis (FMEA)**
  - Systematically identifies potential failure points, assigns severity scores, and prioritizes mitigation actions.

- **Hazard Analysis and Critical Control Points (HACCP)**
  - Used in clinical laboratories, applicable for identifying critical safety checkpoints in AI workflows.

- **Probabilistic Risk Assessment (PRA)**
  - Quantifies risks by estimating probabilities of adverse events and their impact.

## Table: Sample FMEA for AI-driven Sepsis Detection Agent

| Failure Mode | Severity | Likelihood | Detectability | Risk Priority | Mitigation Strategy |
|---|---|---|---|---|---|
| False negative (missed sepsis) | High | Medium | Medium | High | Human-in-loop confirmation, redundancy with EHR CDS |
| False positive (unnecessary alert) | Medium | High | High | Medium | Alert suppression rules, user feedback loops |
| Data latency > 5 min | High | Medium | High | High | Real-time monitoring, failover to backup feeds |
| Unauthorized data access | High | Low | High | Medium | RBAC, encryption, audit logging |

## Auditing and Traceability

Auditing and traceability are essential in healthcare AI to guarantee that every decision can be reconstructed with precision and accountability. This begins with rigorous decision logging, where all inputs, intermediate reasoning steps, and final outputs are systematically recorded. To protect the integrity of this information, logs must be immutable and stored in compliance with healthcare data retention policies, ensuring they remain reliable records for future audits.

Model version control adds another layer of traceability by documenting the exact versions of models in use, along with their training data sources and any parameter adjustments. This level of detail ensures that regulatory filings or compliance reviews can reference specific configurations, making it possible to link outcomes directly to the technical environment in which they were produced.

Complementing these measures are explainability reports, which summarize how decisions are reached. Whether through feature attribution techniques or structured decision pathway descriptions, these reports must be formatted in a way that clinicians can readily interpret. By making the reasoning behind AI outputs transparent and clinically meaningful, healthcare systems can reinforce trust, meet regulatory standards, and ensure that AI remains a responsible partner in patient care.

## Incident Response and Risk Mitigation

Incidents in AI-driven healthcare environments must be managed systematically:

- **Detection**: Monitor for anomalies such as performance degradation, unexpected outputs, or security events.

- **Containment**: Immediately suspend or disable affected modules without disrupting core clinical workflows.

- **Analysis**: Conduct root cause investigations involving both technical and clinical experts.

- **Corrective Action**: Update models, retrain with corrected datasets, or adjust decision thresholds.

- **Regulatory Reporting**: Notify relevant authorities (e.g., FDA, EMA) if incidents meet reporting thresholds.

## Example: Risk Mitigation in Medication Reconciliation

Consider an AI agent supporting medication reconciliation during patient admission:

1. **Data Integration**: The agent ingests medication histories from multiple sources.

2. **Risk Check**: It detects potential drug-drug interactions and allergy conflicts.

3. **Safety Control**: Recommendations are displayed to pharmacists, not directly applied.

4. **Validation**: The pharmacist validates, edits, or rejects suggestions.

5. **Compliance Logging**: All decisions and overrides are stored in the EHR with timestamps.

This layered approach ensures that the agent improves efficiency while remaining safe, auditable, and compliant.

## Best Practices for Risk Mitigation

- **Adopt Incremental Rollouts**: Deploy agents in shadow mode before granting active decision-making authority.

- **Engage Clinical Governance Committees**: Involve physicians, nurses, and compliance officers in evaluation.

- **Maintain Continuous Post-Market Surveillance**: Monitor for emergent risks once agents are live.

- **Document Risk Management Processes**: Ensure that every mitigation step aligns with ISO 14971.

Healthcare AI systems require robust safety, compliance, and risk mitigation frameworks. By adhering to regulations such as HIPAA, GDPR, and MDR, and implementing technical safeguards including fail-safes, validation pipelines, and continuous monitoring, agentic AI can be deployed responsibly. Structured risk assessment methodologies such as FMEA and HACCP provide systematic ways to identify vulnerabilities. Finally, auditing, explainability, and governance mechanisms ensure that systems remain transparent, accountable, and trustworthy in clinical environments.

## Section 3: Evaluation, Deployment, and Lifecycle Management of Healthcare AI Agents

Deployment of agentic AI in healthcare is not a one-time exercise. It requires a structured approach to evaluation, phased introduction into live environments, and continuous lifecycle management to ensure ongoing safety, compliance, and clinical value. Unlike consumer applications, healthcare systems operate in high-stakes settings where reliability, accountability, and traceability are non-negotiable. This section outlines proven methods for validating, deploying, and sustaining LLM-powered healthcare agents in clinical environments.

### Evaluation Principles for Healthcare Agents

Evaluation is the cornerstone of safe deployment. It ensures that AI agents meet predefined standards of accuracy, reliability, and fairness across the populations they serve.

### Key Principles:

1. **Clinical Validity**

   o   Outputs must align with established evidence-based guidelines.

   o   Results should be benchmarked against gold-standard clinical decision support (CDS) systems.

2. **Reliability Under Variability**

   o   Agents must function consistently across different clinical settings, patient demographics, and data sources.

3. **Fairness and Equity**

   o   Systems must be evaluated for potential disparities in recommendations across age, gender, ethnicity, or socioeconomic groups.

4. **Safety Margins**

   o   Agents should default to conservative, clinically safe recommendations when uncertainty is high.

### Evaluation Methodologies

Healthcare AI evaluation requires rigorous multi-layered testing before live deployment.

### 1. Retrospective Validation

- Apply the agent to historical patient data.

- Compare recommendations with actual clinical outcomes.

- Identify false positives, false negatives, and cases requiring escalation.

## 2. Prospective Validation

- Deploy the system in a controlled clinical environment.
- Compare AI-driven recommendations with clinician decisions in real time.
- Use this phase to fine-tune thresholds and workflows.

## 3. Benchmarking Against Standards

- Use established benchmarks such as:
  - **MIMIC-IV dataset** for ICU decision support testing.
  - **PhysioNet Challenges** for physiological signal analysis.
  - **SNOMED CT and LOINC** codes for terminology consistency.

## 4. Simulation-Based Testing

- Employ synthetic datasets to simulate edge cases such as rare diseases or unusual comorbidities.
- Ensure the agent demonstrates robustness to low-frequency, high-impact scenarios.

## 5. User Acceptance Testing (UAT)

- Involve clinicians, nurses, and pharmacists in evaluating the system.
- Collect structured feedback on usability, interpretability, and workflow fit.

### Metrics for Healthcare AI Evaluation

Evaluating healthcare AI requires a broad set of metrics that reflect both clinical effectiveness and operational reliability. Clinical performance metrics are central, as they measure how well the system supports patient care. Sensitivity and specificity provide insight into detection accuracy for conditions such as sepsis or arrhythmia, while positive predictive value and negative predictive value ensure that alerts are dependable. The number needed to alert is also critical, as it quantifies the workload impact by showing how many false alerts occur for every meaningful one, helping to balance safety with efficiency.

System reliability metrics focus on ensuring that AI tools can be trusted in demanding clinical environments. Uptime must exceed 99.9 percent for critical care systems, as even brief downtime can place patients at risk. Latency should remain under a second for bedside monitoring, where delays could jeopardize rapid intervention. Throughput is equally important, as hospital environments require the ability to scale effectively and handle large volumes of data without performance degradation.

Fairness metrics address equity in healthcare delivery. Demographic parity helps determine whether the AI system treats patients consistently across different subgroups, while equalized odds ensure that sensitivity and specificity are balanced across demographics. These measures guard against biases that could exacerbate health disparities.

Usability metrics provide the final layer of evaluation by capturing how well the system integrates into clinical workflows. Task completion rate measures the percentage of clinical activities successfully assisted by AI, while time savings reflect the efficiency gained from reducing repetitive documentation. Clinician override rate offers a reality check; frequent overrides may signal misalignment with professional judgment and highlight areas where the system needs refinement. Together, these metrics create a comprehensive framework for assessing healthcare AI.

## Deployment Strategies for Healthcare AI Agents

### 1. Sandbox Testing

- Deploy agents in a simulated environment using de-identified patient data.
- Validate interoperability with electronic health records (EHRs), lab systems, and imaging repositories.

### 2. Shadow Mode Deployment

- Run agents alongside existing clinical workflows without influencing care decisions.
- Collect performance data and clinician feedback over a defined period.

### 3. Phased Rollouts

- Begin with limited pilot sites or specific clinical departments.
- Gradually it expands based on observed performance and acceptance.

### 4. Controlled Activation

- Configure agents to support narrow, well-defined tasks (e.g., medication reconciliation) before extending to broader domains.

### 5.Human-in-the-Loop Models

- Ensure final decision authority rests with clinicians during early deployment phases.
- Transition to higher autonomy levels only after sufficient evidence of safety.

## Lifecycle Management of Healthcare AI Agents

Once deployed, healthcare agents require continuous management to remain safe, effective, and compliant.

### Model Monitoring

- **Performance Drift**: Track changes in accuracy as new data patterns emerge.
- **Data Drift**: Detect shifts in patient demographics or clinical practices that impact model validity.

### Feedback Loops

- Incorporate clinician feedback directly into system retraining.
- Use structured forms in EHRs to capture override reasons.

### Model Updates

- Schedule regular retraining cycles using updated datasets.
- Validate new versions against prior versions before release.
- Maintain backward compatibility with audit and compliance systems.

### Audit and Logging

- Record every decision with timestamps, inputs, and outputs.

- Store logs in compliance with HIPAA, GDPR, or regional equivalents.

**Governance Committees**

- Establish multidisciplinary governance groups to review system performance and risk reports.

- Ensure accountability across clinical, technical, and regulatory domains.

**Incident Management and Post-Market Surveillance**

Healthcare AI systems must have robust mechanisms for identifying and addressing incidents:

1. **Incident Detection**

   o Automated alerts for abnormal error rates, system downtime, or anomalous outputs.

2. **Root Cause Analysis**

   o Joint reviews by technical teams and clinical experts to trace failure points.

3. **Corrective and Preventive Actions (CAPA)**

   o Update training datasets, refine thresholds, or adjust access controls.

4. **Regulatory Reporting**

   o Submit adverse event reports to regulatory authorities as required under MDR or FDA guidelines.

**Example Deployment: AI Agent for Radiology Workflow**

**Context**

- Task: Automating prioritization of radiology images based on suspected critical findings (e.g., intracranial hemorrhage).

**Evaluation**

- Retrospective testing against annotated datasets.

- Sensitivity > 95 percent for critical findings required before live testing.

**Deployment**

1. Shadow mode integration with PACS (Picture Archiving and Communication System).

2. Alerts displayed only to radiologists for feedback collection.

3. Transition to active use once false positive rates were within acceptable thresholds.

**Lifecycle Management**

- Continuous monitoring of case-level performance.

- Quarterly review of outcomes by a governance committee.

- Annual model retraining with new data from hospital archives.

**Best Practices for Sustainable Healthcare AI Deployment**

1. **Adopt Staged Validation Pipelines**: Move progressively from retrospective validation to prospective and live shadow testing.

2. **Prioritize Interoperability**: Ensure compatibility with major EHRs, laboratory systems, and imaging standards.

3. **Maintain Continuous Monitoring**: Deploy dashboards that track accuracy, latency, and fairness metrics in real time.

4. **Document Lifecycle Changes**: Version control, release notes, and audit trails must be strictly maintained.

5. **Embed Governance Structures**: Clinical, technical, and compliance experts must share responsibility for ongoing oversight.

Evaluation, deployment, and lifecycle management of healthcare AI agents require structured, multi-phase processes to ensure safety, reliability, and clinical value. By combining retrospective and prospective validation with real-world shadow testing, organizations can establish confidence before full-scale deployment. Once live, continuous monitoring, governance, and post-market surveillance are necessary to adapt to evolving clinical practices and patient populations. Sustainable deployment is achieved through rigorous oversight, transparent auditability, and iterative improvement cycles.

# Chapter 12: Agentic AI in Finance

## Section 1: Core Applications of Agentic AI in Financial Services

The financial sector has been one of the earliest adopters of artificial intelligence, largely because financial processes are highly data-driven, time-sensitive, and heavily regulated. The introduction of agentic AI extends this adoption by enabling systems that can not only analyze information but also plan, adapt, and act within defined constraints. Unlike narrow automation systems, agentic AI agents can operate across multiple data sources, coordinate sequential decision-making, and maintain ongoing goals aligned with business objectives. This section examines established applications where these capabilities deliver measurable outcomes.

### Algorithmic and Autonomous Trading

One of the most mature areas of AI application in finance is algorithmic trading. Traditionally, quantitative trading relied on rule-based systems with preprogrammed strategies. Agentic AI extends these systems by enabling dynamic adaptation.

Key characteristics include:

- **Market Data Ingestion**: Continuous analysis of high-frequency data streams from exchanges, economic indicators, and news sources.

- **Adaptive Strategy Selection**: Agents can adjust trading strategies in response to volatility, liquidity conditions, or unexpected market events.

- **Execution Optimization**: Fine-tuning order placement across venues to minimize slippage and transaction costs.

For example, an agent can monitor liquidity fragmentation across exchanges and automatically rebalance order routing to minimize exposure to adverse price movements. The critical consideration is latency since most trading venues impose strict execution timing requirements.

### Risk Modeling and Stress Testing

Risk modeling and stress testing are fundamental requirements in financial institutions, where regulators mandate thorough evaluations of capital adequacy and exposure across a variety of economic conditions. Agentic AI strengthens this process by orchestrating multiple models, integrating both structured and unstructured data, and automating the creation of stress scenarios. This allows institutions to move beyond static models and embrace more adaptive, dynamic forms of analysis.

One of the core capabilities lies in portfolio risk aggregation, where exposures are continuously monitored across asset classes, geographies, and counterparties. This provides a consolidated view of vulnerabilities and ensures that no single source of risk goes unnoticed. Scenario generation further expands the system's capabilities by automatically constructing stress conditions rooted in real-world events, such as sudden interest rate hikes, market crashes, or geopolitical disruptions. These scenarios can be simulated rapidly, offering a more proactive way to evaluate resilience.

Another key feature is adaptive rebalancing. When predefined thresholds are breached, agents can suggest strategic portfolio adjustments, helping institutions maintain compliance with risk limits while minimizing potential losses. In the regulatory context, these systems also play an important role in reporting. By integrating data from trading systems, credit exposure platforms, and external economic databases, agents can automate the preparation of stress test documentation. This not only reduces the manual workload placed on risk teams but also ensures that reports are delivered on time and in accordance with regulatory standards. Through these capabilities, agentic AI makes risk modeling more comprehensive, efficient, and responsive to changing market conditions.

## Fraud Detection and Financial Crime Prevention

Fraud detection has long relied on statistical anomaly detection methods. Agentic AI provides additional functionality by integrating multiple monitoring channels and adapting detection thresholds dynamically.

Applications include:

- **Transaction Monitoring**: Agents continuously evaluate transaction streams for abnormal activity relative to customer profiles.

- **Cross-Channel Correlation**: Linking card transactions, wire transfers, and login activity to detect coordinated fraud attempts.

- **Dynamic Response**: Triggering escalation procedures, blocking suspicious transactions, or alerting compliance officers.

Fraud detection agents must be explainable. Each alert generated should provide rationale, feature contributions, and supporting evidence so that human investigators can act on it.

### Traditional vs. Agentic AI Fraud Detection

| Feature | Traditional Systems | Agentic AI Systems |
|---|---|---|
| Detection Rules | Fixed thresholds, static patterns | Adaptive, context-sensitive |
| Data Sources | Isolated (e.g., card-only) | Integrated (multi-channel, multi-source) |
| Response | Alert-only | Alert plus automated containment actions |
| Explainability | Limited | Enhanced through structured reasoning logs |

## Compliance Monitoring and Regulatory Reporting

Financial institutions operate under extensive regulatory requirements, including anti-money laundering (AML), know-your-customer (KYC), and market abuse prevention. Agentic AI agents can serve as compliance monitors that integrate multiple data sources and enforce policies in real time.

Practical functions include:

1. **KYC Document Analysis**: Automating verification of structured forms and unstructured documents such as contracts.

2. **Transaction Surveillance**: Monitoring for violations of trading restrictions or unusual behavior patterns.

3. **Regulatory Reporting**: Preparing standardized reports in formats required by supervisory bodies, reducing manual compliance overhead.

For example, under MiFID II transaction reporting requirements, an agent can ensure that trade data is captured, validated, and submitted within the required times while maintaining audit trails.

## Customer Service and Personalized Financial Advisory

Financial service providers are deploying conversational agents and autonomous advisors to assist customers directly. These differ from general-purpose chatbots in that they operate as autonomous financial assistants capable of:

- Providing account insights in natural language.

- Recommending savings or investment actions based on customer goals.

- Coordinating multi-step actions, such as fund transfers followed by portfolio allocation.

In wealth management, autonomous advisory agents can support portfolio rebalancing decisions, aligning with customer preferences and risk tolerance. While final execution may require human confirmation, the agent reduces workload for advisors and enables scalable personalization.

## Portfolio Optimization and Asset Allocation

Portfolio management requires a careful balance between achieving expected returns and adhering to risk constraints, and agentic AI provides a powerful framework for optimizing this process. By continuously monitoring portfolio performance, these agents can assess alternative allocations and generate timely suggestions for adjustments, ensuring that portfolios remain aligned with both strategic objectives and market realities.

Dynamic rebalancing is one of the central mechanisms, allowing the system to detect when market movements cause allocations to drift outside of established thresholds. Instead of relying solely on periodic reviews, the agent can intervene proactively, keeping portfolios within desired parameters. Multi-objective optimization further enhances decision-making by incorporating liquidity requirements, transaction costs, and regulatory restrictions into the allocation process, balancing performance with practical constraints.

Scenario evaluation adds another dimension of intelligence, enabling agents to simulate the impact of potential shifts such as changes in interest rates, commodity prices, or currency fluctuations. These simulations help institutions anticipate vulnerabilities and prepare strategies that can withstand diverse economic conditions.

In practice, such AI agents are often deployed in institutional settings, where they integrate with existing portfolio management platforms. Their recommendations are typically presented to investment committees, offering data-driven insights that support strategic decision-making while maintaining human oversight. This collaborative model ensures that portfolios are optimized not only for financial performance but also for resilience in the face of uncertainty.

## Credit Scoring and Loan Underwriting

Credit scoring systems benefit from agentic AI by integrating multiple data types and dynamically adjusting models based on macroeconomic trends. Instead of static scoring formulas, agents can:

1. Incorporate alternative data sources (e.g., payment histories, transaction behavior).

2. Adapt thresholds based on updated risk factors.

3. Provide explainability to meet regulatory fairness requirements.

This application is critical for extending credit access responsibly while maintaining compliance with fairness regulations such as the Equal Credit Opportunity Act.

## Summary of Core Applications

Agentic AI in finance spans multiple domains, each with specific operational, regulatory, and technical constraints. A unifying feature is the requirement for agents to operate under high levels of accountability and transparency, given the potential financial and systemic risks involved.

- Autonomous trading agents improve execution efficiency but must meet latency and auditability requirements.

- Risk modeling agents support regulatory compliance through adaptive scenario generation and reporting.

- Fraud detection agents integrate multiple data sources and provide explainable alerts.

- Compliance agents automate monitoring and reporting in alignment with strict regulatory standards.

- Customer-facing agents provide personalized financial insights while requiring oversight.

- Portfolio and credit agents enhance optimization and risk management while ensuring fairness and accountability.

## Section 2: Technical Architectures and Integration with Financial Infrastructure

Deploying agentic AI in finance requires more than building advanced models. Financial systems demand reliability, latency guarantees, integration with legacy infrastructure, and adherence to strict compliance frameworks. This section examines the architectural approaches and integration practices that enable safe and effective deployment of agentic AI in financial environments.

### Layered Architecture for Agentic AI in Finance

Financial applications benefit from a layered architecture that separates concerns, improves maintainability, and ensures compliance.

This structure ensures that sensitive functions, such as compliance and reporting, remain isolated yet interoperable with agentic reasoning components.

### Data Infrastructure and Integration

Data is the foundation of financial AI systems. Integration challenges arise from the diversity of data formats, latency requirements, and security controls.

Key considerations:

1. **Real-Time Market Data**: Feeds from exchanges and news providers require ultra-low-latency handling.

2. **Transactional Data**: Banking and payment systems generate large volumes that must be captured reliably.

3. **Regulatory Data Stores**: Maintaining auditable records that can be used for reporting or investigations.

4. **Data Quality Assurance**: Automated checks for missing values, outliers, or inconsistencies.

A critical principle is **data segregation by sensitivity**. Personally identifiable information (PII) must be protected with encryption and access controls, while aggregated market data may be more openly shared across agents.

### Model and Tool Integration

Agentic AI systems in finance rarely rely on a single model. Instead, they integrate multiple specialized models and tools, orchestrated by reasoning layers.

Examples:

- **Trading Agents**: Combine predictive models, execution optimizers, and risk limiters.

- **Fraud Detection Agents**: Use anomaly detection models, rule-based filters, and identity verification services.

- **Compliance Agents**: Connect to regulatory reporting engines, transaction monitoring tools, and audit loggers.

Integration approaches include:

- **API Gateways**: Standardize communication between agents and external systems.

- **Containerization**: Deploy models as services for scalability and fault isolation.

- **Model Versioning**: Ensure reproducibility and traceability of outputs for compliance.

## Orchestration and Reasoning Layer

The agent orchestration layer coordinates workflows, plans multi-step actions, and ensures compliance with operational constraints.

Key functions:

1. **Task Planning**: Decomposing high-level goals (e.g., "minimize portfolio risk") into tool-level actions.

2. **Constraint Enforcement**: Ensuring that actions comply with risk limits, trading rules, or legal requirements.

3. **Audit Logging**: Capturing decision rationale for post-event analysis and regulatory inspections.

In financial environments, this layer is often implemented with strict guardrails. For example, an execution agent may propose trades, but an automated risk limiter must validate exposure before orders are placed.

## Security and Access Control

Security is central to financial systems. Agentic AI introduces new risks, such as model misuse or unauthorized tool access, which require systematic controls.

Recommended practices:

- **Role-Based Access Control (RBAC)**: Restrict which agents or users can access sensitive data or perform critical operations.

- **Key Management**: Secure handling of API keys, cryptographic credentials, and tokens used by agents.

- **Isolation**: Deploying agents in sandboxes when interacting with unverified external data sources.

- **Monitoring**: Continuous tracking of agent activities to detect deviations or misuse.

## Reliability and Latency Considerations

In finance, system reliability and execution speed directly impact outcomes. Architecture must address these constraints explicitly.

1. **Low-Latency Execution**: Trading systems often require responses within microseconds to milliseconds. Agents must integrate with optimized execution engines.

2. **High Availability**: Redundant agents and failover systems ensure uninterrupted service during outages.

3. **Consistency**: Risk calculations and compliance checks must produce identical results across distributed systems.

4. **Recovery Protocols**: Agents must have predefined behaviors in case of data feed disruptions or hardware failures.

## Integration with Legacy Financial Systems

Many financial institutions rely on mainframes and legacy transaction systems. Agentic AI must interoperate without disrupting existing workflows.

Approaches include:

- **Middleware Layers**: Wrapping legacy systems with APIs for secure interaction.

- **Message Queues**: Asynchronous communication between modern agents and older batch systems.

- **Data Bridges**: Scheduled synchronization between agent-driven systems and traditional reporting databases.

Compatibility testing is essential to avoid introducing risks in production environments.

## Compliance and Auditability in System Design

Architecture must be designed for transparency and accountability. Regulators often require evidence that AI-driven decisions can be explained and reconstructed.

Key measures:

1. **Decision Logs**: Storing structured records of each action, including input, reasoning, and outputs.

2. **Version Tracking**: Recording which model version and parameter set was used in each decision.

3. **Audit Interfaces**: Providing compliance officers with dashboards for investigation.

For example, a fraud detection system should allow investigators to trace a flagged transaction back through the reasoning process, model outputs, and underlying data sources.

## Deployment Patterns

Financial institutions typically use deployment patterns that balance scalability, resilience, and control.

Common approaches:

- **On-Premises with Secure Extensions**: For high-security contexts such as central banking.

- **Hybrid Cloud**: Market data processing in cloud environments combined with on-premises storage of sensitive customer data.

- **Federated Deployment**: Distributing agent capabilities across subsidiaries while maintaining centralized compliance oversight.

Architectural design in finance emphasizes resilience, transparency, and controlled integration. Agentic AI must be embedded into existing infrastructures without compromising regulatory compliance or operational safety.

- Layered architecture separates data, models, orchestration, and interfaces.

- Secure data infrastructure ensures quality and protects sensitive information.

- Orchestration layers manage planning, compliance enforcement, and auditing.

- Security mechanisms prevent misuse and enforce access control.

- Reliability, latency, and high availability are mandatory in production environments.

- Integration with legacy systems requires middleware and compatibility testing.

- Compliance and auditability must be built into system design from the start.

The final section will examine **evaluation, governance, and risk management practices** for ensuring that agentic AI deployments in finance remain safe, effective, and compliant throughout their lifecycle.

## Section 3: Risk Management, Compliance, and Lifecycle Governance of Financial AI Agents

The financial industry is governed by strict standards of reliability, transparency, and accountability. Introducing agentic AI into such environments requires not only technical rigor but also disciplined risk management and governance frameworks. This section provides detailed guidance on designing, deploying, and maintaining agent-based systems in finance while meeting regulatory and operational requirements.

**Principles of Risk Management in Financial AI**

Risk management for agentic AI must align with established financial principles while accounting for AI-specific concerns. Key categories of risk include:

1. **Operational Risk**: Failures in infrastructure, orchestration, or dependencies.

2. **Model Risk**: Errors, biases, or instability in predictive models.

3. **Regulatory Risk**: Non-compliance with rules such as MiFID II or Basel III.

4. **Security Risk**: Unauthorized access, adversarial inputs, or misuse of tools.

5. **Reputational Risk**: Loss of client trust due to system failures or unexplained actions.

**Table: Mapping of Risks to Controls**

| Risk Category | Example Issue | Recommended Control |
|---|---|---|
| Operational | System downtime during trading | High availability, failover mechanisms, redundancy |
| Model | Biased credit scoring outputs | Model validation, bias detection, regular retraining |
| Regulatory | Incomplete transaction reporting | Automated compliance checks, audit logs |
| Security | API key leakage | Encryption, key rotation, RBAC |
| Reputational | Customer dispute over denial | Explainable AI, transparent documentation |

**Model Risk Management (MRM)**

Financial regulators increasingly emphasize **Model Risk Management** as defined in supervisory guidance (e.g., SR 11-7 in the United States). Agentic AI systems must adopt structured MRM processes.

Core practices:

1. **Model Inventory**: Maintain a registry of all models, their purpose, and version history.

2. **Validation**: Independent review of assumptions, inputs, and outputs before deployment.

3. **Stress Testing**: Evaluate models under extreme but plausible conditions, such as market volatility spikes.

4. **Performance Monitoring**: Continuous measurement of accuracy, stability, and drift.

5. **Decommissioning**: Formal retirement procedures for outdated or high-risk models.

For agents that combine multiple models, each component must be validated both individually and within the integrated workflow.

## Compliance Requirements

Agentic AI must operate within the bounds of global and regional regulatory frameworks. Some key obligations include:

- **Basel III and IV**: Capital adequacy and risk exposure calculations must be transparent and traceable.
- **MiFID II (Europe)**: Algorithmic trading agents must include controls for order throttling, market abuse prevention, and kill switches.
- **Dodd-Frank (United States)**: Reporting of derivatives and risk exposures requires auditable workflows.
- **GDPR and Data Privacy Laws**: Customer data used by agents must be handled with consent, minimization, and security controls.

Architectural designs must integrate compliance enforcement mechanisms rather than treating them as post-deployment add-ons.

## Auditability and Explainability

Auditability is critical for both regulators and internal governance teams. Every decision made by an agent must be reconstructable.

Key requirements:

1. **Decision Logging**: Capturing inputs, model versions, reasoning steps, and outputs.
2. **Explainability Interfaces**: Tools that provide human-understandable justifications for actions.
3. **Immutable Records**: Use of secure storage and cryptographic hashes to prevent tampering.

For example, if a credit agent denies a loan, the system should provide a structured explanation that references credit history features, thresholds, and regulatory criteria.

## Monitoring and Incident Management

Agentic AI systems must be continuously monitored to detect anomalies, failures, or compliance breaches.

Recommended practices:

- **Real-Time Dashboards**: Track system health, model accuracy, and key risk indicators.
- **Threshold Alerts**: Automated notifications when metrics exceed acceptable ranges.
- **Incident Protocols**: Predefined escalation steps for outages, anomalous trades, or compliance violations.
- **Post-Mortem Reviews**: Structured analysis of failures with corrective action plans.

Monitoring should cover not only technical metrics but also business impact, such as unusual trading activity or customer complaints.

## Lifecycle Governance

Lifecycle governance ensures that agentic AI systems remain reliable, compliant, and aligned with organizational goals over time.

Governance framework components:

1. **Development Stage**: Model validation, security reviews, and compliance design.

2. **Deployment Stage**: Controlled rollout, backtesting, and contingency planning.

3. **Operational Stage**: Ongoing monitoring, retraining, and regulatory reporting.

4. **Retirement Stage**: Safe decommissioning and archival of logs for future audits.

This lifecycle should be documented in alignment with enterprise risk management (ERM) frameworks already used by financial institutions

## Human Oversight and Control

Although agentic AI can operate autonomously, human oversight is necessary to satisfy regulatory and ethical requirements.

Common mechanisms:

- **Pre-Trade Controls**: Humans approve trades above a certain threshold.

- **Dual-Control Systems**: Sensitive operations require approval from two independent operators.

- **Override Functions**: Kill switches or manual intervention capabilities.

- **Governance Committees**: Periodic review of AI systems by risk, compliance, and IT stakeholders.

Oversight should balance efficiency with accountability, ensuring that agents enhance productivity without compromising governance.

## Security Governance

Security practices must extend beyond infrastructure to include model and orchestration layers.

Essential measures:

- **Threat Modeling**: Identify potential attack vectors such as data poisoning or adversarial inputs.

- **Access Reviews**: Regular audits of who can access which systems and data.

- **Change Management**: Approval of workflows for modifying models or updating orchestration rules.

- **Resilience Testing**: Simulated attacks or penetration tests to validate defenses.

These practices ensure that AI systems do not introduce vulnerabilities into mission-critical financial environments.

## Summary of Governance Practices

Financial AI agents demand rigorous governance to manage risks, ensure compliance, and maintain trust.

- Risk management must address operational, model, regulatory, security, and reputational risks.

- Model Risk Management (MRM) practices, including validation and monitoring, are mandatory.

- Compliance must be built into system design, not retrofitted after deployment.

- Auditability requires structured decision logging and explainability.

- Continuous monitoring and structured incident management are essential.

- Lifecycle governance ensures long-term reliability and regulatory alignment.

- Human oversight and control mechanisms safeguard accountability.

- Security governance addresses model-specific and orchestration-layer threats.

- Cross-border operations require harmonization of global and local requirements.

Agentic AI in finance presents opportunities for efficiency, insight, and automation, but it must be deployed with caution and discipline. The integration of autonomous reasoning into financial systems requires architectures that prioritize security, compliance, and resilience. More importantly, governance frameworks must provide continuous oversight, ensuring that agents remain reliable and trustworthy throughout their lifecycle. By combining advanced AI techniques with established risk management principles, financial institutions can safely harness the capabilities of agentic systems while maintaining alignment with regulatory and fiduciary responsibilities.

## Section 1: Architectures for Agentic AI Integration in Robotic Systems

Designing and deploying agentic AI in robotics requires well-structured system architectures that balance the unique constraints of physical machines with the adaptive reasoning capabilities of large language models (LLMs) and agentic control layers. Unlike purely digital systems, robots interact directly with the physical environment, which introduces variability, uncertainty, and safety-critical requirements. This section provides a structured review of integration approaches, control hierarchies, and orchestration methods for embedding agentic AI within robotic systems.

### Foundations of Robotic System Architectures

Robotic systems typically follow layered architectures that separate perception, planning, and actuation. Each layer is designed to handle tasks with different temporal and computational requirements:

- **Perception Layer**: Processes sensor inputs such as vision, LiDAR, or tactile data. Generates a structured representation of the environment.

- **Planning Layer**: Converts environmental data and task goals into executable action sequences. Includes path planning, decision-making, and task allocation.

- **Actuation Layer**: Executes low-level control commands for motors, joints, or effectors. Ensures adherence to physical dynamics and stability requirements.

Agentic AI primarily enhances the **planning layer**, with extensions into perception (through multimodal reasoning) and actuation (via adaptive control selection).

This layered approach ensures separation of concerns, allowing LLM-powered agents to operate at a higher abstraction level while delegating time-critical execution to deterministic controllers.

### Integration of Agentic AI with Robotics Middleware

Most robotics systems depend on middleware to coordinate communication among components, with ROS and ROS 2 serving as the dominant frameworks. They provide publish–subscribe messaging, modular packaging, and rich simulation tools, which together form a stable substrate for perception, planning, and control. To embed agentic AI into this ecosystem, interfaces must translate between language-model decisions and the message-oriented world of ROS so that high-level intent can drive reliable, low-level execution.

A dedicated agent interface node acts as the bridge. It receives natural-language or symbolic task directives from LLM-based modules and converts them into well-formed ROS messages, topics, and service calls. Above this, a task orchestration layer tracks progress, decomposes broad goals into executable steps, and issues the corresponding ROS requests while enforcing safety limits and resource budgets. This layer ensures that agent plans are realized as orderly sequences compatible with robot capabilities and operational constraints.

Closed-loop adaptation comes from a structured feedback cycle. Sensor streams, status updates, and execution reports flow back through ROS into compact summaries the agent can ingest, allowing the LLM to reassess plans, adjust parameters, or escalate fallbacks when conditions change. With this pattern-language to ROS messages, orchestrated execution, and measured feedback-agentic AI can integrate cleanly with robotics middleware and make decisions that remain transparent, safe, and responsive.

### Example Flow

- A human operator specifies: "Organize items on the table by size."

- The **LLM agent** decomposes this into subtasks: detect items, classify by size, plan grasp trajectories, place objects.

- Each subtask is delegated through ROS nodes that handle perception (object detection), planning (motion paths), and actuation (arm movement).

- Feedback is continuously fed back to the agentic layer for error handling.

## Centralized vs Distributed Architectures

When deploying multiple robots or complex systems, a key architectural decision is whether agentic control should be centralized or distributed.

## Centralized Architectures

- **Structure**: A single agentic AI module coordinates all decision-making for the system.

- **Advantages**:
    - Simplified coordination.
    - Easier to enforce global policies.
    - Reduced redundancy in training and resource usage.

- **Limitations**:
    - Single point of failure.
    - Potential communication bottlenecks.
    - Limited scalability in large fleets.

## Distributed Architectures

- **Structure**: Each robot or subsystem has its own agentic controller, with peer-to-peer communication.

- **Advantages**:
    - Greater fault tolerance.
    - Scalability across fleets.
    - Local autonomy allows faster responses.

- **Limitations**:
    - More complex coordination mechanisms are required.
    - Risk of inconsistent decision-making across agents.

## Hybrid Approaches

Many production systems adopt hybrid models, where **local agents manage execution** while a **central coordinator enforces global policies** such as safety rules, resource allocation, or shared task scheduling

## Orchestration Between Perception, Reasoning, and Action

One of the most difficult challenges in robotics is ensuring smooth orchestration between perception, reasoning, and action. Agentic AI architectures are designed to bridge the gap between symbolic reasoning and the continuous control required for physical systems. The first link in this chain is the perception–reasoning bridge, where raw sensor inputs must be abstracted into symbolic descriptions that a language model can interpret. Instead of handing over dense LiDAR point clouds, for example, the system might provide a higher-level message such as "obstacle detected at 2.5 meters, left of trajectory." This allows reasoning modules to work with structured information rather than overwhelming raw data.

The next stage is the reasoning–action bridge. Here, the symbolic plans produced by an LLM must be translated into executable commands that the robot can carry out. An instruction like "grasp nearest red object" cannot remain abstract-it must be mapped into concrete motion plans, including inverse kinematics trajectories that move the robot arm precisely to the object while accounting for constraints like reachability and collision avoidance. This step ensures that high-level reasoning is grounded in low-level control.

Finally, feedback integration closes the loop between planning and reality. Continuous monitoring of execution allows the system to detect discrepancies and adjust accordingly. For instance, if an object slips from the robot's grasp, the perception system updates the agent, which then replans the action to correct the error. This iterative process allows agentic AI systems to maintain adaptability and robustness, ensuring that symbolic reasoning and physical control remain aligned in dynamic environments.

**Design Trade-offs in Agentic AI Robotics**

System architects must evaluate trade-offs when embedding agentic AI into robotic platforms.

- **Abstraction Level**
    - Higher abstraction (natural language goals) improves usability.
    - Lower abstraction (direct control policies) ensures predictability and determinism.

- **Latency vs Autonomy**
    - LLM reasoning introduces latency.
    - Safety critical tasks (e.g., collision avoidance) must remain in deterministic controllers.

- **Explainability vs Efficiency**
    - Symbolic task decomposition enhances explainability.
    - Pure reinforcement learning methods may achieve efficiency but lack transparency.

- **Resource Allocation**
    - Running LLM agents requires significant computing.
    - Embedded deployment may require model compression, edge-cloud partitioning, or hybrid setups.

Architectures for incorporating agentic AI into robotics must adhere to the limitations of real-world settings, where dependability and safety are of utmost importance. When connected to current middleware frameworks like ROS, LLM-driven reasoning layers function best. This lets perception, planning, and actuation all operate together in a modular way. There are pros and cons to centralized, distributed, and hybrid models, and orchestration systems must make sure that abstract reasoning and concrete control can switch between them easily.

Engineers may add agentic AI to robotic systems while keeping them strong, scalable, and easy to understand by using layered architecture with clear interfaces.

## Section 2: Operational Workflows and Multi-Agent Coordination in Robotics

Operational workflows in robotics specify the decomposition, allocation, and execution of tasks in both single-agent and multi-agent systems. When agentic AI is added, these workflows go beyond just planning and include higher-level thinking, adaptation, and working together to get things done. This part looks at how robotic operational workflows are set up, how to coordinate in multi-agent systems, and how to make sure that numerous autonomous units work together reliably.

**Task Decomposition and Execution in Agentic Robotics**

The integration of LLM-powered agents introduces an additional reasoning layer that reshapes traditional task execution.

**Task Lifecycle in Agentic Robotics**

1. **Goal Interpretation**

   o   Inputs may come from human operators, external systems, or environmental triggers.

   o   The LLM agent translates these into structured tasks.

   o   Example: "Deliver the package to Room 3B" is decomposed into navigation, obstacle avoidance, and handoff subtasks.

2. **Task Decomposition**

   o   The Agentic AI layer structures the goal into sequential or parallel subtasks.

   o   Dependencies between subtasks are mapped explicitly.

   o   Example: An industrial robot tasked with assembling a component decomposes into retrieving parts, positioning them, fastening, and verification.

3. **Planning and Scheduling**

   o   Subtasks are assigned execution slots, accounting for resource constraints such as battery, manipulator availability, or workspace usage.

   o   Scheduling can be centralized or distributed depending on system architecture.

4. **Execution and Monitoring**

   o   Control is delegated to low-level controllers and middleware nodes.

   o   Real-time monitoring captures deviations from planned behavior.

5. **Feedback and Adaptation**

   o   Errors trigger re-planning or task reallocation.

   o   Example: If a part is missing, the LLM agent can query an inventory system and adjust the workflow.

This structured lifecycle ensures that agentic reasoning enhances flexibility without compromising deterministic execution.

**Multi-Agent Coordination Models**

In multi-robot systems, coordination is critical for efficiency and safety. Agentic AI enables dynamic negotiation, reasoning over shared goals, and adaptive reallocation of resources.

**Coordination Models**

1. **Hierarchical Coordination**
   - A central controller or supervisory agent allocates tasks to subordinate robots.
   - Suitable for structured environments such as warehouses.
   - Pros: Simplifies optimization, ensures policy consistency.
   - Cons: Scalability challenges, potential single point of failure.

2. **Market-Based Coordination**
   - Robots bid for tasks based on cost functions such as energy usage, distance, or task complexity.
   - Inspired by auction mechanisms, this model allows distributed allocation.
   - Pros: Scales well in heterogeneous fleets.
   - Cons: Requires well-designed cost metrics to prevent inefficiencies.

3. **Consensus-Based Coordination**
   - Agents iteratively update their state and converge on a shared plan through distributed algorithms.
   - Common in swarm robotics for coverage or formation control.
   - Pros: No central bottleneck, resilient to failures.
   - Cons: Communication overhead and slower convergence.

4. **Hybrid Coordination**
   - Combines central oversight with distributed autonomy.
   - Example: Central server allocates zones, while local robots self-organize within their zone.

**Communication and Synchronization in Multi-Agent Systems**

Effective coordination requires structured communication mechanisms.

**Modes of Communication**

- **Direct Peer-to-Peer**: Agents exchange status and plans directly.
- **Message Bus via Middleware**: Agents communicate through shared channels such as ROS2 topics.
- **Blackboard Systems**: A shared repository stores knowledge, allowing agents to post and read updates.

**Synchronization Mechanisms**

- **Time-Triggered Synchronization**: Actions occur at defined intervals. Useful for periodic tasks like area scanning.

- **Event-Driven Synchronization**: Triggered by events such as "object detected" or "task completed."
- **Hybrid Synchronization**: Combines periodic checks with event-driven responses.

## Conflict Resolution in Multi-Agent Workflows

When multiple robots interact in the same space, conflicts arise in task allocation, motion planning, or resource usage. Agentic AI systems must handle these systematically.

## Conflict Types

- **Resource Conflicts**: Two robots attempt to use the same manipulator station.
- **Path Conflicts**: Navigation paths intersect in narrow corridors.
- **Task Conflicts**: Multiple agents attempt overlapping goals.

## Resolution Strategies

1. **Priority Assignment**
   - Tasks are ranked, and higher-priority agents proceed first.
   - Simple but may reduce overall efficiency.

2. **Negotiation Mechanisms**
   - Agents negotiate through bidding or exchange mechanisms to determine task ownership.

3. **Dynamic Replanning**
   - Conflicts trigger localized replanning, ensuring minimal disruption.

4. **Rule-Based Arbitration**
   - Predefined safety and operational rules determine outcomes.
   - Example: "Yield to loaded transport robots."

## Workflow Case Study: Warehouse Logistics

Consider a warehouse where multiple robots collaborate under an agentic AI system.

## Workflow Example

1. **Goal Assignment**: LLM agent receives a request to "restock aisle 4 with product batch X."
2. **Task Decomposition**: Breaks into retrieving batch X, navigating to aisle 4, and placing items.
3. **Agent Selection**:
   - Robot A closest to the loading dock retrieves batch X.
   - Robot B clears the aisle for accessibility.
   - Robot C verifies stock placement.
4. **Execution**: Each robot follows local controllers for navigation and manipulation.

5. **Coordination**:
   - ○ Conflict arises as Robot A and B approach the same corridor.
   - ○ Priority is assigned based on task urgency.
   - ○ Robot A proceeds, Robot B waits.
6. **Completion**: Robot C validates with perception data and updates the central knowledge base.

This structured workflow illustrates how agentic AI ensures both efficiency and adaptability in multi-robot operations.

## Monitoring and Performance Metrics

Operational workflows require systematic monitoring to ensure reliability.

## Key Metrics

- **Task Completion Rate**: Percentage of assigned tasks successfully completed.
- **Mean Task Latency**: Average time from task assignment to completion.
- **Coordination Overhead**: Time spent on negotiation or synchronization.
- **Collision Rate**: Frequency of near misses or collisions.
- **Resource Utilization**: Efficiency of shared resource allocation.

## Monitoring Infrastructure

- Centralized dashboards aggregate data from all robots.
- Event logs capture execution history for traceability.
- Alerts flag abnormal patterns, such as repeated deadlocks.

## Design Principles for Multi-Agent Workflows

Practical deployments of multi-agent systems highlight several design principles that ensure reliability, safety, and efficiency. One of the most important is modular task design, which allows complex objectives to be broken down into independent units that can be executed in parallel. This decomposition not only improves efficiency but also enables better fault isolation, since individual tasks can be reassigned or retried without disrupting the entire workflow.

Safety-first arbitration is another essential principle, emphasizing that collision avoidance and hazard prevention must always take precedence over efficiency or speed. In environments where multiple agents operate simultaneously, prioritizing safety ensures system stability and prevents cascading failures.

To further strengthen resilience, adaptive reallocation mechanisms must be built in. When an agent encounters delays or failures, its tasks should be automatically reassigned to others, minimizing downtime and ensuring continuity of operation. Complementing this is the principle of minimal communication assumptions. Since real-world systems are vulnerable to delays, interference, or partial failures in communication, workflows should be designed to tolerate interruptions without breaking down entirely.

Finally, traceability of decisions is critical for both accountability and long-term maintainability. Structured logs of task allocations, arbitration outcomes, and reassignments provide a transparent record that can be audited later. This not only supports debugging and compliance but also helps refine future deployments. Together, these principles form a robust framework for orchestrating multi-agent workflows in complex, dynamic environments.

Operational workflows in agentic robotics extend traditional robotics pipelines by embedding reasoning-driven task decomposition and adaptive coordination. Multi-agent systems can operate under hierarchical, market-based, or consensus-driven models, each with distinct trade-offs. Reliable execution depends on structured communication, synchronization, and conflict resolution strategies.

Through systematic monitoring and adherence to safety-focused design principles, multi-agent coordination in robotics can scale from single collaborative tasks to complex industrial operations, ensuring both robustness and adaptability.

## Section 3: Safety, Reliability, and Evaluation of Agentic Robotics Workflows

Ensuring the safe and reliable operation of agentic robotics systems is critical for adoption in real-world environments. Unlike isolated software systems, robotic agents interact with the physical world, which amplifies the consequences of errors. This section details engineering practices for safety assurance, reliability mechanisms, and systematic evaluation frameworks specific to agentic AI in robotics.

### Safety Foundations in Agentic Robotics

Safety mechanisms must be embedded into the design of workflows, communication channels, and decision-making layers.

### Safety Layers

1. **Physical Safety Controls**

    o   Emergency stop buttons, kill switches, and isolation zones.

    o   Hardware interlocks to prevent dangerous actuator movements.

2. **Software Safety Policies**

    o   Rule-based safety constraints are integrated into planning and reasoning layers.

    o   Examples: maximum speed limits, restricted zones, collision avoidance rules.

3. **Supervisory Oversight**

    o   Human-in-the-loop mechanisms for approval of high-risk actions.

    o   Supervisory monitoring of agentic reasoning outputs.

4. **Fail-Safe Defaults**

    o   If uncertain, agents default to a safe halt or rollback state.

A layered approach ensures that failure in one domain does not propagate unchecked.

### Risk Analysis and Hazard Mitigation

Before deploying autonomous or multi-agent systems, a structured risk analysis process is essential to ensure safety and resilience. The first step is hazard identification, where potential risks such as collisions, payload drops, or communication breakdowns are cataloged. This provides a clear picture of the vulnerabilities that could compromise operations.

Once hazards are mapped, failure mode and effects analysis (FMEA) is applied to study how each failure might propagate through the system. For instance, a navigation system malfunction could lead to missed obstacle detection, ultimately resulting in a collision. Tracing these chains of events makes it easier to understand both direct and indirect consequences of component failures.

Risk prioritization follows, where each identified hazard is scored according to its severity, likelihood, and detectability. This ranking ensures that mitigation efforts target the most critical risks rather than spreading resources thinly across low-impact issues. By focusing on high-priority vulnerabilities, the system is better protected against failures with the greatest potential harm.

Finally, mitigation planning translates analysis into action. Strategies may include building redundancies into critical subsystems, defining safe fallback behaviors when anomalies occur, or enhancing monitoring to catch risks before they escalate. Through this systematic process, risk analysis and hazard mitigation create a foundation of safety and preparedness for real-world deployment.

### Example Mitigation Strategies

- **Collision risk**: Deploy redundant lidar and vision sensors.

- **Task conflict risk**: Add arbitration rules that prevent unsafe concurrent execution.

- **Communication loss**: Introduce timeout protocols and autonomous safe states.

### Reliability Mechanisms for Robust Operation

Reliability in autonomous systems is about maintaining consistent performance even when operating in unpredictable or dynamic environments. One of the key strategies to achieve this is fault tolerance. By incorporating redundant sensors and actuators, critical functions are supported through multiple input channels, reducing the risk of single points of failure. In addition, systems should be designed for graceful degradation, where partial functionality is preserved even if one subsystem fails. This allows the system to continue operating at a reduced capacity rather than shutting down entirely.

Recovery mechanisms further reinforce reliability by providing ways to restore stability after disruptions. Checkpointing and rollback processes enable the system to return to the last known safe state whenever errors or failures occur, minimizing the impact of unexpected problems. Similarly, task reassignment ensures continuity in multi-agent settings; if one agent becomes unavailable, others can absorb its responsibilities without significant delays. Together, these mechanisms create a robust operational framework that allows autonomous systems to perform dependably over time, even in the face of failures.

### Robustness in Multi-Agent Systems

- **Consensus Protocols**: Prevent inconsistent states across agents.

- **Adaptive Task Allocation**: Rebalances workload in case of performance degradation.

### Testing Frameworks for Agentic Robotics

Testing robotics systems requires both simulated and physical environments.

### Simulation-Based Testing

- **Digital Twins**: High-fidelity replicas of physical environments used for validation.

- **Stress Testing**: Evaluate performance under extreme scenarios, such as sensor noise or high agent density.

- **Scenario-Based Evaluation**: Predefined test cases, for example, obstacle-rich navigation paths.

### Hardware-in-the-Loop Testing

- Combines real sensors and actuators with simulated environments.
- Validates both control algorithms and physical safety mechanisms.

### Field Testing

- Gradual rollout in controlled environments before full deployment.
- Example: Introducing robots into a production line during off-peak hours.

## Metrics for Safety and Reliability Evaluation

Quantitative evaluation ensures that systems meet deployment standards.

### Core Metrics

1. **Mean Time Between Failures (MTBF)**
   - Track's reliability over long-term operation.
2. **Failure Recovery Time (FRT)**
   - Measures responsiveness to failures.
3. **Task Success Rate**
   - Percentage of tasks executed without safety violations or manual intervention.
4. **Collision Avoidance Rate**
   - Ratio of successful avoidance maneuvers to detect collision risks.
5. **Human Intervention Frequency**
   - Indicator of system autonomy maturity.

### Multi-Agent Specific Metrics

- **Coordination Latency**: Time taken to resolve task conflicts.
- **Deadlock Frequency**: Occurrence of agents stalling due to circular dependencies.
- **Scalability Efficiency**: Performance retention as the number of agents increases.

## Continuous Monitoring and Runtime Verification

Safety and reliability cannot rely solely on pre-deployment testing. Continuous runtime monitoring is necessary.

### Runtime Verification Components

- **Health Monitoring**: Tracks sensor data integrity, actuator performance, and network stability.
- **Policy Compliance Checking**: Validates that decisions adhere to safety constraints.
- **Anomaly Detection**: Identifies deviations from normal operational patterns.

## Monitoring Infrastructure

- **Centralized Dashboards**: Aggregate telemetry from all robots.
- **Event Logging Systems**: Provide forensic traceability after incidents.
- **Automated Alerts**: Notify operators when thresholds are exceeded.

## Human-in-the-Loop and Ethical Oversight

In safety-critical contexts, human supervision remains indispensable.

- **Gates**: High-risk actions, such as handling hazardous materials, require human authorization.
- **Override Controls**: Operators must have immediate authority to interrupt agentic workflows.
- **Transparency**: Agents should log decision pathways for human auditing.

## Case Example: Safe Deployment in Hospital Robotics

In a hospital environment, robotic agents may handle deliveries, sanitation, and patient support tasks.

- **Hazards**: Potential collisions in crowded hallways, misdelivery of critical supplies, or equipment malfunction.
- **Safety Layers**: Low-speed limits, restricted access zones, and human override controls.
- **Reliability Measures**: Redundant navigation sensors, health monitoring dashboards, and reallocation of tasks if a robot halts.
- **Evaluation**: Metrics include delivery accuracy, incident-free operating hours, and staff override frequency.

This structured deployment approach ensures that hospital staff can trust the robotic system to operate without compromising safety or reliability.

## Design Principles for Safety and Reliability

Safety and reliability in autonomous systems depend on a set of disciplined design principles that guide both development and deployment. Redundancy across critical functions is essential to avoid single points of failure, ensuring that if one component malfunctions, others can take over seamlessly. Alongside this, systems should adopt fail-safe defaults, where the preferred response to uncertainty is a controlled stop rather than risky continuation, prioritizing the protection of people and assets.

Reliability also requires iterative validation. Before wide-scale deployment, agents should undergo extensive simulation and carefully staged field testing to uncover weaknesses under controlled conditions. Transparent decision records add another layer of security by maintaining detailed logs that allow engineers to trace errors and analyze how decisions were reached, providing accountability and improving future iterations.

Finally, continuous adaptation is necessary as environments and requirements evolve. Safety rules and evaluation parameters should be updated regularly to reflect new data, lessons learned, and changing operational contexts. Together, these principles create a resilient foundation that allows autonomous systems to operate safely, reliably, and responsibly over time.

Safety, reliability, and systematic evaluation are foundational to agentic robotics. By applying structured risk analysis, embedding fail-safes, and using robust testing frameworks, organizations can deploy autonomous systems with confidence. Continuous monitoring, human oversight, and quantitative evaluation ensure that workflows remain dependable across varied conditions.

Through disciplined engineering practices, agentic AI can augment robotics while maintaining the standards required for safety-critical and industrial-grade applications.

Designing agentic AI for business and operations requires a structured approach that balances autonomous decision-making with enterprise integration, reliability, and governance. This section outlines core architectural patterns, components, and system integration strategies that ensure agentic AI can operate effectively in complex business environments.

## Core Architectural Components

Agentic business systems are composed of multiple interacting modules. Understanding their roles is critical for building scalable and maintainable solutions.

## Decision Engine

The decision engine serves as the central component of an autonomous system, responsible for evaluating incoming information and producing either recommended or fully autonomous actions. Its role begins with data ingestion, where both structured and unstructured business data are processed and normalized into a usable format. This ensures that information from diverse sources can be effectively compared and interpreted.

Once the data is prepared, the reasoning stage applies a combination of predefined rules, predictive models, or large language model–driven logic to evaluate options and determine the most appropriate course of action. This step allows the engine to balance efficiency, accuracy, and adaptability in complex decision-making scenarios.

The final stage is action execution, where the chosen decision is put into practice. This may involve triggering downstream processes, updating automated workflows, or escalating alerts to human operators when intervention is required. By integrating these functions, the decision engine enables systems to move seamlessly from raw data to informed action, forming the core of intelligent automation.

## Workflow Orchestration

- Coordinates the sequence of operations across multiple agents, systems, and human actors.
- Typical features:
    - Scheduling and prioritization of tasks.
    - Dependency management, ensuring sequential or conditional operations are executed correctly.
    - Error handling and rollback mechanisms to maintain business continuity.

## Integration Layer

The integration layer connects agentic AI systems with the broader enterprise ecosystem, ensuring smooth interaction with platforms such as ERP, CRM, HR, and finance systems. Its purpose is to bridge diverse technologies and data formats so that the AI can operate effectively within existing workflows.

To achieve this, the integration layer offers standardized APIs that enable bidirectional communication, allowing information to flow seamlessly between the AI system and enterprise applications. It also handles data normalization, converting heterogeneous inputs from multiple sources into a consistent format that can be readily processed by decision-making modules. In addition, event-driven triggers allow the system to respond dynamically to real-time operational changes, ensuring that actions are timely and contextually relevant.

Through these capabilities, the integration layer provides the foundation for interoperability, enabling agentic AI to extend its intelligence into complex business environments without disrupting established systems.

## Knowledge and Memory Module

The knowledge and memory module is a core component that strengthens agent decision-making by maintaining historical and contextual information. Its purpose is not only to store past interactions but also to provide continuity and learning, allowing the system to improve performance over time.

This module incorporates operational logs, which serve as a foundation for auditing and compliance, ensuring that every action can be traced back to its origin. It also leverages knowledge graphs that map relationships among business entities, processes, and governing rules, enabling the agent to reason more effectively about complex interactions. In addition, persistent memory captures recurrent patterns and exceptions, allowing the system to recognize familiar situations and respond with greater accuracy and efficiency.

By combining these elements, the knowledge and memory module ensures that agentic AI systems operate with context, adaptability, and accountability, ultimately leading to smarter and more reliable outcomes.

## Human-in-the-Loop Interfaces

Human-in-the-loop interfaces play a vital role in ensuring that AI-driven systems remain safe, accountable, and aligned with organizational goals, especially in high-risk or complex scenarios. These interfaces create structured opportunities for human oversight and intervention, balancing automation with professional judgment.

One of their key functions is supporting approval workflows for critical decisions, where automated recommendations are reviewed by human operators before execution. This prevents unintended consequences in sensitive contexts. They also provide alerting and dashboard systems that allow continuous monitoring of agent activity, giving users visibility into performance, anomalies, and operational status in real time.

Equally important are feedback mechanisms, which enable humans to supply corrections, guidance, or contextual knowledge that the system can incorporate into future reasoning. Over time, this loop fosters continuous improvement, making the agent more aligned with real-world needs and expectations. By combining oversight, transparency, and adaptability, human-in-the-loop interfaces ensure that intelligent systems remain trustworthy and effective.

## Architectural Patterns

Several architectural patterns have emerged as effective in business contexts, balancing autonomy with control.

## Single-Agent Decision Engine

A single-agent decision engine represents a centralized approach where one agent is responsible for processing all business data and issuing corresponding actions. This design offers the advantage of simplified control and monitoring, since all decision-making is concentrated in a single system. It also makes auditing more straightforward, as decision pathways can be easily traced within one unified framework.

However, this architecture comes with notable limitations. As data volume and complexity increase, scalability becomes a significant challenge, with the centralized agent struggling to keep pace with rising demands. In addition, reliance on a single point of control creates vulnerability; if the system fails or encounters errors, the entire decision-making process is disrupted. These risks highlight the trade-offs inherent in single-agent architectures, making them suitable for smaller-scale operations but less effective for environments requiring robustness and high scalability.

## Multi-Agent Collaborative Network

A multi-agent collaborative network distributes responsibilities across several specialized agents, each focused on a distinct domain such as finance, coordination, or customer support. By allowing these agents to operate in parallel, the system gains scalability, as workloads are divided rather than concentrated in a single point of processing. This architecture also enables domain-specific optimization, with each agent designed to incorporate expertise and rules tailored to its functional area.

To maintain coherence, coordination mechanisms are essential. Shared knowledge graphs provide a common contextual framework, ensuring that agents operate with consistent information about entities, processes, and relationships. When conflicting actions arise, consensus protocols help the agents negotiate and converge on an acceptable decision. Arbitration modules further refine collaboration by managing dependencies, sequencing tasks appropriately, and preventing resource conflicts.

Together, these mechanisms allow multi-agent networks to combine efficiency with specialization, creating systems that are both scalable and adaptable. This design is particularly well-suited for complex enterprise environments where diverse workflows must be managed simultaneously without compromising accuracy or consistency.

Table example: Agent responsibilities in a multi-agent business system

| Agent | Domain | Responsibilities | Dependencies | Human Oversight Points |
|-------|--------|------------------|--------------|------------------------|
| Finance Agent | Accounts payable/receivable | Evaluate transactions, approve payments | ERP, bank systems | Approval for high-value transfers |
| Supply Agent | Inventory management | Reorder stock, monitor deliveries | ERP, warehouse sensors | Intervention for critical shortages |
| Customer Support Agent | Service requests | Prioritize tickets, suggest responses | CRM, knowledge base | Escalation for complaints |

**Human-in-the-Loop Hybrid Architecture**

A human-in-the-loop hybrid architecture integrates autonomous agents with structured human oversight, striking a balance between automation and accountability. In this setup, the system operates with a blend of independent decision-making and human intervention, ensuring both efficiency and safety.

A key design consideration is the clear definition of boundaries between actions that can be executed automatically and those that require explicit human approval. This distinction ensures that high-risk or sensitive operations remain under human control, while routine processes can be handled by agents without delay. To guard against bottlenecks, fallback procedures must also be established in case human input is delayed or unavailable, allowing the system to maintain continuity while still prioritizing safety.

Equally important is the maintenance of detailed audit trails. Every decision, whether automated or human-approved, must be logged in a transparent and verifiable way to support regulatory compliance and provide accountability. By combining autonomy with oversight, this hybrid architecture ensures that agentic systems remain both effective in real time and trustworthy in high-stakes environments.

**Data Management and Pipeline Architecture**

Agentic business systems rely on high-quality data streams. Robust pipeline design ensures operational efficiency.

**Data Ingestion and Preprocessing**

Data ingestion and preprocessing form the foundation of any intelligent system, ensuring that raw inputs are both reliable and usable for downstream reasoning. Sources often include transactional databases, external APIs, sensor streams, and direct customer interactions, each contributing data in different formats and levels of structure.

Before analysis, preprocessing steps are essential to guarantee quality and compliance. Data integrity must first be validated to detect and correct inconsistencies or errors. Following this, inputs are transformed into standardized formats, allowing heterogeneous sources to be integrated seamlessly. Where privacy regulations apply, anonymization is performed to protect sensitive information while still preserving the utility of the data.

Through these processes, the system establishes a clean, consistent, and regulation-compliant dataset, enabling agents to operate on a trustworthy information base for decision-making.

## Contextual Knowledge Integration

Contextual knowledge integration enhances decision-making by combining real-time operational data with historical context, ensuring that actions are not only responsive but also informed by past experience. This approach allows systems to move beyond reactive responses and toward predictive, context-aware reasoning.

For example, inventory levels can be linked to past demand trends, enabling more accurate forecasting and proactive restocking decisions. Similarly, client interactions can be associated with historical service outcomes, allowing the system to tailor responses based on patterns of past success or failure. By embedding this contextual layer, agentic AI systems provide richer insights and more precise recommendations, ultimately improving both efficiency and reliability in dynamic environments.

## Action Execution Pipelines

Action execution pipelines define the processes through which agent decisions are transformed into concrete business operations. They serve as the bridge between decision-making and real-world impact, ensuring that outputs are not only accurate but also actionable.

A key component of these pipelines is transaction management, which often includes rollback capabilities to restore systems to a safe state in case of failure. This safeguards data integrity and prevents cascading errors. In addition, pipelines commonly involve API calls to third-party systems, allowing agents to trigger actions across diverse platforms and integrate seamlessly with existing enterprise infrastructure.

Another important element is communication with human stakeholders. Notifications and alerts keep relevant personnel informed about critical actions, exceptions, or required approvals, ensuring transparency and oversight. By combining automation with reliability and accountability, action execution pipelines ensure that agentic AI systems drive business processes both effectively and safely.

## System Resilience and Reliability Patterns

Business-critical systems must remain reliable under high load and unexpected conditions.

## Redundancy and Failover

- Redundant agents or modules ensure continuity if a component fails.
- Load balancing between agents maintains system responsiveness.

## Error Handling and Recovery

- Predefined fallback actions in case of exceptions.

- Rollback procedures for transactions or task sequences.

**Monitoring and Observability**

- Continuous logging of agent actions and decision outcomes.

- Metrics dashboards to track throughput, task completion, and error rates.

- Alerting systems for operational anomalies or performance degradation.

**Integration with Enterprise Governance and Compliance**

Agentic systems in business environments must comply with regulations and internal policies.

- **Role-Based Access Controls (RBAC)**: Limit agent actions according to permission levels.

- **Audit Logging**: Detailed records of all decisions and actions.

- **Compliance Checks**: Continuous validation against internal policies and external regulations.

Example: A finance agent processing invoices includes checks for regulatory compliance, approval from authorized personnel, and maintains immutable logs for auditing purposes.

Architectural patterns for agentic business systems combine autonomous reasoning, modular design, workflow orchestration, and human oversight. Core components include decision engines, integration layers, memory modules, and observability infrastructure. Effective deployment relies on clear architectural selection, robust data pipelines, error handling mechanisms, and compliance integration. By adhering to these patterns, organizations can build scalable, reliable, and auditable agentic AI systems that augment operational decision-making across complex business environments.

## Section 2: Operational Applications Across Core Business Domains

Deploying agentic AI in business environments requires careful alignment with operational goals, process structures, and domain-specific requirements. This section examines practical applications across core business domains, detailing how agentic systems enhance efficiency, decision quality, and responsiveness. Structured examples illustrate inputs, workflows, and measurable outcomes in each domain.

**Supply Chain Management**

Supply chain operations involve multi-step processes, high-volume data, and real-time decision requirements, making them well-suited for agentic AI applications.

**Inventory Optimization**

Inventory optimization uses intelligent agents to balance supply with demand, reducing inefficiencies and ensuring smooth operations. By continuously monitoring inventory levels alongside historical demand patterns, agents can detect trends and anticipate future needs with greater accuracy.

A core function of this process is predictive stock replenishment, which minimizes both understocking and overstocking by aligning orders with expected demand. Agents can also automate ordering workflows by factoring in vendor lead times and adjusting purchases dynamically as demand shifts. This reduces manual oversight while improving responsiveness to market changes.

To maintain consistency across the organization, these agents integrate directly with ERP systems, synchronizing inventory data across multiple warehouses and distribution centers. This ensures that stock levels remain accurate in real time, enabling better coordination and preventing costly discrepancies. Together, these functions create a smarter, more adaptive inventory management process that improves efficiency and reduces risk.

## Logistics and Routing

Logistics and routing agents play a crucial role in streamlining transportation by calculating optimal delivery paths that balance cost, time, and efficiency. Their primary function is to design schedules and routes that ensure goods reach their destinations promptly while minimizing operational expenses.

To achieve this, agents draw on a wide range of inputs. Real-time traffic data and live shipment locations provide the foundation for dynamic route adjustments, ensuring that delays are avoided whenever possible. Delivery deadlines and priority levels are factored in to guarantee that urgent shipments are handled with the required speed and precision. At the same time, fuel consumption and environmental considerations are incorporated to reduce costs and support sustainability goals.

By integrating these diverse inputs, logistics and routing agents not only optimize daily operations but also contribute to long-term efficiency and environmental responsibility. This results in a smarter, more adaptable supply chain that can respond effectively to changing conditions.

## Supplier Coordination

- Agents manage supplier interactions, including order confirmations, performance tracking, and anomaly detection.

- Automated alerts for delays or non-compliance improve response time and reduce operational risk.

Table: Supply chain agentic workflows

| Process | Agent Function | Data Inputs | Outputs | Human Oversight |
|---------|----------------|-------------|---------|-----------------|
| Inventory | Predict demand, reorder | ERP inventory, historical sales | Purchase orders, stock updates | Approve high-value orders |
| Delivery | Route optimization | GPS, traffic, delivery schedule | Delivery schedules, route assignments | Intervene for exceptional delays |
| Supplier | Performance monitoring | Supplier KPIs, contract terms | Alerts, recommendations | Confirm corrective actions |

## Customer Service and Experience

Agentic AI systems enhance customer support by providing consistent, rapid, and contextually aware responses.

## Automated Ticket Triage

- Agents categorize and prioritize support tickets based on urgency and customer history.

Workflow:

1. Receive support requests from CRM or email system.

2. Classify issue type and severity using NLP models.

3. Assign ticket to appropriate agent or automated resolution workflow.

## Decision Augmentation for Agents

- Agents suggest responses or next actions for human support staff.

- Provides contextual insights from previous cases, policies, and product documentation.

## Performance Monitoring

- Metrics tracked include first response time, resolution rate, and customer satisfaction scores.

- Continuous feedback loops allow the agent to refine prioritization and suggested actions.

## Financial Operations

Finance and accounting are heavily rule-based, structured, and data-intensive, making them ideal for agentic automation.

## Transaction Processing

Transaction processing agents streamline financial workflows by automating key tasks such as invoice validation, payment execution, and account reconciliation. Their role is to ensure accuracy, security, and efficiency in handling financial operations that are often repetitive yet critical.

One of their core features is automated validation, where invoices are cross-checked against purchase orders and contracts to confirm legitimacy and compliance before payment is released. When anomalies or discrepancies arise, the system routes them into exception handling workflows, allowing human review while preventing delays in standard transactions.

These agents also integrate with banking APIs to carry out secure payments, ensuring compliance with financial regulations and safeguarding sensitive data. By combining automation, oversight, and secure connectivity, transaction processing agents reduce manual workload while improving reliability in financial operations.

## Forecasting and Planning

- Agents generate financial projections based on historical trends, market data, and internal KPIs.

- Supports budget planning, cash flow management, and scenario analysis.

Table: Finance Agentic Applications

| Function | Agent Capability | Input Sources | Output | Human Oversight |
|----------|------------------|---------------|--------|-----------------|
| Accounts Payable | Invoice validation, payment processing | ERP, supplier invoices | Payment approvals, reconciled accounts | High-value approvals |
| Risk Monitoring | Fraud detection, compliance alerts | Transactions, external regulations | Alerts, reports | Compliance officer review |
| Forecasting | Cash flow projections, budget planning | Historical data, market indices | Financial forecasts, planning scenarios | CFO review |

## Compliance and Regulatory Monitoring

Business operations are subject to internal policies and external regulations. Agentic AI can provide real-time monitoring and enforce compliance standards.

## Policy Enforcement

- Agents check operational actions against internal business rules.

- Examples: employee expense approvals, contract terms adherence, operational thresholds.

## Regulatory Surveillance

- Agents monitor transactions and processes to detect regulatory breaches.
- Key features:
    - Event-driven alerts for suspicious activity.
    - Automated reporting for regulatory authorities.
    - Integration with audit systems to maintain verifiable records.

## Continuous Auditing

- Agents maintain audit trails of actions and decisions.
- Supports internal review cycles and external audits without disrupting daily operations.

## Workforce Coordination and Productivity

Agentic AI can assist in scheduling, task allocation, and resource optimization for operational teams.

## Task Assignment

- Agents dynamically assign tasks based on skills, availability, and priority.
- Reduces manual scheduling effort and ensures balanced workloads.

## Performance Tracking

- Agents monitor progress, identify bottlenecks, and provide recommendations to managers.
- Metrics include task completion rates, average handling times, and efficiency scores.

## Resource Optimization

- Agents evaluate operational needs, optimizing staffing, equipment allocation, and shift planning.
- Improves utilization rates while reducing operational costs.

Table: Workforce agentic operations

| Activity | Agent Function | Inputs | Outputs | Oversight |
|---|---|---|---|---|
| Task Assignment | Allocate tasks dynamically | Employee schedules, skills, task priorities | Task list for each employee | Manager approval for exceptions |
| Performance Tracking | Monitor KPIs, detect delays | Task completion data, workflow logs | Progress dashboards, alerts | Management intervention |
| Resource Allocation | Optimize staffing/equipment | Demand forecasts, inventory | Optimized schedules, assignments | HR or operations review |

Across supply chain, customer service, finance, compliance, and workforce management, agentic AI provides measurable benefits through automation, decision augmentation, and real-time monitoring. Effective deployment requires alignment with domain-specific processes, integration with existing enterprise systems, and structured human oversight. By applying agentic systems to these operational domains, organizations can achieve efficiency gains, risk reduction, and improved decision quality, while maintaining control and compliance.

Effective deployment of agentic AI in business operations requires not only robust architecture and operational integration but also rigorous governance, reliability assurance, and systematic performance evaluation. This section provides detailed guidance on establishing governance frameworks, monitoring system reliability, implementing fail-safe mechanisms, and evaluating agentic AI impact using measurable metrics.

## Governance Frameworks for Agentic Business Systems

Governance ensures that agentic AI operates within defined organizational policies, regulatory requirements, and ethical boundaries.

## Policy Definition and Enforcement

Policy definition and enforcement form the backbone of governance in agentic AI systems, ensuring that autonomy operates within safe and accountable boundaries. Governance begins with the articulation of clear operational policies that outline how agents should function. These include defining decision authority limits to specify which actions agents can take independently, establishing workflow boundaries and escalation protocols to handle exceptions, and setting strict rules for data usage, privacy, and security.

Enforcement mechanisms bring these policies into practice. Automated policy checks embedded within the decision engine ensure that agents operate within their defined constraints, preventing unauthorized actions from being executed. For high-risk or critical activities, human review acts as an additional safeguard, providing oversight and accountability. By combining automated enforcement with human judgment, policy definition and enforcement create a structured framework that maintains compliance, enhances trust, and supports responsible deployment of agentic AI systems.

## Role-Based Access Controls (RBAC)

- Assigns permission based on role responsibilities.
- Ensure that agents only execute actions appropriate to their domain or level of authority.
- Supports compliance by preventing unauthorized operations and providing an audit trail of agent activity.

## Audit and Traceability

- Maintains detailed logs of decisions, data access, and actions executed by agents.
- Enables review of past operations to ensure regulatory compliance and operational accountability.
- Logs can be structured as immutable records stored in enterprise databases or blockchain-based ledgers for tamper resistance.

## Human Oversight Protocols

- Identify decision points where human approval is mandatory.
- Implement dashboards and alert systems to provide visibility into agent activity.
- Enable corrective intervention in real-time or post-execution analysis to ensure operational safety and accountability.

## Reliability and Fault-Tolerance Mechanisms

Reliability in agentic AI is critical for business continuity, especially in high-stakes operations such as finance or supply chain management.

**Redundancy and Failover Architecture**

- Redundant agents or modules prevent single points of failure.

- Failover systems automatically transfer responsibilities to backup agents in the event of operational failure.

- Load balancing ensures consistent response times under varying workloads.

**Error Handling and Recovery Strategies**

- Define clear exception handling protocols for all operational workflows.

- Implement rollback mechanisms for transactional operations to maintain data consistency.

- Include contingency procedures for external system failures, such as ERP or CRM downtime.

**Monitoring and Observability**

- Continuous monitoring of agent performance, task completion, and error rates.

- Observability tools track both operational metrics and agent decision pathways.

- Alerts and automated remediation triggers allow rapid detection and correction of anomalies.

Table: Reliability mechanisms

| Mechanism | Purpose | Implementation | Example |
|-----------|---------|----------------|---------|
| Redundancy | Preventing single point of failure | Parallel agents or backup modules | Finance agent failover during high-volume transaction processing |
| Rollback | Maintain consistency | Transactional checkpoints | Reversing automated payment processing errors |
| Monitoring | Detect anomalies | Dashboards and alerts | Alert on supply chain route deviation |

**Performance Evaluation Metrics**

Evaluating the performance of agentic AI ensures that business objectives are met and provides data for continuous improvement.

**Operational Metrics**

- **Task completion rate**: Percentage of tasks successfully executed by agents.

- **Cycle time**: Duration from reception input to output delivery.

- **Introduction**: Number of tasks handled per unit of time.

- **Error rate**: Frequency of incorrect or failed actions.

**Business Impact Metrics**

- **Cost savings**: Reduction in operational expenses due to automation.

- **Revenue impact**: Improvements in sales, order processing, or service outcomes.

- **Customer satisfaction**: Measured through surveys, NPS scores, or service response times.
- **Compliance adherence**: Number of regulatory or policy violations prevented by agent oversight.

## Model and Decision Quality Metrics

- **Accuracy**: Correctness of agent predictions or recommendations.
- **Precision and recall**: Particularly relevant in risk detection or anomaly identification.
- **Decision latency**: Time required for agents to generate actionable outputs.

## Continuous Improvement and Feedback Loops

To maintain operational excellence, agentic AI systems require structured feedback mechanisms.

## Feedback Collection

- Collect data from human supervisors, operational outcomes, and system logs.
- Categorize feedback into:
    - Corrective actions for errors or inefficiencies.
    - Enhancements for process optimization.
    - Compliance updates to reflect regulatory changes.

## Iterative Refinement

- Integrate feedback into agent models or rule sets.
- Update decision engines to improve accuracy and operational alignment.
- Maintain version control and testing procedures to ensure that updates do not introduce regressions.

## Benchmarking Against Standards

- Compare agentic system performance against industry or internal benchmarks.
- Metrics such as SLA adherence, processing times, and error rates can validate system effectiveness.

Table: Continuous improvement cycle

| Step | Description | Responsible Component |
|---|---|---|
| Feedback Collection | Gather operational and human input | Monitoring dashboards, human operators |
| Analysis | Identify gaps or areas for improvement | Analytics module |
| Update | Refine models, rules, or workflows | Decision engine, workflow orchestrator |
| Validation | Test changes against benchmarks | QA or simulation environments |

## Risk Management and Compliance Integration

## Risk Identification

- Agents analyze operational data to identify potential risks in finance, supply chain, or service processes.
- Techniques include statistical anomaly detection, rule-based triggers, and scenario analysis.

**Mitigation Strategies**

- Automated alerts and escalation protocols for high-risk events.

- Predefined fallback actions, including human intervention or process halts.

- Contingency planning for system failures or external disruptions.

**Compliance Tracking**

- Agents continuously validate that actions adhere to legal, regulatory, and internal policies.

- Reports and dashboards provide audit-ready documentation of compliance adherence.

Governance, reliability, and performance evaluation are critical to operationalizing agentic AI in business workflows. Implementing role-based access control, audit logging, and human oversight ensures policy compliance and accountability. Redundancy, failover mechanisms, and monitoring increase system reliability under real-world conditions. Performance evaluation through operational, business, and model-specific metrics enables data-driven assessment and continuous improvement. By integrating these practices, organizations can deploy agentic AI systems that are safe, robust, compliant, and measurable, delivering predictable business value while maintaining operational integrity.

# PART IV: GOVERNANCE, RISK, AND HUMAN FACTORS

As agentic AI systems move from prototypes to production environments, governance and human oversight become as critical as technical performance. This part addresses the legal, ethical, and organizational dimensions of deploying autonomous agents at scale. It explores risk management strategies, regulatory frameworks, and the role of human supervision in ensuring safety and accountability. Readers will gain a structured understanding of how to align technical architecture with compliance requirements and how to design systems that remain transparent, trustworthy, and resilient in real-world use.

## Section 1: Regulatory Frameworks and Compliance Requirements

The deployment of agentic AI systems requires strict adherence to legal and regulatory frameworks to ensure lawful operation and organizational accountability. These frameworks encompass international, national, and industry-specific standards that govern data handling, AI behavior, and operational responsibilities. Understanding these requirements is critical for software engineers, system architects, and product leads when designing and scaling LLM-powered autonomous agents.

### International and National Regulations

### Data Protection and Privacy

- **General Data Protection Regulation (GDPR):** Applies to AI systems processing personal data of European Union residents. Requirements include data minimization, purpose limitation, and the ability to provide data subjects with access, rectification, or erasure rights.

- **California Consumer Privacy Act (CCPA):** Similar requirements for California residents, emphasizing transparency, consent, and opt-out mechanisms.

- **Implementation Considerations:** Agents must incorporate privacy-preserving mechanisms such as pseudonymization, secure storage, and audit logging. Automated data handling processes should maintain traceability and compliance verification.

### Sector-Specific Regulations

- **Healthcare:** HIPAA (U.S.) mandates secure handling of Protected Health Information (PHI). Agentic AI systems performing diagnostics, scheduling, or monitoring must integrate secure transmission, encryption, and access controls.

- **Finance:** Anti-Money Laundering (AML) and Know Your Customer (KYC) regulations govern transaction monitoring, reporting, and risk management. Agents interacting with financial systems must include audit trails and anomaly detection to maintain regulatory compliance.

- **Transportation and Utilities:** Safety-critical regulations (e.g., aviation, automotive, and energy sector standards) require real-time monitoring, fail-safe mechanisms, and reporting capabilities. Agentic AI must interface with existing control systems while meeting reliability and safety requirements.

### AI-Specific Regulatory Initiatives

- **AI Act (European Union):** Establishes risk-based classification of AI systems. High-risk systems, including autonomous decision-making in healthcare or finance, must undergo rigorous conformity assessments, documentation, and transparency measures.

- **Algorithmic Accountability Acts (various districts):** Require organizations to evaluate automated decision systems for bias, fairness, and impact on consumers.

- **Implementation Strategies:** Design AI agents to log decision processes, allow external auditing, and provide explainable outputs that support regulatory inspection.

### Compliance Strategies for Agentic AI

### Integrating Regulatory Requirements into System Design

- **Privacy by Design:** Embed data protection measures into AI architecture from initial design stages.
- **Security Controls:** Implement encryption, authentication, and access control layers to prevent unauthorized access to sensitive data.
- **Auditability:** Maintain detailed logs of agent actions, input/output transactions, and decision rationale to demonstrate compliance during regulatory reviews.

**Continuous Monitoring and Automated Compliance Checks**

- Agents can incorporate real-time monitoring modules to verify adherence to operational rules.
- Automated compliance dashboards can track data usage, policy adherence, and system anomalies.
- Regular updates and configuration management ensure agents remain aligned with evolving legal requirements.

**Legal Accountability and Liability**

- **Organizational Responsibility:** Companies deploying agentic AI retain ultimate legal accountability for system behavior, even when operations are automated.
- **Operator and Developer Roles:** Clearly defined responsibilities for developers, system integrators, and operational teams reduce ambiguity in liability cases.
- **Contracts and Terms of Use:** Explicitly define limits of liability, obligations for oversight, and escalation procedures for incidents involving autonomous agents.

**Implementation Checklist**

| Compliance Area | Action Item | Verification Method |
|---|---|---|
| Data Privacy | Implement pseudonymization and encryption | Periodic audits and privacy impact assessments |
| Sectoral Regulations | Align system functions with HIPAA, AML, or safety standards | Internal and external compliance reviews |
| Logging & Audit | Maintain detailed operational logs | Automated audit dashboards and manual inspections |
| Transparency | Provide explainable outputs for high-risk decisions | Evaluation by legal and compliance teams |
| Continuous Monitoring | Real-time compliance verification | System alerts and anomaly detection reports |

## Section 2: Ethical Principles and Responsible Design Practices

Ethical considerations are central to the design, deployment, and management of agentic AI systems. While compliance with legal frameworks ensures that autonomous agents operate within regulatory boundaries, ethical practices ensure that these systems behave responsibly, minimize harm, and maintain public trust. This section outlines the core ethical principles, practical strategies for implementation, and methods for monitoring ethical alignment in LLM-powered autonomous agents.

**Core Ethical Principles**

**Fairness**

- Agents must treat all users and stakeholders equitably, avoiding bias based on demographic, socioeconomic, or contextual factors.
- Techniques for fairness assessment include statistical parity, disparate impact analysis, and fairness-aware modeling.
- Fairness measures should be integrated at multiple stages, including data collection, model training, and decision execution.

## Transparency

- Systems should provide clear, interpretable outputs that explain their reasoning and actions.
- Explainability techniques for LLM-based agents include attention visualizations, decision trees for post-hoc analysis, and natural language justifications.
- Transparency supports auditability, trust, and accountability, particularly in high-stakes domains such as healthcare, finance, and legal services.

## Accountability

- Human stakeholders retain ultimate responsibility for agent decisions.
- Accountability structures require documentation of agent actions, decision rationale, and operational context.
- Governance frameworks define roles and responsibilities across developers, operators, and oversight personnel.

## Privacy and Data Protection

- Ethical design incorporates privacy beyond legal mandates.
- Techniques include differential privacy, anonymization, and secure multi-party computation.
- Agents should minimize data retention and provide mechanisms for user consent and data access.

## Bias Detection and Mitigation

## Sources of Bias

- Training data may reflect historical inequities, systemic biases, or incomplete representation.
- Model architecture and parameterization can inadvertently amplify certain patterns or correlations.
- Interaction patterns from users may introduce feedback loops that reinforce undesirable behavior.
- **Mitigation Strategies**
- Preprocessing: Curate datasets to remove or balance biased samples.
- In-processing: Apply fairness constraints during model training.
- Post-processing: Adjust outputs to correct identified biases without compromising overall system integrity.
- Continuous evaluation: Deploy monitoring pipelines to detect emergent bias during real-world operation

## Human-in-the-Loop Design

- Incorporating human oversight ensures critical decisions are reviewed by qualified personnel.

- Supervisory agents can approve, modify, or veto actions proposed by autonomous systems.

- Multi-level review structures allow different levels of oversight depending on risk assessment, system autonomy, and operational context.

- Examples include clinical review in healthcare applications, financial risk assessment approvals, and legal case triage.

## Ethical Evaluation Frameworks

## Audit and Assessment Protocols

- Periodic ethical audits evaluate adherence to fairness, transparency, and accountability principles.

- Assessment may involve scenario testing, stress testing for bias, and outcome validation against societal or organizational norms.

## Ethical Scorecards

- Quantitative measures track ethical compliance across multiple axes such as fairness indices, transparency levels, and human intervention frequency.

- Scorecards support decision-making on system deployment, updates, and scaling.

## Cross-Functional Oversight

- Integrating legal, technical, and ethical review teams ensure holistic evaluation.

- Governance committees monitor alignment between system behavior, organizational values, and societal expectations.

## Aligning AI Behavior with Organizational and Societal Values

- Agents should operate within clearly defined ethical boundaries that reflect both corporate policy and public standards.

- Normative constraints may include prohibitions on harmful content generation, avoidance of discriminatory practices, and prioritization of safety-critical outcomes.

- Behavioral alignment is reinforced through:

  o Rule-based constraints are embedded in decision logic.

  o Reinforcement of learning objectives that penalize unethical actions.

  o Continuous feedback from human stakeholders and user communities.

## Implementation Checklist

| Ethical Principle | Implementation Strategy | Verification Method |
| --- | --- | --- |
| Fairness | Preprocessing, in-processing, and post-processing bias mitigation | Statistical audits, scenario testing |
| Transparency | Explainable outputs, decision rationale reporting | Human review and automated analysis |
| Accountability | Document agent actions, define oversight roles | Audit trails, incident investigations |

| Privacy | Differential privacy, consent management, minimal retention | Compliance checks, system monitoring |
| --- | --- | --- |
| Human Oversight | Multi-level approval structures | Workflow review, supervisory interventions |

By systematically integrating these ethical principles into the design, operation, and evaluation of agentic AI, organizations can ensure that autonomous systems operate responsibly, maintain public trust, and complement regulatory compliance. These practices provide the foundation for reliable, accountable, and socially aligned AI deployment.

## Section 3: Risk Management, Liability, and Governance in Agentic AI

Effective risk management, clearly defined liability structures, and robust governance frameworks are essential for safely deploying agentic AI systems. While regulatory compliance and ethical practices provide external and internal guardrails, systematic risk management ensures operational resilience, reduces exposure to legal or financial penalties, and supports the sustained reliability of autonomous agents. This section presents practical frameworks, processes, and organizational strategies for managing risk and enforcing accountability in LLM-powered AI systems.

**Mitigation Strategies**

**Technical Safeguards**

- **Redundancy and Fail-Safes:** Implement backup processes, fallback models, and error-handling mechanisms to maintain functionality during failures.

- **Robust Data Pipelines:** Validate inputs, enforce schema conformity, and detect anomalies to prevent corrupted data from affecting agent decisions.

- **Monitoring and Alerts:** Continuous system monitoring with automated alerts for abnormal behavior or performance deviations.

**Procedural Safeguards**

- **Human-in-the-Loop Oversight:** Supervisory approval for high-risk or high-impact decisions.

- **Operational Checkpoints:** Integrate review stages, threshold-based decision-making, and rollback procedures.

- **Incident Response Plans:** Predefined protocols for identifying, documenting, and mitigating incidents, including communication strategies with stakeholders.

**Organizational Safeguards**

- **Defined Roles and Responsibilities:** Assign clear accountability for developers, system integrators, operational teams, and oversight committees.

- **Cross-Functional Governance:** Ensure collaboration between legal, technical, and ethical oversight teams for holistic risk management.

- **Training and Awareness:** Educate staff on operational, ethical, and regulatory risks associated with agentic AI deployment.

**Liability Frameworks**

**Organizational Liability**

- Companies remain responsible for system behavior, even when actions are automated.

- Liability agreements should be embedded in contracts with vendors, developers, and third-party service providers.

**Risk Transfer Mechanisms**

- **Insurance Policies:** Tailored AI liability insurance can mitigate financial exposure from operational or legal incidents.

- **Contractual Indemnification:** Clear terms assigning responsibility for data breaches, system errors, or decision harms.

**Documentation and Traceability**

- Maintain comprehensive logs of system inputs, decisions, and human interventions.

- Traceability supports legal defense, post-incident analysis, and compliance verification.

Effective risk management begins with systematically identifying, classifying, and quantifying potential hazards that LLM-powered autonomous agents may encounter. Agentic AI systems operate in dynamic environments, interact with diverse data sources, and make high-impact decisions, making comprehensive risk assessment critical. This section presents structured methodologies for uncovering operational, technical, ethical, and regulatory risks, and outlines standardized approaches to classify and quantify them.

## Operational Risk Identification

Operational risks arise from the practical functioning of agentic systems in real-world environments. Identifying these risks requires a holistic understanding of system components, data flows, and dependencies. Key operational risks include:

### System Failures

- **Hardware Failures:** Agents running on physical devices may be affected by hardware malfunctions, network interruptions, or infrastructure degradation.

- **Software Errors:** Bugs in code, memory leaks, or improper exception handling can lead to system crashes or inconsistent behavior.

- **Latency and Throughput Issues:** High computational demand may introduce latency, reduce real-time responsiveness, or cause incomplete task execution.

### Data-Related Risks

- **Data Corruption:** Inputs that are incomplete, malformed, or inconsistent can trigger erroneous outputs.

- **Data Drift:** Changes in data distribution over time may degrade model performance and decision reliability.

- **External Data Dependencies:** Agents relying on third-party APIs or external databases can be exposed to outages, inaccuracies, or delayed updates.

### Integration and Interoperability Risks

- **API Misalignment:** Incorrect assumptions about input/output formats can result in failed communications with external systems.

- **Version Conflicts:** Upgrades or changes in dependent systems may cause incompatibility.

- **Unexpected Interactions:** Agents interacting with other autonomous systems may create emergent behaviors that were not anticipated during design.

## Technical Risk Assessment

Technical risks pertain to model-specific and computational challenges inherent in LLM-powered agents. Proper identification requires monitoring both model behavior and system performance under diverse operational scenarios.

### Model Drift and Degradation

- Over time, language models may produce less accurate outputs due to shifts in input patterns or contextual changes.

- Monitoring model performance metrics, such as accuracy, consistency, and completion rates, is critical for early detection.

## Adversarial and Malicious Inputs

- Agents may be susceptible to inputs designed to manipulate outputs, including prompt injection, data poisoning, or API misuse.

- Detection mechanisms include anomaly scoring, input validation, and behavior consistency checks.

## Robustness Limitations

- Models may fail under edge cases or out-of-distribution scenarios.

- Stress-testing with rare or extreme inputs is essential to understand operational boundaries.

By systematically identifying, classifying, and quantifying risks, organizations can establish a solid foundation for mitigation strategies, safety protocols, and governance. Early and continuous risk assessment enables controlled deployment of agentic AI systems while minimizing operational, technical, ethical, and regulatory exposure

## Section 2: Mitigation Strategies, Safety Protocols, and Incident Response

Once risks have been systematically identified, classified, and quantified, the next critical step in managing agentic AI systems is implementing robust mitigation strategies, establishing comprehensive safety protocols, and preparing incident response frameworks. These measures ensure that LLM-powered autonomous agents operate reliably, minimize adverse outcomes, and maintain compliance with regulatory and organizational standards. This section provides a structured, evidence-based approach to designing and operationalizing these mechanisms.

### Technical Mitigation Strategies

Technical mitigation focuses on system-level safeguards that reduce the likelihood and impact of operational and model-related risks. These strategies are implemented across design, deployment, and runtime stages.

### Redundancy and Fail-Safes

- **Redundant Architectures:** Deploying multiple agent instances or parallel systems ensures continuity in case of individual component failures.

- **Fail-Safe Mechanisms:** Systems are designed to revert to a safe state upon encountering errors, such as pausing operations or defaulting to human review.

- **Circuit Breakers:** Automatic detection of abnormal behavior triggers temporary halts to prevent cascading failures.

### Input Validation and Filtering

- Ensures that agents process only well-formed, authorized inputs.

- Implement boundary checks, schema validation, and anomaly detection to prevent model exploitation.

- Protects against adversarial attacks, such as prompt injections, malicious API calls, or corrupted datasets.

### Continuous Monitoring and Logging

- Real-time monitoring of agent performance metrics (latency, accuracy, throughput) identifies anomalies early.

164

- Detailed logs of agent decisions, inputs, and outputs support traceability and post-incident analysis.
- Alerts and dashboards can trigger human intervention for high-severity anomalies.

## Controlled Access and Environment Segmentation

- Segregation of development, staging, and production environments reduces the risk of unintended cross-system impacts.
- Role-based access control ensures that only authorized personnel can modify agent behavior or access sensitive data.

## Procedural Safeguards

Procedural safeguards complement technical measures by embedding human oversight and structured operational practices into agent workflows.

## Human-in-the-Loop (HITL)

- Critical or high-impact decisions require human review before execution.
- HITL mechanisms can be fully integrated for task approval, partial review for confidence thresholds, or advisory-only feedback depending on operational risk.

## Threshold-Based Approvals

- Agents can be configured to automatically escalate decisions that exceed predefined confidence or risk thresholds.
- Examples include financial transaction limits, healthcare dosage recommendations, or legal document review alerts.

## Operational Checkpoints and Workflow Segmentation

- Breaking complex tasks into discrete checkpoints allows for verification at intermediate stages.
- Checkpoints reduce the likelihood of error propagation and facilitate targeted debugging.

## Cross-Functional Oversight

- Engineering, compliance, and operations teams collaborate to review agent outputs, monitor performance, and evaluate risk exposure.
- Structured review cycles, such as weekly or monthly audits, ensure ongoing alignment with safety objectives.

## Incident Response Planning

Even with preventive measures, unanticipated incidents can occur. Effective response protocols minimize damage, maintain trust, and support rapid recovery.

## Detection and Alerting

- Automated monitoring detects anomalies, deviations, and potential breaches in real-time.
- Alerts are prioritized based on severity, enabling appropriate escalation paths.

### Containment and Isolation

- Systems should allow rapid isolation of affected components to prevent propagation of errors.

- Containment strategies may include switching traffic to redundant agents, suspending agent actions, or rolling back to stable configurations.

### Root Cause Analysis (RCA)

- Post-incident RCA identifies the underlying source of failure, whether technical, procedural, or environmental.

- Documentation of findings informs mitigation updates and prevents recurrence.

### Communication Protocols

- Internal communication ensures that all stakeholders, including operations, engineering, and compliance teams, are aware of incidents promptly.

- External communication protocols maintain transparency with customers, regulators, and partners when appropriate.

## Testing and Validation for Safety Assurance

Testing and validation are essential to confirm that safety mechanisms and risk mitigation strategies perform effectively under both expected and edge-case conditions. Rigorous evaluation ensures that agentic AI systems remain stable, resilient, and trustworthy in real-world deployments. Stress Testing evaluates system stability by exposing agents to high-load conditions, rare input cases, and adversarial scenarios. Key metrics such as task completion rates, error propagation, and recovery times are tracked to measure robustness and resilience under pressure.

Simulation Scenarios recreate controlled, real-world-like environments to test agent behavior in complex, multi-step tasks. These simulations enable verification of human-in-the-loop processes, fail-safe mechanisms, and contingency protocols, ensuring that systems respond safely when unexpected events occur. Controlled Rollouts introduce agentic AI systems gradually using techniques such as canary releases or phased regional deployments. This strategy reduces systemic risk by monitoring performance in a limited scope before full-scale adoption, allowing organizations to validate safety mechanisms and mitigation strategies in production-like settings. Automated Regression Testing provides continuous validation that updates, patches, or model fine-tuning do not introduce new vulnerabilities. When integrated into CI/CD pipelines, regression tests enforce safety standards throughout iterative development, ensuring that innovation does not compromise reliability.

### Feedback Loops for Continuous Improvement

Safety and risk mitigation are ongoing processes. Continuous feedback loops capture operational data and lessons learned to refine strategies.

- **Monitoring Metrics:** Track safety KPIs such as incident frequency, resolution time, system uptime, and model confidence intervals.

- **Periodic Audits:** Formal assessments of agent behavior, risk logs, and mitigation effectiveness ensure adherence to safety objectives.

- **Update Cycles:** Incorporate findings from simulations, RCA, and operational monitoring into model retraining, system updates, and procedural enhancements.

- **Cross-Team Reviews:** Encourage knowledge sharing and collaborative problem-solving to enhance overall system resilience.

**Integration into Organizational Practice**

- Establish clear roles and responsibilities for safety management across engineering, operations, and compliance teams.

- Maintain detailed documentation of mitigation strategies, checkpoints, incident procedures, and test results.

- Embed risk and safety review cycles within standard development sprints or operational planning sessions.

- Align safety practices with industry standards, such as ISO 31000 for risk management and IEC 61508 for functional safety in software-controlled systems.

By combining technical safeguards, procedural protocols, and structured incident response frameworks, organizations can reduce the probability and impact of failures in agentic AI systems. Continuous testing, controlled deployment, and feedback-driven improvement create a resilient operational environment that supports reliable, safe, and compliant autonomous agent behaviour.

## Section 3: Governance, Compliance, and Continuous Safety Management

Effective risk management in agentic AI systems extends beyond technical safeguards and operational protocols. Comprehensive governance, regulatory compliance, and continuous safety oversight are essential to ensure that autonomous agents operate reliably, ethically, and within organizational and legal boundaries. This section details structured frameworks and practices for governing LLM-powered agents, integrating compliance into development and operations, and sustaining continuous safety management.

**Governance Frameworks for Agentic AI**

Governance establishes accountability, decision-making structures, and oversight mechanisms that guide agentic AI development and deployment.

**Roles and Responsibilities**

- **Chief AI Officer (CAIO) or equivalent:** Provides strategic oversight, defines policies, and ensures alignment with organizational risk appetite.

- **AI Risk Committee:** Cross-functional team including engineering, operations, legal, and compliance representatives to review agentic system risks and mitigation plans.

- **System Owners and Engineers:** Responsible for day-to-day implementation of governance policies, monitoring agent performance, and enforcing safety protocols.

- **Human-in-the-Loop Operators:** Oversee critical decision points and maintain operational control in high-risk scenarios.

**Policy Development**

- Define organizational policies for agentic AI usage, including permissible tasks, operational boundaries, and escalation protocols.

- Policies should address ethical considerations, data privacy, operational transparency, and model reliability requirements.

- Establish procedures for documenting deviations, exceptions, and mitigations to maintain accountability.

**Audit and Review Cycles**

- Conduct periodic audits to evaluate system compliance with internal policies and external regulations.
- Review incident logs, risk metrics, and system performance data to identify gaps in governance practices.
- Ensure governance processes evolve with model updates, architectural changes, or regulatory developments.

**Regulatory Compliance**

Compliance ensures that agentic AI systems meet legal, industry, and ethical standards, reducing organizational exposure to liability and enhancing trust.

**Data Privacy and Protection**

- Adhere to regulations such as GDPR, HIPAA, or equivalent local standards governing the collection, storage, and processing of personal and sensitive data.
- Implement data minimization, anonymization, and secure storage protocols to limit exposure.
- Maintain detailed audit trails to demonstrate regulatory compliance during inspections or legal reviews.

**Industry-Specific Regulations**

- Finance: Compliance with SEC, FINRA, or equivalent mandates on automated trading, transaction monitoring, and auditability.
- Healthcare: Alignment with FDA, HIPAA, and clinical safety standards for diagnostic support, patient data handling, and autonomous decision support.
- Manufacturing and Robotics: Adherence to ISO 10218 (robotics safety), ISO 13849 (control systems), and functional safety requirements for autonomous operations.

**Ethical and Responsible AI Guidelines**

- Implement fairness, transparency, and accountability principles.
- Ensure that autonomous decisions can be interpreted, reviewed, and corrected when necessary.
- Establish procedures for monitoring bias, discriminatory outcomes, or unintended consequences, integrating mitigation protocols into operational workflows.

**Continuous Safety and Risk Management**

Sustaining safety in agentic AI requires continuous monitoring, iterative improvement, and dynamic adaptation to evolving risks.

By integrating governance frameworks, compliance requirements, and continuous safety management into the lifecycle of agentic AI systems, organizations can achieve operational resilience, ethical integrity, and regulatory alignment. This structured approach ensures that LLM-powered autonomous agents function predictably, mitigate risks proactively, and maintain trust among stakeholders.

# Chapter 17: Human-Agent Collaboration and

## Section 1: Frameworks for Human-Agent Interaction and Oversight

Human-agent collaboration and supervision are foundational to the design of reliable, safe, and effective autonomous systems. In complex, real-world applications, fully autonomous decision-making without human oversight is often impractical or unsafe. This section establishes the conceptual and practical frameworks that engineers, architects, and product leads can use to integrate human oversight into agentic AI systems. The focus is on proven design principles, structured interaction models, and evaluative criteria that optimize both task performance and safety.

### Taxonomies of Human-Agent Interaction

Human-agent collaboration can be classified according to the role humans play relative to the agent:

1. **Supervisory Control**: In this model, the human oversees multiple autonomous agents, monitoring their outputs and intervening selectively. Humans typically maintain high-level control, such as approving decisions, assigning tasks, or modifying objectives. Supervisory control is common in industrial robotics, air traffic management, and coordination, where agents perform routine or repetitive tasks, but human judgment is essential for exceptions.

2. **Peer-Level Collaboration**: Here, the human and agent operate as functional peers, sharing responsibility for task execution. Both human and agent contribute to decision-making, often iterating through a shared workflow. Examples include medical decision support systems and collaborative software development tools. Peer-level collaboration requires real-time communication channels, well-defined task boundaries, and explicit coordination protocols to prevent conflicts.

3. **Intervention-Based Models**: In this framework, agents operate autonomously but humans maintain the ability to intervene in critical situations. Intervention may be triggered by predefined thresholds, anomaly detection, or system uncertainty. Examples include automated financial trading systems and self-driving vehicles, where humans are not involved in routine operation but retain the authority to stop, override, or adjust agent behavior in high-risk scenarios.

Each taxonomy has implications for system design, resource allocation, and risk management. Supervisory models emphasize human workload management, peer-level models focus on communication protocols and coordination, and intervention-based models prioritize monitoring and rapid response capabilities.

### Principles of Effective Oversight

Designing effective human-agent collaboration requires adherence to several core principles:

- **Transparency**: Agents must provide interpretable outputs that clearly indicate reasoning, confidence levels, and operational state. Transparency enables humans to understand agent behavior, anticipate errors, and make informed interventions. Techniques include structured output formats, probabilistic confidence indicators, and visualization of agent reasoning paths.

- **Interpretability**: Interpretability ensures that humans can map agent outputs to real-world implications. This is particularly critical in high-stakes domains such as healthcare, aviation, and critical infrastructure. Model-agnostic approaches, such as SHAP (SHapley Additive exPlanations) values or counterfactual analysis, support interpretability without requiring full access to model internals.

- **Controllability**: Human agents must retain actionable control over autonomous systems. Controllability encompasses the ability to adjust parameters, halt or redirect workflows, and override automated decisions.

Control interfaces should be designed to minimize latency, reduce cognitive load, and support situational awareness.

- **Responsiveness**: Human-agent systems must support timely responses to both agent-generated alerts and environmental changes. Responsiveness is achieved through efficient monitoring architecture, automated alert prioritization, and clearly defined escalation paths.

**Design Patterns for Human-in-the-Loop Systems**

Human-in-the-loop (HITL) systems integrate humans directly into the agent workflow to enhance reliability, safety, and adaptability. Established design patterns provide practical guidance:

1. **Approval Loops**: Agents propose decisions or actions that require explicit human approval before execution. This pattern is widely used in content moderation, clinical decision support, and critical infrastructure management.

2. **Advisory Systems**: Agents provide recommendations along with supporting evidence, but humans retain ultimate decision authority. This pattern supports peer-level collaboration and is effective when human expertise is essential for context-sensitive interpretation.

3. **Corrective Feedback Loops**: Humans can correct agent outputs during or after task execution. These corrections are then fed back into the system to improve future performance. This pattern supports continuous learning and is commonly implemented in machine learning pipelines with active learning components.

4. **Escalation Protocols**: Agents identify situations that exceed operational thresholds or confidence limits and escalate them to human oversight. Escalation can be triggered by anomalies, uncertainty, or predefined risk conditions.

**Evaluation Criteria for Collaboration Effectiveness**

Human-agent collaboration must be quantitatively and qualitatively assessed to ensure reliability and safety. Key evaluation dimensions include:

- **Task Performance**: Measures the effectiveness and efficiency of the combined human-agent system in achieving operational objectives. Metrics include completion time, accuracy, and error rates.

- **Error Mitigation**: Evaluates how well the human-agent system detects, prevents, and corrects errors. This includes assessing false positive/negative rates, intervention success rates, and resilience to unexpected inputs.

- **Decision Quality**: Focuses on the appropriateness, rationality, and consistency of decisions produced by the human-agent team. This metric is particularly critical in high-stakes applications, such as clinical diagnostics or automated trading.

- **Human Workload**: Assesses cognitive, temporal, and physical demands placed on human operators. Techniques such as the NASA Task Load Index (NASA-TLX) or structured observational studies can quantify workload and inform system adjustments.

- **Trust and Usability**: Evaluates whether human operators perceive the system as reliable, understandable, and supportive. Metrics can include standardized questionnaires, task completion success under supervision, and frequency of override interventions.

**Trade-Offs Between Human Workload and Agent Autonomy**

Optimizing human-agent collaboration requires balancing autonomy with oversight. Key trade-offs include:

- **Autonomy vs. Situational Awareness**: High agent autonomy can reduce human workload but may reduce situational awareness and increase the risk of undetected errors.

- **Human Bandwidth vs. Task Coverage**: Supervising multiple agents increases operational efficiency but can overload human operators if interfaces or monitoring systems are poorly designed.

- **Responsiveness vs. Cognitive Load**: Frequent alerts and interventions improve system responsiveness but can overwhelm human operators, leading to fatigue and reduced intervention quality.

Designing for these trade-offs requires systematic assessment of task complexity, environmental variability, and operator capacity. Simulation-based testing and phased deployment can provide empirical evidence to calibrate autonomy levels against human supervision needs.

**Layered Interaction Model**

To clarify the relationships among human roles, agent decision-making layers, and feedback loops, consider a layered interaction model:

- **Layer 1: Autonomous Agent Layer** – Performs task execution, generates recommendations, and monitors operational parameters.

- **Layer 2: Human Oversight Layer** – Receives agent outputs, monitors system state, intervenes when necessary, and provides feedback.

- **Layer 3: Feedback Integration Layer** – Integrates human corrections and supervisory inputs into agent learning pipelines or control logic.

- **Layer 4: Environment Layer** – Represents the external context, including dynamic task conditions, external signals, and operational constraints.

This model emphasizes bidirectional communication: agents report status and confidence to humans, while humans provide approvals, corrections, or escalations that refine agent behavior. It highlights the structured, layered approach necessary for safe, efficient human-agent collaboration.

Frameworks for human-agent interaction and oversight provide the foundational structure for designing systems that combine human judgment with autonomous decision-making. By categorizing interaction models, adhering to core principles of transparency, interpretability, controllability, and responsiveness, and applying structured HITL design patterns, practitioners can optimize both safety and performance. Evaluating collaboration effectiveness through task performance, error mitigation, decision quality, workload assessment, and trust metrics ensures that systems are operationally robust. Understanding the trade-offs between autonomy and human workload allows for calibrated supervision that supports reliability without overburdening human operators. Layered interaction models provide a clear blueprint for integrating human oversight into agentic systems while maintaining operational efficiency and safety.

## Section 2: Mechanisms for Monitoring, Feedback, and Intervention

Effective human-agent collaboration relies on robust mechanisms for monitoring agent behavior, providing timely feedback, and executing interventions when necessary. These mechanisms ensure operational reliability, reduce error propagation, and maintain human trust in autonomous systems. This section presents evidence-based practices for designing monitoring architectures, feedback loops, and intervention strategies, with a focus on measurable outcomes and operational clarity.

## Continuous Monitoring Architectures

Monitoring agentic AI systems requires structured mechanisms to observe both system outputs and their surrounding context. Several architectural approaches can be used to ensure reliability, compliance, and operational transparency.

**Centralized Monitoring Dashboards** aggregate real-time data from multiple agents into a single interface. These dashboards display operational metrics, agent confidence levels, anomaly indicators, and task status, allowing supervisors to quickly detect deviations or critical events without manually inspecting individual logs.

**Distributed Monitoring Systems** spread monitoring responsibilities across multiple human operators or automated subsystems. This model is particularly effective in large-scale, multi-agent environments where a single dashboard cannot provide adequate situational awareness. Hierarchical reporting structures allow local monitors to generate aggregated insights and escalate them to higher-level supervisors for action.

**Anomaly Detection Modules** apply statistical or machine learning techniques to detect unusual agent behavior. Methods such as threshold-based triggers, time-series analysis, and probabilistic modeling support early identification of risks. By flagging deviations in real time, these modules enable human operators to intervene before errors escalate into failures.

**Logging and Audit Trails** provide detailed records of agent decisions, environmental observations, and system inputs. These logs, which should include timestamped events, confidence scores, decision rationales, and records of human interventions, serve as a foundation for compliance audits, post-incident reviews, and continuous system improvement.

Together, these monitoring architectures provide enterprises with the visibility and control needed to maintain trustworthy, resilient agentic AI operations.

## Feedback Loops

Feedback loops enable human supervisors to communicate corrections, adjustments, or guidance to agents efficiently. Effective feedback design maximizes learning and adaptation while minimizing operational disruptions. Key elements include:

- **Corrective Feedback**: Humans identify errors or suboptimal decisions and provide structured corrections to the agent. This feedback can be incorporated into learning pipelines for reinforcement or supervised learning.

- **Confidence-Based Alerts**: Agents communicate uncertainty levels for decisions or predictions. Humans prioritize interventions based on confidence thresholds, focusing attention on high-risk or ambiguous outputs.

- **Performance Scoring**: Supervisors rate agent outputs according to predefined criteria such as accuracy, timeliness, and compliance with rules. Scores inform adaptive system adjustments or retraining cycles.

- **Iterative Learning Cycles**: Human-provided feedback is fed back into model training pipelines, supporting continuous improvement. Feedback loops should maintain traceability to identify which input influenced model updates.

## Intervention Strategies

Intervention is a critical component of safe human-agent collaboration, providing mechanisms for human operators to correct, redirect, or halt agent actions. Intervention strategies are classified based on immediacy and scope:

1. **Real-Time Overrides**:

    o Humans immediately halt or adjust agent actions when unsafe or incorrect behavior is detected.

    o Requires low-latency interfaces and clear status indicators to minimize intervention delays.

2. **Escalation Protocols**:

    o Agents automatically escalate tasks to humans when operational thresholds are exceeded.

    o Escalation triggers include anomalies, confidence below defined levels, or contextual risks.

    o Protocols must define human responsibilities, response time expectations, and fallback measures.

3. **Dynamic Authority Assignment**:

    o Adjusts the degree of agent autonomy based on task complexity, environmental conditions, or human availability.

    o Reduces unnecessary human workload in routine tasks while ensuring oversight in critical scenarios.

4. **Delayed or Post-Hoc Intervention**:

    o Humans review agent decisions after execution, providing corrective guidance for future iterations.

    o Effective for lower-risk tasks or systems where immediate intervention is impractical.

## Integrating Explainable AI Outputs

Explainable AI (XAI) enhances human comprehension and trust, improving both monitoring and intervention effectiveness. Practical integration strategies include:

- **Structured Rationale Presentation**: Agents present decision explanations in a standardized format, highlighting key features, confidence scores, and decision paths.

- **Visualizations and Dashboards**: Use charts, heat maps, or dependency graphs to convey complex information efficiently. For example, a clinical diagnostic system might highlight relevant patient features contributing to prediction.

- **Counterfactual Analysis**: Display alternative outcomes if certain inputs were different, allowing humans to assess decision robustness.

- **Alert Prioritization**: XAI outputs can be combined with anomaly detection to focus human attention on high-impact decisions or errors.

## Metrics and KPIs for Monitoring and Intervention

Quantitative metrics are essential for evaluating monitoring and intervention systems. Commonly used metrics include:

- **Detection Rate**: Percentage of agent errors or anomalies correctly identified by monitoring systems.

- **Intervention Success Rate**: Percentage of interventions that result in corrected or prevented errors.

- **Time to Intervention**: Duration between detection of an issue and successful human intervention.

- **False Positive/Negative Rates**: Measures reliability of monitoring alerts and escalation triggers.

- **System Responsiveness**: Latency of feedback loops, agent adaptation speed, and human response time.

- **Operational Load Metrics**: Measures of human cognitive and temporal burden associated with monitoring tasks.

**Table: Mapping Agent Behaviors to Supervision Interventions**

| Agent Behavior | Recommended Supervision Intervention | Monitoring Method | Feedback Mechanism |
|---|---|---|---|
| High uncertainty in decision | Escalate to human | Confidence-based alerts | Corrective feedback |
| Anomalous output | Real-time override | Anomaly detection | Structured rationale review |
| Repeated errors in task execution | Dynamic authority adjustment | Performance scoring | Iterative learning cycle |
| Low-risk, routine task | Minimal supervision | Dashboard summaries | Post-hoc review |
| Critical operation in variable environment | Immediate human approval | Combined anomaly + confidence monitoring | Corrective guidance + escalation |

This table provides a practical mapping of agent behaviors to human supervision mechanisms, enabling engineers to implement structured intervention strategies in operational systems.

**Practical Implementation Considerations**

When designing monitoring, feedback, and intervention mechanisms, engineers must address several practical factors:

- **Interface Design**: Interfaces should minimize cognitive load, clearly communicate agent state, and provide actionable controls. Standardized layouts and prioritization of high-risk alerts improve effectiveness.

- **Scalability**: Systems must support multiple agents, distributed supervision teams, and integration with enterprise monitoring infrastructure.

- **Latency and Performance**: Monitoring and intervention systems must operate with low latency to prevent delayed responses that could compromise task safety.

- **Data Integration**: Systems should aggregate agent logs, environmental data, and human inputs to provide a unified operational picture. Structured data storage facilitates post-hoc analysis and compliance reporting.

- **Training and Protocols**: Human supervisors require standardized training in intervention protocols, feedback mechanisms, and interpretation of agent outputs. Operational protocols should define thresholds, roles, and escalation paths clearly.

To keep human-agent collaboration safe and effective, it's important to have ways to monitor, give feedback, and step in when necessary. Centralized dashboards, distributed systems, and anomaly detection are all examples of continuous monitoring designs that provide you with a full picture of what's going on. Structured feedback loops that include corrective input, confidence-based alarms, and performance assessment guarantee that human instruction is delivered and used efficiently. Intervention solutions, such as real-time overrides, escalation processes, dynamic authority assignment, and post-hoc corrections, make operations more flexible and safer in all situations. Adding explainable AI outputs makes things clearer, understandable, and trustworthy, which helps people make smart choices.

Quantitative metrics and operational KPIs allow for systematic evaluation and optimization of human-agent supervision, making sure that both the burden of the human and the performance of the agent are balanced for dependable results. Finally, actual implementation issues including interface design, scalability, latency, data integration, and human training make up the operational foundation needed to put these processes into real-world systems.

## Section 3: Governance, Risk Management, and Operational Protocols

Human-agent collaboration requires more than technical integration; it necessitates structured governance, risk management, and operational protocols to maintain system reliability, safety, and compliance. Without formalized procedures, even well-designed monitoring and intervention mechanisms can fail under real-world operational complexity. This section provides practical frameworks for organizational oversight, risk assessment, procedural standardization, and continuous operational improvement.

### Risk Assessment Frameworks for Human-Agent Workflows

Managing risk in agentic AI deployments requires structured methods for identifying and analyzing potential points of failure. Several established frameworks can be applied to human-agent workflows to ensure safety, reliability, and accountability.

**Failure Mode and Effects Analysis (FMEA)** provides a systematic way to identify failure modes, assess their impact, and prioritize them for mitigation. By assigning severity ratings, occurrence probabilities, and detectability scores, teams can calculate a Risk Priority Number (RPN) to guide corrective action. This method is particularly useful for multi-agent workflows, supervisory control interfaces, and feedback loops.

**Hazard and Operability Analysis (HAZOP)** focuses on deviations from standard operating conditions that may cause unsafe or suboptimal outcomes. In human-agent systems, HAZOP highlights potential hazards such as delayed human intervention, misinterpretation of outputs, or inconsistent agent behavior, enabling proactive safeguards.

**Quantitative Risk Assessment (QRA)** employs statistical modeling to estimate both the likelihood and impact of adverse events. This approach supports informed decision-making about acceptable levels of autonomy, monitoring thresholds, and escalation protocols in critical workflows.

**Scenario-Based Risk Analysis** explores risk under dynamic, real-world conditions by modeling operational scenarios that combine environmental variability, agent behavior, and human responses. These scenarios help organizations test escalation pathways, evaluate dynamic authority assignment, and assess multi-agent coordination strategies.

Together, these frameworks provide a comprehensive toolkit for identifying risks, mitigating failures, and ensuring that human-agent workflows operate safely and effectively.

Key components include:

- **Role Definitions**: Clearly specify which tasks are agent-driven, which require human oversight, and which are shared responsibilities.

- **Escalation Protocols**: Define conditions under which human intervention is mandatory, including thresholds, confidence scores, and anomaly triggers.

- **Approval Workflows**: Standardize decision review processes, specifying when and how humans must approve or correct agent outputs.

- **Intervention Procedures**: Document step-by-step actions for overrides, corrections, or system shutdowns, including fallback options.

- **Communication Protocols**: Specify channels, formats, and frequencies for agent-human and human-human coordination, particularly in distributed supervision environments.

SOPs should be regularly reviewed and updated based on operational experience, performance metrics, and post-incident analyses. Compliance with SOPs is critical for minimizing errors, ensuring accountability, and supporting regulatory requirements.

## Auditing and Compliance Requirements

Regulated industries and mission-critical systems require robust auditing and compliance structures. Auditing ensures that human-agent interactions meet predefined safety, performance, and ethical standards. Practices include:

- **Operational Logs**: Maintain detailed records of agent decisions, human interventions, alerts, and feedback. Logs must be timestamped, structured, and auditable.

- **Periodic Compliance Reviews**: Evaluate adherence to SOPs, intervention protocols, and monitoring standards. Include both quantitative metrics and qualitative assessments.

- **Traceability**: Ensure that every agent's action and human intervention can be traced to a specific workflow, operator, or event. Traceability supports accountability, post-incident analysis, and regulatory reporting.

- **Regulatory Alignment**: Align operational practices with industry-specific standards, such as ISO 13485 for medical devices, ISO/IEC 27001 for information security, or FAA guidelines for aviation automation.

Auditing not only ensures compliance but also provides structured feedback for system improvement, risk mitigation, and evidence-based decision-making regarding agent autonomy.

## Scalability Considerations

Scaling human-agent systems introduces additional complexity, particularly when multiple agents or supervisors operate in distributed environments. Key considerations include:

- **Multi-Agent Coordination**: Establish rules and communication protocols to manage inter-agent dependencies and prevent conflict. Ensure that supervisory mechanisms can handle aggregated agent outputs efficiently.

- **Distributed Oversight**: Design supervision hierarchies that allocate human attention according to task criticality, agent confidence, and operational risk. Avoid overloading individual operators.

- **Workload Balancing**: Use quantitative metrics to monitor human operator workload, adjusting supervision assignments dynamically to maintain effectiveness and prevent fatigue.

- **Automation of Routine Oversight**: Implement automated monitoring and alerting for low-risk tasks, reserving human attention for high-risk or ambiguous situations.

Putting governance into everyday operations cuts down on the need for ad hoc decision-making, makes things more consistent, and makes the whole system more reliable.

Governance, risk management, and operational norms are necessary for keeping human-agent collaboration safe and reliable. Structured risk assessment frameworks, such as FMEA, HAZOP, and scenario-based analysis, offer evidence-based methodologies for identifying and mitigating failures. Standard operating procedures spell out who is responsible for what, how to handle problems, and how to communicate, making sure that everyone is on the same page and accountable. Auditing and compliance processes help with traceability, following the rules, and making operations clear.

Scalability concerns include coordinating multiple agents, overseeing distributed systems, and balancing workloads. These concerns allow systems to grow without putting safety at risk. Continuous improvement techniques, which are based on post-incident analysis, performance data, and revisions to standard operating procedures (SOPs), make sure that lessons learned from operations are always used in future deployments. Finally, layered governance workflows give you a practical plan for putting up a system that includes human oversight, automated agents, operational protocols, and organizational review that can keep dependability, safety, and performance at scale.

## Section 1: Organizational and Cultural Barriers to AI Integration

Enterprise adoption of agentic AI systems extends beyond technical deployment; it involves aligning organizational processes, culture, and human resources with new operational paradigms. Successful integration requires a systematic assessment of organizational readiness, identification of adoption barriers, and implementation of structured strategies to overcome resistance. This section provides a detailed framework for understanding cultural and organizational challenges that can impede AI integration and offers practical approaches for addressing these issues.

### Resistance to Change and Adoption of Inertia

A primary barrier in enterprise AI adoption is organizational resistance to change. Employees may perceive agentic AI systems as disruptive, threatening existing roles, or overly complex to operate. Common factors include:

- **Perceived Threats to Job Security**: Employees may fear displacement or reduction in responsibilities due to automation.

- **Operational Disruption**: Integration of new AI systems may require changes to established workflows, which can generate resistance from teams accustomed to traditional processes.

- **Insufficient Awareness**: Lack of understanding of AI capabilities, limitations, and practical applications can reduce engagement and willingness to adopt.

Mitigation strategies include early stakeholder engagement, transparent communication of AI capabilities and objectives, and aligning AI adoption with clearly defined business benefits. Phased deployment and pilot programs allow employees to experience incremental change, reducing the perceived risk of disruption.

### Alignment of AI Capabilities with Organizational Processes

Misalignment between AI capabilities and organizational processes is a critical challenge. Agentic AI systems are most effective when integrated into workflows that can leverage autonomous decision-making, predictive analysis, or task automation. Factors to consider include:

- **Task Suitability**: Identify operational tasks where agentic AI can provide measurable benefits, such as repetitive analysis, decision support, or large-scale data synthesis.

- **Process Mapping**: Examine existing workflows to determine where AI outputs can enhance decision-making without creating bottlenecks or redundancies.

- **Interdepartmental Dependencies**: Agentic AI adoption requires coordination across departments; siloed operations can impede effective integration.

Practical approaches include conducting process audits, establishing AI task alignment matrices, and developing workflow redesign plans that clearly define agentic AI roles, responsibilities, and handoff points.

### Leadership, Stakeholder Engagement, and Internal Advocacy

Leadership and active stakeholder engagement are fundamental to overcoming adoption barriers. Senior management must provide strategic vision, resource allocation, and advocacy for AI integration. Effective practices include:

- **Executive Sponsorship**: Assigning executive sponsors ensures organizational accountability and provides authority for decision-making.

- **Cross-Functional Steering Committees**: Committees comprising representatives from technical, operational, and business teams facilitate alignment and coordination across departments.

- **Internal AI Champions**: Identifying and empowering internal advocates can promote awareness, address concerns, and demonstrate practical benefits to colleagues.

Leadership must maintain continuous engagement with employees, provide consistent messaging, and establish clear goals to prevent skepticism and maintain adoption momentum.

## Cultural Readiness and Employee Trust

Organizational culture strongly influences AI adoption success. Cultural readiness refers to the extent to which employees are willing to adopt AI tools, trust automated outputs, and collaborate effectively with agentic systems. Key components include:

- **Trust in AI Systems**: Employees must perceive AI outputs as reliable, explainable, and aligned with organizational objectives. Trust can be fostered through transparency, interpretability, and effective feedback mechanisms.

- **Collaboration Practices**: Successful adoption requires integration of AI outputs into human decision-making processes rather than viewing AI as a replacement. Establishing clear roles and responsibilities enhances cooperative workflows.

- **Training and Education**: Comprehensive training programs improve AI literacy, provide procedural guidance, and reduce fear of system errors or misuse.

Organizational readiness assessments, cultural audits, and targeted training initiatives can identify gaps in trust and preparedness, enabling focused interventions to promote cultural alignment with AI

## Impact of Siloed Departments and Lack of Cross-Functional Integration

Enterprise organizations often operate in departmental silos, which can inhibit the flow of information required for effective AI deployment. Challenges include:

- **Data Fragmentation**: Isolated data systems reduce the quality, consistency, and availability of inputs for AI models.

- **Communication Barriers**: Limited interdepartmental collaboration impedes workflow integration, delays decision-making, and reduces adoption efficiency.

- **Duplication of Effort**: Without coordinated deployment strategies, multiple teams may independently implement AI tools, creating inefficiencies and inconsistencies.

Overcoming silo-related challenges requires structured cross-functional governance, centralized data management, and shared adoption goals. Establishing enterprise AI committees and cross-departmental working groups ensures alignment, facilitates knowledge sharing, and prevents fragmented adoption efforts.

## Change Management Strategies for Cultural Integration

Structured change management is essential to reduce resistance and embed AI adoption into organizational culture. Effective strategies include:

- **Communication Plans**: Clearly articulate AI objectives, expected benefits, and operational impacts to all levels of the organization.

- **Phased Rollout**: Introduce AI systems gradually, beginning with pilot projects in well-defined domains before enterprise-wide deployment.

- **Feedback Loops**: Encourage employee feedback to identify challenges, clarify expectations, and refine processes.

- **Performance Recognition**: Recognize teams and individuals who demonstrate effective AI integration and adoption practices, reinforcing positive behavior.

Change management frameworks, such as Kotter's 8-Step Process for Leading Change or ADKAR (Awareness, Desire, Knowledge, Ability, Reinforcement), provide structured guidance for managing organizational adaptation to AI systems.

**Organizational Readiness Heatmap**

A heatmap can illustrate adoption readiness across departments and hierarchical levels:

- **X-axis**: Departments or functional units (e.g., IT, operations, marketing, finance).

- **Y-axis**: Adoption of readiness dimensions (e.g., trust in AI, process alignment, technical familiarity, leadership support).

- **Color Scale**: Low (red), moderate (yellow), high (green) readiness.

These visuals enable stakeholders to identify areas requiring targeted interventions, prioritize training, and allocate resources effectively to address cultural and organizational barriers.

Organizational and cultural factors play a critical role in enterprise adoption of agentic AI systems. Resistance to change, misalignment between AI capabilities and operational processes, insufficient leadership engagement, and siloed organizational structures are primary barriers. Addressing these challenges requires structured approaches, including stakeholder engagement, internal advocacy, targeted training, and phased deployment strategies. Cultural readiness, employee trust, and collaboration practices must be assessed and developed to integrate AI systems effectively into workflows. Visual tools, such as organizational readiness heatmaps, provide actionable insights for prioritizing interventions. By systematically addressing organizational and cultural barriers, enterprises can create an environment conducive to successful AI adoption, laying the foundation for technical integration and operational scalability.

## Section 2: Technical and Infrastructure Challenges

Enterprise adoption of agentic AI systems is strongly influenced by technical and infrastructure readiness. Even when organizational and cultural factors are addressed, technical limitations can hinder performance, reliability, and scalability. This section examines core technical obstacles, including data integration, computational infrastructure, system scalability, and security, and provides evidence-based approaches to mitigate these challenges in enterprise environments.

### Data Quality, Availability, and Integration

High-quality and accessible data is a cornerstone of successful agentic AI deployment. Many enterprises struggle with fragmented, incomplete, or inconsistent datasets, which can undermine model performance and increase error rates. Ensuring data quality requires validation pipelines, duplication checks, and automated cleansing processes to eliminate inaccuracies and maintain consistency. Data availability is another common challenge, as legacy systems often store information in isolated silos that are difficult to access for training or inference. Centralized data lakes or enterprise data warehouses can help consolidate these sources. Data integration adds further complexity, especially when harmonizing structured and unstructured data such as transaction logs, documents, and sensor outputs. Standardizing formats, schemas, and ontologies is essential for building reliable integrations. Best practices include adopting an enterprise-wide data governance framework, enforcing standardization protocols, automating ETL pipelines, and defining clear ownership and stewardship roles to safeguard long-term data integrity.

## Computational Infrastructure Requirements

Agentic AI systems demand significant computational resources to support training, inference, and real-time decision-making. Enterprises must balance performance, cost efficiency, and operational reliability when designing infrastructure. Processing power is critical, as complex models-particularly LLM-powered agents-depend on high-performance CPUs, GPUs, or specialized accelerators. Workload profiling helps determine whether a cloud, on-premises, or hybrid deployment is most appropriate. Storage and bandwidth requirements also grow as datasets and models scale, necessitating distributed storage systems and high-speed networking to reduce latency. The choice between cloud and on-premises infrastructure depends on business priorities: cloud solutions offer elasticity and scalability, while on-premises environments provide greater control over data privacy, compliance, and latency. A hybrid approach often balances the benefits of both, aligning performance with regulatory and operational needs.

Mitigation strategies include workload profiling, capacity planning, and infrastructure monitoring to prevent resource bottlenecks and ensure consistent system performance.

## Scalability, Latency, and Reliability

Agentic AI deployment must address operational requirements for scale, responsiveness, and fault tolerance:

- **Scalability**: Systems should accommodate growth in data volume, user interactions, and agent instances. Horizontal scaling (adding nodes) and vertical scaling (increasing hardware capacity) are commonly used strategies. Microservice architecture facilitates modular deployment and distributed scalability.

- **Latency**: Low-latency responses are essential for real-time decision-making. Network optimization, caching strategies, and model optimization (e.g., quantization or pruning) reduce response times without compromising accuracy.

- **Reliability**: High availability and fault tolerance are critical for enterprise operations. Implement redundancy, failover mechanisms, and monitoring to minimize downtime and ensure continuity during hardware or software failures.

Simulation and load testing provide empirical evidence of system performance under expected operational loads, informing infrastructure scaling and optimization decisions.

## Integration with Existing Workflows and Enterprise Software

Seamless integration of agentic AI systems with existing enterprise applications and workflows is essential for operational efficiency:

- **API Compatibility**: Ensure AI systems can communicate with ERP, CRM, and other enterprise software via standardized APIs or middleware layers.

- **Workflow Embedding**: Integrate AI outputs into decision-making processes without introducing bottlenecks or redundant steps. For example, agentic recommendations should appear within familiar dashboards and operational tools.

- **Interoperability**: Support data exchange between legacy systems and new AI components, including handling different data formats, protocols, and operational conventions.

- **Change Management in Technical Integration**: Introduce system modifications incrementally, validate integration points, and provide rollback mechanisms to mitigate operational risk during deployment.

Effective integration requires collaboration between IT, operations, and AI teams, supported by clear documentation, interface standards, and testing protocols.

**Table: Technical Challenges and Mitigation Strategies**

| Technical Challenge | Impact on Adoption | Mitigation Strategy | Responsible Teams |
|---|---|---|---|
| Fragmented data sources | Reduced model performance | Centralized data warehouse, ETL pipelines | Data engineering, IT |
| Limited computational resources | Slow inference, training bottlenecks | Capacity planning, cloud, or hybrid infrastructure | IT, AI engineering |
| High latency in real-time workflows | Delayed decision-making | Model optimization, caching, network optimization | AI engineering, operations |
| Security and compliance gaps | Regulatory risk, data breaches | Encryption, access control, auditing | IT security, compliance |
| Workflow integration issues | Operational inefficiency | API standardization, middleware, phased deployment | IT, operations, AI teams |
| Scalability constraints | Restricted system growth | Horizontal/vertical scaling, microservice architecture | IT, AI engineering |

This table provides a structured mapping between technical obstacles, their operational impact, mitigation approaches, and responsible enterprise teams. It serves as a practical guide for managing enterprise-level AI adoption challenges.

**Practical Implementation Considerations**

Several practical considerations must be addressed to ensure technical and infrastructure readiness:

- **Monitoring and Observability**: Deploy monitoring systems for resource usage, latency, error rates, and system health to detect and resolve issues proactively.

- **Version Control and Model Management**: Maintain versioned AI models, configuration files, and deployment artifacts to support reproducibility and rollback capability.

- **Testing and Validation**: Conduct rigorous functional, integration, and performance testing in controlled environments before production deployment.

- **Documentation and Knowledge Management**: Maintain detailed technical documentation, integration guides, and troubleshooting procedures for operational continuity.

- **Cross-Functional Collaboration**: Coordinate AI engineering, IT operations, and business teams throughout deployment to ensure alignment and rapid issue resolution.

Technical and infrastructure challenges present critical barriers to enterprise adoption of agentic AI systems. Data quality, availability, and integration must be addressed through governance frameworks, ETL pipelines, and standardized data practices. Computational infrastructure, including processing, storage, and deployment models, must support scalable, low-latency, and reliable AI operations. Security, privacy, and compliance constraints require integration into system design to prevent regulatory and operational risks. Seamless integration with existing workflows and enterprise software ensures efficiency and usability, while structured monitoring, testing, and documentation support operational reliability. By proactively addressing technical and infrastructure challenges, enterprises can create a foundation for scalable, secure, and performant AI deployment.

## Section 3: Governance, Risk Management, and Change Management in Enterprise Adoption

Effective enterprise adoption of agentic AI systems requires structured governance, comprehensive risk management, and disciplined change management. Even when cultural and technical barriers are addressed, enterprises risk operational failures, regulatory non-compliance, and inefficiencies without clear oversight and procedural frameworks. This section provides evidence-based guidance on implementing governance structures, assessing, and mitigating risks, and managing organizational change to ensure sustainable AI adoption.

### Change Management Strategies for Enterprise Adoption

Change management ensures that technical and procedural adoption of AI systems translates into effective operational use. Enterprises should adopt structured methodologies to guide transition and maintain employee engagement:

- **Phased Deployment**: Implement AI systems incrementally, starting with pilot projects in controlled environments. Evaluate performance, refine workflows, and expand deployment gradually.

- **Stakeholder Communication**: Maintain consistent messaging about AI objectives, operational impact, and performance expectations. Communication should target executives, technical teams, and end-users.

- **Training Programs**: Provide comprehensive training on AI system operation, monitoring, intervention protocols, and decision interpretation. Training reduces resistance and increases operational confidence.

- **Feedback and Iteration Loops**: Capture user feedback to identify bottlenecks, clarify procedures, and improve system usability. Iterative refinement strengthens adoption outcomes.

- **Performance Incentives**: Recognize teams and individuals who demonstrate effective AI utilization and operational integration, reinforcing adoption behaviors.

Structured change management minimizes disruption, accelerates operational acceptance, and ensures that enterprise AI adoption delivers measurable value.

### Metrics and Key Performance Indicators (KPIs)

Measuring enterprise adoption of agentic AI requires objective and meaningful metrics that capture performance, operational impact, and effectiveness. Adoption rate tracks the percentage of target users actively using AI tools within workflows, while system reliability reflects error frequency, downtime, and performance degradation. Intervention frequency indicates how often human oversight is required per task or workflow, highlighting areas for improvement in automation. Operational efficiency gains measure reductions in task completion time, throughput improvements, and decision accuracy. Finally, user satisfaction and trust-often gathered through surveys-provide insights into employee confidence in AI outputs and overall usability. Together, these KPIs guide governance decisions, risk management, and change management, ensuring AI adoption aligns with enterprise goals and operational expectations.

### Continuous Improvement and Feedback Mechanisms

Long-term success in AI adoption depends on structured feedback loops and continuous improvement practices. Post-incident analysis helps identify the root causes of errors, near misses, or system failures, enabling corrective action. Regular performance review cycles integrate key operational metrics to assess system reliability, adoption progress, and risk exposure. Updates to standard operating procedures (SOPs) and process refinements are then implemented based on these insights, keeping operations aligned with evolving needs. Additionally, knowledge sharing across teams ensures lessons learned are disseminated widely, supporting cross-functional learning and reinforcing adoption momentum. These mechanisms sustain trust, optimize workflows, and maintain alignment with enterprise objectives.

Feedback mechanisms should be structured, traceable, and integrated into daily operations to ensure that insights from real-world deployment inform continuous system improvement.

**Enterprise Adoption Governance Workflow**

A layered workflow illustrates governance and risk management integration:

- **Layer 1: Strategic Oversight** – Executive steering committees define objectives, resource allocation, and adoption priorities.

- **Layer 2: Operational Governance** – AI oversight teams monitor system performance, manage deployments, and coordinate cross-functional integration.

- **Layer 3: Risk Assessment and Intervention** – Continuous evaluation of operational risks, intervention protocols, and compliance checks.

- **Layer 4: Change Management and Feedback Loops** – Employee training, adoption tracking, iterative process improvement, and communication channels reinforce organizational adoption.

This layered model provides a structured framework for combining governance, risk management, and changing management into a cohesive operational strategy.

**Practical Implementation Considerations**

Practical considerations for effective governance, risk, and change management include:

- **Documentation**: Maintain detailed records of governance policies, SOPs, risk assessments, and training programs.

- **Cross-Functional Coordination**: Align IT, AI engineering, operations, and business teams to prevent misalignment and duplication of effort.

- **Audit Readiness**: Ensure traceable logs and structured reporting facilitate internal and external audits.

- **Scalable Frameworks**: Design governance and change management processes to accommodate multiple departments, distributed teams, and future AI deployments.

- **Operational Resilience**: Implement contingency plans and rollback procedures to mitigate unforeseen failures or operational disruptions.

These measures provide practical guidance for embedding governance and risk management into enterprise operations, ensuring that AI adoption remains controlled and effective.

Enterprise adoption of agentic AI systems requires structured governance, systematic risk management, and disciplined change management. Governance structures, including executive steering committees, oversight teams, and SOPs, ensure accountability, strategic alignment, and operational control. Risk assessment frameworks, such as FMEA and scenario-based analysis, identify potential failure points and guide mitigation strategies. Change management practices, including phased deployment, stakeholder communication, training, and feedback loops, reduce resistance and enhance operational integration. Metrics and KPIs provide evidence-based insights into adoption effectiveness, system performance, and operational efficiency. Continuous improvement processes ensure that lessons from real-world deployment inform iterative refinement of policies, procedures, and workflows. Integrating governance, risk management, and changing management into cohesive operational frameworks allows enterprises to achieve safe, scalable, and sustainable adoption of agentic AI systems.

# PART V: TOOLS, FRAMEWORKS, AND ECOSYSTEM

To build analyzed AI, you need more than just theoretical models. You need a developing ecosystem of frameworks, libraries, and open-source projects that can be used to build real-world applications. This section looks at the most popular tools and talks about their pros and cons, as well as how to integrate them. It gives engineers and architects a useful map of the existing ecosystem, which helps them make smart choices about which technologies to use and how to construct systems. Practitioners can speed up development, make sure everything works together, and build on proven foundations instead of beginning from scratch by knowing about the frameworks and community-driven resources that are out there.

## Section 1: Core Architectural Patterns and Design Principles

Agentic AI frameworks provide structured environments for designing, building, and operating autonomous agents. Understanding the core architectural patterns and design principles is critical for engineers, system architects, and product leads to implementing scalable, reliable, and maintainable systems. This section outlines the foundational components, modular design approaches, and widely recognized architectural patterns employed in agentic AI frameworks.

### Layered Agent Architectures

A common architectural paradigm in agentic AI is the layered model, which separates system functionality into distinct modules or layers to simplify design, promote maintainability, and enable modular extension. Standard layers include:

1. **Perception Layer**: Responsible for data ingestion and preprocessing. This layer interfaces with external inputs such as databases, APIs, sensors, or user commands. Functions include natural language processing, structured data parsing, and contextual interpretation.

2. **Reasoning Layer**: Handles decision-making and inference. Core capabilities include knowledge representation, logical reasoning, probabilistic inference, and planning. This layer often integrates symbolic and statistical reasoning approaches.

3. **Planning and Execution Layer**: Converts decisions into actionable sequences. It includes task decomposition, workflow scheduling, and resource allocation. The execution layer may manage interactions with external systems or human operators.

4. **Action Layer**: Interfaces directly with the operational environment. It executes planned tasks, triggers tool usage, or communicates results to downstream systems or users.

A layered design supports separation of concerns, allowing developers to update or replace individual components without impacting other system layers.

### Design Principles for Agentic AI Frameworks

Key design principles guide the development of robust and scalable frameworks:

- **Modularity**: Components such as planners, reasoners, and memory managers are decoupled to facilitate independent development, testing, and replacement.

- **Extensibility**: Frameworks should allow integration of new modules, tools, or APIs to adapt to evolving requirements.

- **Scalability**: Architectural patterns must support growth in data volume, number of agents, and interaction complexity. Distributed or microservice-based designs enable horizontal scaling.

- **Interoperability**: Frameworks should be compatible with standard data formats, APIs, and enterprise systems to minimize integration overhead.

- **Maintainability**: Clear interfaces, documentation, and standardized module structures support long-term operational sustainability.

- **Human-in-the-Loop Integration**: Systems should support supervisory control, intervention, and feedback mechanisms to balance autonomy with human oversight.

## Reactive, Deliberative, and Hybrid Agent Models

Agentic AI frameworks implement various interaction and reasoning paradigms to meet specific operational objectives:

- **Reactive Agents**: Operate primarily on immediate stimuli without maintaining long-term internal models. Reactive architecture provides fast, low-latency responses suitable for operational tasks requiring high responsiveness.

- **Deliberative Agents**: Maintain internal models, perform planning, and reason about future states before acting. These agents are suitable for complex decision-making, multi-step workflows, and strategic problem-solving.

- **Hybrid Agents**: Combine reactive and deliberate capabilities. The hybrid approach enables real-time responsiveness for routine tasks while supporting planned, strategic actions for complex scenarios.

Choosing the appropriate agent model depends on system objectives, environmental constraints, and performance requirements. Frameworks may provide built-in support for one or multiple agent paradigms.

## Memory and State Management

Memory and state management are central to the effectiveness of agentic AI systems, allowing them to sustain context and continuity across interactions. Short-term memory supports immediate decision-making by retaining recent interactions, system states, and temporary knowledge that is relevant only for the current task or session. This enables the agent to respond fluidly in real time without losing track of ongoing processes.

Long-term memory, by contrast, maintains persistent knowledge that extends across multiple interactions. It records historical exchanges, domain-specific expertise, and accumulated experience, providing the foundation for reasoning, learning, and adaptation over time. This persistence allows agents to improve their performance and maintain consistency in complex or recurring workflows.

Contextual memory adds another layer of sophistication by preserving task-specific information such as user preferences, workflow history, and operational constraints. This ensures that the system tailors its behavior to the unique requirements of each scenario, enhancing relevance and personalization.

To support these functions, modern frameworks provide standardized memory interfaces, giving developers the tools to manage memory effectively while keeping architectures modular and flexible. This structured approach ensures that agents can operate with continuity, adapt to evolving needs, and deliver reliable outcomes.

## Planning and Task Decomposition

Planning modules in agentic frameworks convert high-level goals into actionable sub-tasks. Key considerations include:

- **Hierarchical Task Decomposition**: Break down complex objectives into smaller, manageable actions with clearly defined dependencies.

- **Dependency Management**: Ensure sub-task execution respects sequential, conditional, or resource-based constraints.

- **Tool Invocation Management**: Plan when and how external tools or APIs should be invoked, ensuring correct sequencing and error handling.

Frameworks may implement planners using symbolic reasoning, heuristic search algorithms, or reinforcement learning methods to optimize task execution.

**Multi-Agent Coordination**

In enterprise or operational contexts, multiple agents may collaborate or compete to achieve shared goals. Frameworks support multi-agent coordination through:

- **Communication Protocols**: Standardized message formats and channels for inter-agent interaction.

- **Task Allocation Mechanisms**: Assign tasks based on agent capabilities, availability, and workload.

- **Conflict Resolution**: Handle conflicts when multiple agents request the same resource or produce overlapping actions.

- **Synchronization and State Sharing**: Ensure consistency of shared state information across agents.

Frameworks designed for multi-agent environments typically provide libraries or modules to manage these coordination mechanisms efficiently.

**Extensibility and Tool Integration**

Agentic AI frameworks often allow integration with external tools, services, and APIs to extend functional capabilities:

- **Tool Abstraction Layers**: Standardize interaction with diverse tools, from database queries to API-driven software.

- **Plugin Architectures**: Enable dynamic addition of modules without modifying core framework code.

- **API-Based Integration**: Allow enterprise systems, dashboards, or external applications to interact with agents seamlessly.

Extensibility ensures that frameworks remain adaptable to evolving business requirements and operational environments.

Core architectural patterns and design principles are the foundation of agentic AI frameworks. Layered architecture separates perception, reasoning, planning, and action functions, enabling modularity and maintainability. Design principles such as extensibility, scalability, interoperability, and human-in-the-loop integration ensure that frameworks can meet enterprise operational requirements. Reactive, deliberative, and hybrid agent models provide flexibility in performance and decision-making approaches. Memory and state management modules maintain context, while planning and task decomposition structures optimize workflow execution. Multi-agent coordination, tool integration, and extensibility mechanisms allow frameworks to support complex enterprise use cases. Understanding these foundational principles enables system architects and engineers to select, extend, and deploy agentic AI frameworks effectively.

## Section 2: Widely Adopted Frameworks and Libraries

Agentic AI frameworks provide standardized environments for designing, building, and deploying autonomous agents. Selecting the appropriate framework is critical to ensure scalability, reliability, and maintainability in enterprise and operational contexts. This section examines widely recognized frameworks and supporting libraries, compares their capabilities, and provides guidance for evaluating framework suitability.

**LangChain Framework**

LangChain is a widely adopted framework for building agentic AI applications that leverage large language models (LLMs). Its key characteristics include:

- **Modularity**: LangChain provides separate modules for LLM integration, memory management, prompt templates, and tool invocation. This modularity supports extensibility and simplifies maintenance.

- **Memory Management**: Offers short-term and long-term memory abstractions for context retention across sessions.

- **Agentic Capabilities**: Supports both single-agent and multi-agent orchestration, enabling task decomposition and autonomous workflow execution.

- **Tool Integration**: Provides standardized interfaces for connecting external APIs, databases, and software tools.

- **Use Cases**: Document analysis, question-answering systems, process automation, and multi-step reasoning tasks.

LangChain emphasizes a structured programming approach, enabling engineers to define agent behaviors, workflows, and decision logic with clarity and precision.

**Haystack Framework**

Haystack is an open-source framework designed for building retrieval-augmented generation (RAG) pipelines and question-answering systems. Its features include:

- **Document Retrieval**: Integrates with multiple storage backends, including Elasticsearch and SQL databases, for high-performance information retrieval.

- **Pipeline Architecture**: Supports modular pipelines for query processing, retrieval, and response generation.

- **Integration with LLMs**: Provides connectors for various large language models, enabling reasoning over retrieved knowledge.

- **Tool Integration**: Supports embedding external APIs and databases into pipelines to extend capabilities.

- **Enterprise Applications**: Knowledge management, customer support automation, and compliance monitoring.

Haystack emphasizes flexibility in constructing pipelines and provides an evaluation framework for measuring retrieval accuracy, response quality, and latency.

**Microsoft Semantic Kernel**

Semantic Kernel (SK) is a framework for integrating AI capabilities into enterprise applications with structured, semantic-aware workflows. Its key characteristics include:

- **Planner and Orchestrator**: Provides built-in task planning and workflow orchestration for multi-step processes.

- **Memory and Context Management**: Supports embedding-based memory storage and retrieval for agent context retention.

- **Integration with Microsoft Ecosystem**: Natively integrates with Azure services, cognitive APIs, and enterprise software.

- **Extensibility**: Offers plugin and skill mechanisms for custom tool integration.

- **Use Cases**: Business process automation, decision support systems, and knowledge-driven workflows.

Semantic Kernel emphasizes enterprise-grade deployment, providing features for secure, scalable, and reliable operations.

## Supporting Libraries for Planning, Reasoning, and Tool Integration

Frameworks are often supplemented by specialized libraries that enhance agentic capabilities:

- **Planning Libraries**: Examples include PyPlanning, PDDL-based planners, and custom workflow engines. They support task decomposition, dependency management, and scheduling.

- **Reasoning Libraries**: Tools such as pyDatalog, Prolog interfaces, and probabilistic programming frameworks provide symbolic and probabilistic reasoning capabilities.

- **Memory and State Libraries**: Persistent storage engines, vector databases (e.g., FAISS, Milvus), and in-memory caches facilitate short-term and long-term context management.

- **Tool Integration Libraries**: Standardized connectors for APIs, databases, and enterprise software support extensibility and interoperability.

Integrating these libraries within a framework allows engineers to build agentic systems that can plan, reason, and act across multiple tasks and domains.

## Criteria for Framework Selection

Selecting a framework involves assessing technical and operational factors relative to organizational requirements:

1. **System Scale and Complexity**: Consider the number of agents, workflow complexity, and expected data volume. Distributed frameworks or those supporting horizontal scaling are preferable for large-scale applications.

2. **Integration Requirements**: Evaluate the framework's compatibility with existing software, APIs, databases, and enterprise infrastructure.

3. **Extensibility and Customization**: Assess how easily custom modules, tools, or connectors can be integrated.

4. **Operational Reliability**: Consider framework support for monitoring, logging, fault tolerance, and human-in-the-loop supervision.

5. **Community Support and Documentation**: Active developer communities, comprehensive documentation, and established best practices reduce implementation risk.

6. **Evaluation and Testing Capabilities**: Frameworks that provide metrics, simulation environments, and test harnesses enable structured performance evaluation.

Applying these criteria ensures that the selected framework aligns with operational objectives, technical constraints, and long-term maintainability.

## Comparative Feature Matrix

The following table provides a comparative view of selected agentic AI frameworks and libraries:

| Feature / Framework | LangChain | Haystack | Semantic Kernel | Notes |
|---|---|---|---|---|
| Modularity | High | Medium | High | LangChain emphasizes modular agent structure |
| Memory Management | Short-term & long-term | Session-based, RAG pipelines | Embedding-based memory | Supports context retention across tasks |
| Multi-Agent Coordination | Supported | Limited | Supported | Multi-agent orchestration for complex workflows |
| Planning & Task Decomposition | Built-in | Pipeline-based | Planner module included | Enables multi-step reasoning |
| Tool Integration | API & database connectors | Pipeline nodes & APIs | Plugins & skills | Supports enterprise tool connectivity |
| Enterprise Readiness | Medium | Medium | High | Semantic Kernel optimized for Azure & enterprise systems |
| Use Cases | Document QA, automation | Knowledge retrieval, QA | Workflow automation, process support | Context-specific adoption |

This matrix provides a structured overview to support framework selection decisions based on technical features, operational capabilities, and enterprise requirements.

**Implementation and Deployment Considerations**

When deploying frameworks in enterprise environments, practical considerations include:

- **Testing and Validation**: Conduct functional, integration, and performance testing in staging environments before production deployment.

- **Monitoring and Observability**: Implement logging, metrics collection, and alerting to track agent behavior, memory usage, tool invocations, and task completion.

- **Security and Compliance**: Ensure frameworks support secure API connections, data privacy, and regulatory compliance.

- **Workflow Integration**: Embed agentic capabilities into existing processes, dashboards, or automation pipelines to maximize operational value.

- **Training and Documentation**: Provide technical teams with detailed guides, example workflows, and operational SOPs to facilitate adoption.

These practices ensure that frameworks are deployed reliably, with minimal operational disruption, and can be scaled according to enterprise needs.

Widely recognized agentic AI frameworks provide structured environments for modular, scalable, and maintainable autonomous agent development. LangChain emphasizes modularity and multi-step reasoning, Haystack focuses on retrieval-augmented pipelines and flexible information processing, and Semantic Kernel provides enterprise-grade orchestration and integration with Microsoft services. Supporting libraries extend planning, reasoning, memory management, and tool integration capabilities. Framework selection requires assessment of system scale, integration requirements, extensibility, reliability, and community support. Comparative analysis and practical deployment considerations guide engineers in selecting frameworks that meet both technical and operational requirements.

Successfully deploying agentic AI frameworks in enterprise environments requires attention to integration, extensibility, and evaluation. Even the most capable frameworks will fail to deliver value if they cannot be integrated with operational workflows, extended to meet evolving requirements, or systematically evaluated for performance and reliability. This section provides evidence-based practices and structured approaches to achieve effective framework deployment.

## Integration into Enterprise Systems

Integrating agentic AI into enterprise systems requires embedding its capabilities within the broader IT infrastructure, existing business applications, and day-to-day operational workflows. A central element of this process is API-based integration, where frameworks provide standardized interfaces-such as REST, gRPC, or GraphQL-that allow seamless communication with enterprise platforms including ERP, CRM, and workflow management systems. These APIs enable interoperability while maintaining consistency across diverse applications.

Data interoperability is another critical requirement, as enterprises often rely on both legacy systems and modern cloud-based tools. To ensure smooth interaction, schema mapping, data transformation, and format standardization must be implemented so that data flows reliably across different sources. This guarantees that agentic AI can operate on clean, compatible information regardless of origin.

Workflow embedding makes AI outputs directly actionable by integrating recommendations into operational dashboards, task queues, or notification systems. This reduces the need for manual intervention and ensures that decisions are reflected immediately within existing processes. To coordinate these interactions at scale, middleware and orchestration layers are employed, managing communication between agent frameworks, databases, and external services while ensuring both reliability and scalability.

In practice, deployment is often phased. Organizations typically begin with pilot modules in controlled environments, allowing for testing and validation before gradually expanding integration to cover full operational scope. This iterative approach reduces risk while enabling enterprises to adapt AI capabilities progressively to their unique requirements.

## Extensibility and Custom Module Development

Extensibility is critical for adapting frameworks to evolving business requirements and domain-specific workflows. Common strategies include:

- **Plugin Architecture**: Leverage frameworks that support modular plugins or "skills" to extend functionality without altering core components.

- **Custom Tool Integration**: Develop connectors for domain-specific APIs, enterprise services, or third-party tools to expand agent capabilities.

- **API Wrappers**: Wrap external services with standardized interfaces to ensure consistent interaction patterns and error handling.

- **Configuration-Driven Behavior**: Use declarative configurations to define agent behaviors, tool usage, and workflow parameters, reducing the need for deep code modifications.

Extensible frameworks allow organizations to evolve agentic systems over time, incorporating new tools, integrating emerging data sources, and refining reasoning strategies while minimizing operational risk.

## Evaluation Methodologies

Systematic evaluation is essential for validating performance, reliability, and operational impact. Established evaluation practices include:

- **Functional Testing**: Verify that agents correctly execute defined tasks, respond accurately to queries, and perform planned sequences of actions.

- **Performance Benchmarking**: Measure response latency, throughput, and system resource utilization under expected operational loads.

- **Reliability Testing**: Simulate failures, interruptions, or data inconsistencies to assess system fault tolerance and recovery mechanisms.

- **Accuracy and Decision Quality**: Evaluate outputs against reference datasets or predefined objectives to quantify correctness and appropriateness of agent reasoning.

- **User and Human-in-the-Loop Assessment**: Collect feedback from end-users and supervisors on agent utility, transparency, and trustworthiness.

Frameworks that provide built-in evaluation tools or testing harnesses reduce implementation complexity and improve reproducibility of assessment results.

## Continuous Monitoring and Lifecycle Management

Ongoing monitoring and management are required to ensure that agentic AI systems maintain performance and compliance over time:

- **Operational Dashboards**: Track task completion rates, error occurrences, tool usage, and memory state in real-time.

- **Automated Alerting**: Trigger notifications for anomalies, system failures, or deviations from expected behavior.

- **Version Control and Deployment Management**: Maintain versioned artifacts for models, configuration files, and integration modules to support reproducibility and rollback.

- **Lifecycle Updates**: Regularly update frameworks, libraries, and external connectors to address security vulnerabilities, performance improvements, and compatibility with enterprise software updates.

Monitoring and lifecycle management practices reduce downtime, improve reliability, and ensure that agentic systems remain aligned with organizational goals.

## Metrics and Key Performance Indicators (KPIs)

Effective evaluation and operational oversight require clear metrics and KPIs:

- **Task Completion Accuracy**: Percentage of tasks executed correctly according to predefined criteria.

- **System Latency**: Average response time for decision-making or tool invocation.

- **Throughput**: Number of tasks completed per unit time.

- **Human Intervention Rate**: Frequency of manual corrections or escalations required during operations.

- **Resource Utilization**: CPU, GPU, memory, and network usage patterns for capacity planning and optimization.

- **User Satisfaction and Trust**: Surveys and feedback measuring perceived reliability, usability, and transparency.

Tracking these KPIs supports continuous improvement, informs governance decisions, and guides resource allocation for scaling or optimizing deployment.

## Feedback Loops and Continuous Improvement

Feedback loops are essential to ensuring that agentic AI systems evolve in line with operational realities and shifting requirements. By embedding structured mechanisms for continuous improvement, these frameworks can become more reliable, efficient, and trusted over time.

The process begins with incident analysis, where root causes of errors, failures, or unexpected behaviors are examined in depth. These investigations highlight whether issues arise from process gaps, misconfigurations, or deeper architectural weaknesses, guiding targeted improvements. Operational review cycles complement this by assessing performance metrics, intervention rates, and user feedback on a regular basis, helping teams fine-tune frameworks and adjust workflows for better alignment with real-world use.

Based on these insights, models, reasoning modules, and tool connectors can be updated incrementally. Such iterative enhancements ensure that the system remains adaptable without destabilizing existing operations. To support transparency and collaboration, thorough documentation is maintained, including technical notes, change logs, and lessons learned. This knowledge sharing not only supports reproducibility but also accelerates cross-functional learning within organizations.

By closing the loop between monitoring, review, and system updates, feedback-driven improvement strengthens reliability, boosts operational efficiency, and builds user confidence in agentic AI deployments.

## Practical Implementation Considerations

Key practical considerations for successful integration, extensibility, and evaluation include:

- **Cross-Functional Collaboration**: Coordinate between AI engineering, IT operations, and business teams to align technical capabilities with operational objectives.

- **Testing and Staging Environments**: Use isolated environments for validating integrations, module extensions, and workflow interactions prior to production deployment.

- **Security and Compliance**: Maintain secure handling of sensitive data, adhere to regulatory requirements, and ensure controlled access to agentic systems.

- **Documentation and Training**: Provide comprehensive guides for developers, operators, and end-users to support adoption, troubleshooting, and system maintenance.

- **Scalability Planning**: Anticipate growth in agent instances, workflow complexity, and data volume to ensure infrastructure and framework readiness.

Addressing these considerations reduces operational risk, improves system reliability, and supports long-term maintainability.

Integration, extensibility, and evaluation practices are critical for the successful deployment of agentic AI frameworks in enterprise environments. Frameworks must be seamlessly embedded into existing workflows and IT infrastructure using standardized APIs, middleware, and data interoperability strategies. Extensibility through plugins, custom modules, and configuration-driven behavior allows organizations to adapt frameworks to evolving requirements without disrupting core functionality. Structured evaluation methodologies, including functional testing, performance benchmarking, reliability assessment, and human-in-the-loop evaluation, provide objective evidence of system effectiveness. Continuous monitoring, lifecycle management, KPI tracking, and feedback loops ensure operational reliability and support iterative improvement. By following these practices, enterprises can deploy agentic AI frameworks that are scalable, maintainable, and aligned with business objectives.

# Chapter 20: Open-Source Projects, APIs, and Ecosystem Tools

## Section 1: Core Open-Source Frameworks and Libraries

Open-source frameworks and libraries form the foundation of agentic AI development, providing reusable modules, standardized interfaces, and community-validated best practices. They enable engineers and system architects to build autonomous agents efficiently while maintaining scalability, modularity, and maintainability. This section examines widely recognized frameworks, their architectural patterns, and core capabilities.

### LangChain

LangChain is a leading open-source framework for creating agentic AI applications that leverage large language models (LLMs). Its key features include:

- **Modular Design**: LangChain separates core components such as LLM integration, memory management, tool invocation, and prompt handling. Modularity enables independent testing, replacement, and extension of components.

- **Memory Management**: The framework supports short-term session memory and long-term persistent memory, enabling agents to maintain contextual continuity across interactions.

- **Agent Capabilities**: LangChain facilitates both single-agent and multi-agent orchestration. Agents can perform sequential task decomposition, tool usage, and reasoning over multi-step workflows.

- **Tool Integration**: Provides standardized interfaces for connecting to APIs, databases, and enterprise software.

- **Typical Use Cases**: Multi-step reasoning, document analysis, automated question answering, and workflow automation.

LangChain emphasizes structured programming, allowing developers to define agent behaviors, orchestrate tools, and manage state consistently.

### Haystack

Haystack is an open-source framework optimized for retrieval-augmented generation (RAG) pipelines and question-answering systems. Its features include:

- **Document Retrieval**: Integrates with backends such as Elasticsearch, SQL databases, and vector stores for high-performance information retrieval.

- **Pipeline Architecture**: Modular pipelines support query processing, document retrieval, ranking, and response generation.

- **LLM Integration**: Connects to multiple LLM providers to perform reasoning over retrieved knowledge.

- **Tool Integration**: Supports inclusion of external APIs or custom connectors within pipelines to extend functionality.

- **Enterprise Applications**: Knowledge management, customer support automation, compliance monitoring, and research workflows.

Haystack emphasizes flexible pipeline construction, allowing engineers to tailor retrieval and generation workflows to specific operational requirements.

## Rasa

Rasa is an open-source framework focused on conversational agents and dialogue management. Its primary capabilities include:

- **Dialogue Management**: Supports rule-based and machine learning-based dialogue policies to control conversation flow.

- **Natural Language Understanding (NLU)**: Provides intent recognition, entity extraction, and context tracking.

- **Action and Tool Integration**: Allows execution of custom actions, API calls, or task triggers in response to user input.

- **Modularity and Extensibility**: Components such as NLU pipelines and custom actions can be modified or extended independently.

- **Use Cases**: Chatbots, customer service automation, and enterprise support systems.

Rasa is well-suited for scenarios requiring structured conversational workflows and contextual understanding in multi-turn dialogues.

## OpenAI API Client Libraries

OpenAI provides official client libraries for integrating large language models into applications. Core features include:

- **LLM Access**: Provides programmatic access to GPT models for text generation, summarization, and reasoning tasks.

- **Fine-Tuning and Prompt Management**: Supports customization of model behavior through prompt engineering or fine-tuning.

- **Tool Invocation**: Can be combined with workflow orchestration frameworks to execute multi-step tasks or API calls.

- **Security and Compliance**: Offers secure authentication mechanisms and usage monitoring to ensure enterprise-grade deployment.

- **Use Cases**: Automated content generation, multi-step reasoning, summarization, and question-answering.

These client libraries complement open-source frameworks, enabling hybrid systems that integrate proprietary LLM capabilities with modular agentic architectures.

## Key Architectural Features Across Frameworks

Despite differences in specialization, widely adopted open-source frameworks share common architectural features:

- **Modularity**: Separation of perception, reasoning, planning, and action modules simplifies testing, maintenance, and extension.

- **Memory and Context Management**: Persistent and session memory components maintain context across tasks, supporting coherent multi-step reasoning.

- **Task Orchestration**: Planning and execution modules manage sequential or parallel workflows, tool invocations, and conditional branching.

- **Extensibility**: Plugin and connector architectures allow integration of domain-specific tools, APIs, and external services.

- **Human-in-the-Loop Integration**: Frameworks often provide interfaces for supervisory control, feedback, or intervention to ensure safety and reliability.

**Comparative Analysis**

Selecting the appropriate framework depends on use case, deployment environment, and operational constraints. The following table summarizes core capabilities and typical use cases:

| Framework / Library | Modularity | Memory Management | Tool Integration | Multi-Agent Support | Use Cases |
|---|---|---|---|---|---|
| LangChain | High | Short & Long-term | APIs & Databases | Supported | Multistep reasoning, automation, document analysis |
| Haystack | Medium | Session-based | Pipelines & APIs | Limited | Knowledge retrieval, question-answering, RAG pipelines |
| Rasa | High | Session & Context | Custom Actions | Limited | Conversational agents, chatbots, dialogue management |
| OpenAI API Client Libraries | Medium | External memory via framework | APIs & Workflow connectors | Limited | LLM integration, summarization, content generation, multi-step reasoning |

This comparative view provides engineers with a structured framework for evaluating which open-source projects best align with technical requirements and operational goals.

**Integration Patterns and Best Practices**

Effective utilization of open-source frameworks requires standard integration patterns and engineering practices:

- **Layered Architecture**: Implement perception, reasoning, planning, and action modules in a layered manner to simplify updates and maintenance.

- **Middleware Abstraction**: Use middleware to manage communication between agents, external APIs, and enterprise systems, ensuring consistent interfaces.

- **Memory and State Standardization**: Adopt unified interfaces for short-term and long-term memory to support context retention and reasoning consistency.

- **Tool Wrappers and Connectors**: Standardize interactions with external services using wrapper modules to handle authentication, rate limits, and error handling.

- **Testing and Validation**: Conduct functional testing of modular components, integration testing with enterprise systems, and simulation-based evaluation for multi-step workflows.

Open-source frameworks and libraries provide the foundational components for building agentic AI systems. LangChain, Haystack, Rasa, and OpenAI client libraries are widely adopted for their modular design, memory management, task orchestration, and integration capabilities. Core architectural patterns across frameworks emphasize separation of perception, reasoning, planning, and action, enabling modularity, extensibility, and maintainability. Standard integration patterns, middleware use, memory standardization, and testing practices ensure reliable deployment in enterprise environments. Understanding these frameworks, their capabilities, and best practices allows engineers and architects to select, extend, and operationalize open-source agentic AI projects effectively.

## Section 2: APIs and Service Integrations for Agentic AI

Application Programming Interfaces (APIs) and service integrations are critical components in the development of agentic AI systems. They provide standardized mechanisms to extend framework capabilities, access external services, and integrate agents into operational workflows. This section examines widely used APIs, integration strategies, and best practices for secure, reliable, and efficient service interaction. **LLM APIs**

Large language model APIs provide programmatic access to pretrained models capable of natural language understanding, reasoning, and generation. Key characteristics include:

- **Model Access**: APIs provide endpoints for text generation, summarization, question-answering, and multi-step reasoning tasks.

- **Scalability**: Cloud-based APIs handle dynamic request loads, enabling enterprise-scale deployments without requiring local model hosting.

- **Customizability**: Many APIs support prompt engineering, fine-tuning, or parameter adjustment to tailor model outputs to specific tasks.

- **Security**: Authentication mechanisms, usage monitoring, and encrypted communication ensure secure integration in enterprise systems.

Commonly used LLM APIs include OpenAI, Cohere, and Anthropic, which are widely integrated into agentic AI frameworks for reasoning, planning, and natural language processing tasks.

### Knowledgebase and Data APIs

Agentic AI systems rely on access to both structured and unstructured data sources to generate accurate and contextually relevant outputs. Knowledgebase APIs provide standardized interfaces for retrieving this information, supporting reasoning and retrieval-augmented generation. These APIs typically offer query interfaces for searching databases, document repositories, or knowledge graphs. Results are returned in consistent formats such as JSON or XML, ensuring compatibility with downstream reasoning and planning modules. Features like rate limiting and pagination maintain predictable performance under high-load conditions. Common examples include the Wikidata API for structured knowledge, enterprise GraphQL endpoints for internal systems, and semantic search APIs for document retrieval. By integrating knowledge APIs, agents can access reliable context, improve accuracy, and strengthen decision-making processes.

### Tool Invocation and Workflow APIs

In addition to data access, agentic AI systems must often execute actions, invoke external tools, or trigger enterprise workflows. Tool and workflow APIs provide the standardized interfaces necessary for these interactions. Execution endpoints allow agents to call external services, perform computations, or initiate workflow events. Monitoring and status reporting capabilities ensure that agents can validate task completion, handle errors gracefully, and retry operations when required. Security is enforced through mechanisms such as authentication tokens, role-based access control, and encrypted communications. Examples include REST or gRPC endpoints for service execution, CI/CD pipeline triggers, database update APIs, or ERP workflow integrations. By leveraging these APIs, agentic AI frameworks can perform multi-step reasoning, orchestrate complex workflows, and integrate seamlessly into enterprise operations.

## Best Practices for API Integration

Effective API integration ensures reliable, secure, and scalable agentic AI operations. Recommended practices include:

- **Authentication and Authorization**: Use secure tokens, OAuth2, or API keys to restrict access and ensure compliance with organizational policies.

- **Rate Limiting and Throttling**: Implement mechanisms to manage request volumes, prevent API overuse, and maintain system stability.

- **Error Handling and Retry Policies**: Design robust handling of transient failures, network timeouts, and service unavailability, including exponential backoff strategies.

- **Monitoring and Logging**: Track request success rates, latency, errors, and tool usage to identify operational bottlenecks and optimize performance.

- **Data Standardization**: Transform and validate API responses to ensure compatibility with internal frameworks and reasoning modules.

Applying these practices reduces operational risk, enhances reliability, and simplifies maintenance of integrated systems.

## Evaluation of API Performance

Enterprise-grade deployment requires systematic evaluation of APIs to ensure efficiency and reliability:

- **Latency Measurement**: Assess average response time and variability to determine suitability for time-sensitive workflows.

- **Throughput Analysis**: Evaluate how many requests can be handled per unit time without degradation in performance.

- **Error Rate Assessment**: Monitor the frequency of API failures, incorrect responses, or timeouts to identify risks.

- **Consistency and Accuracy**: Validate API outputs against expected results or reference datasets to ensure correctness.

- **Operational Impact**: Measure how API integration affects overall agent performance, task completion rates, and system resource utilization.

Evaluation metrics provide evidence-based insights that guide selection, scaling, and optimization of API integrations.

## Comparative Feature Matrix of Key APIs

The table below provides a structured comparison of representative APIs for agentic AI integration:

| API Type | Key Features | Latency | Scalability | Security & Compliance | Use Cases |
|---|---|---|---|---|---|
| | | | | | |

| LLM APIs (OpenAI, Cohere) | Text generation, reasoning, summarization | Low | High | TLS, API keys | Multi-step reasoning, content generation, question-answering |
|---|---|---|---|---|---|
| Knowledge-Base APIs | Structured retrieval, semantic search | Medium | High | TLS, OAuth2 | Knowledge retrieval, decision support, RAG pipelines |
| Workflow & Tool APIs | Task execution, workflow orchestration | Low | High | TLS, role-based access | Automation, process orchestration, multi-agent coordination |
| Enterprise Data APIs | Query endpoints, database access | Medium | Medium | TLS, RBAC | Data-driven reasoning, reporting, system integration |

This matrix helps engineers evaluate API suitability based on latency, scalability, security, and operational requirements.

**Integration Patterns for Agentic AI APIs**

Standard integration patterns support reliable agentic AI operations:

- **Synchronous Calls**: Suitable for low-latency tasks where immediate results are required.

- **Asynchronous Calls**: Used for long-running workflows or non-critical operations to avoid blocking agent execution.

- **Event-Driven Triggers**: Agents respond to external events, webhook notifications, or system signals to initiate tasks dynamically.

- **Middleware Abstraction**: Centralizes API calls, authentication, and error handling, ensuring consistency across multiple agents and tools.

- **Caching and State Management**: Reduce repeated API requests by storing recent responses or precomputed results, improving efficiency and reliability.

Applying these patterns ensures predictable, scalable, and maintainable API interactions within agentic AI systems.

APIs and service integrations are essential for extending agentic AI frameworks with reasoning, knowledge access, and workflow orchestration capabilities. LLM APIs provide flexible natural language understanding and generation, knowledge-based APIs enable retrieval-augmented reasoning, and workflow/tool APIs allow multi-step task execution within enterprise systems. Effective integration relies on authentication, error handling, rate management, monitoring, and data standardization. Systematic evaluation of latency, throughput, accuracy, and operational impact ensures APIs meet enterprise requirements. Security and compliance practices, including encryption, access control, and audit logging, are critical to protecting sensitive data and maintain regulatory adherence. Standard integration patterns such as synchronous/asynchronous calls, event-driven triggers, middleware abstraction, and caching provide a robust foundation for scalable and maintainable agentic AI deployments.

## Section 3: Ecosystem Tools for Development, Monitoring, and Deployment

The agentic AI ecosystem extends beyond frameworks and APIs to include tools for development, testing, monitoring, and deployment. These ecosystem tools provide engineers with structured environments to build, evaluate, and operationalize autonomous agents while maintaining reliability, scalability, and maintainability. This section examines key tools, integration practices, and lifecycle management strategies for enterprise-grade agentic AI systems.

## Development Tools and IDEs

Effective agentic AI development requires a combination of integrated development environments (IDEs) and specialized tooling:

- **IDEs**: Tools such as Visual Studio Code, PyCharm, and IntelliJ IDEA provide code editing, debugging, and project management features.

- **Version Control**: Git-based systems manage source code, configuration files, and model artifacts, supporting collaboration, reproducibility, and rollback.

- **Dependency Management**: Package managers such as pip, conda, and poetry ensure consistent library versions across development and production environments.

- **Unit and Integration Testing Frameworks**: PyTest, unittest, and custom test harnesses allow modular and pipeline testing of agentic AI components.

Structured development tooling enables rapid iteration, reproducibility, and systematic validation of agentic systems.

## Simulation and Testing Environments

Simulation and testing tools provide controlled environments to evaluate agent behavior before production deployment:

- **Sandbox Environments**: Isolated test environments mimic operational conditions without impacting live systems.

- **Scenario Simulation**: Frameworks such as OpenAI Gym, custom workflow simulators, or Rasa test harnesses allow evaluation of multi-step reasoning and tool orchestration.

- **Load and Stress Testing**: Measure system performance, latency, and resource utilization under expected operational loads.

- **Edge Case Testing**: Simulate unexpected inputs, API failures, and workflow deviations to validate agent robustness.

Simulation and testing environments reduce deployment risk by identifying functional, performance, and reliability issues early in the development lifecycle.

## Observability, Monitoring, and Logging

Continuous monitoring is essential for operational reliability, troubleshooting, and performance optimization:

- **Metrics Collection**: Track KPIs such as task completion rate, response latency, human intervention frequency, and resource utilization.

- **Logging**: Capture agent interactions, tool invocations, API responses, and error events to support root cause analysis and auditability.

- **Visualization Dashboards**: Platforms such as Grafana, Kibana, or custom dashboards display real-time metrics and historical trends.

- **Alerting Systems**: Implement notifications for anomalies, failures, or threshold breaches to facilitate rapid response.

Observability ensures agents operate as intended, maintains accountability, and provides actionable insights for continuous improvement. **Deployment and Orchestration Tools**

Deployment and orchestration tools ensure agents are reliably executed in production environments:

- **Containerization**: Docker and Podman enable encapsulation of frameworks, dependencies, and configurations for consistent deployment.

- **Orchestration Platforms**: Kubernetes and Docker Swarm manage scaling, load balancing, and failover for multiple agent instances.

- **Continuous Integration/Continuous Deployment (CI/CD)**: Jenkins, GitLab CI, and GitHub Actions automate testing, packaging, and deployment pipelines.

- **Environment Configuration Management**: Tools such as Ansible, Terraform, and Helm charts standardize deployment across environments and support reproducibility.

Using these tools ensures agents can be deployed at scale, maintained efficiently, and updated with minimal operational disruption.

### Lifecycle Management and Version Control

Sustaining agentic AI systems over time requires structured lifecycle management to ensure stability and reproducibility. Versioning is critical, allowing teams to track changes across code, models, configurations, and integration modules, which supports rollback and consistent reproduction of results. Continuous updates-covering models, libraries, and connectors-help maintain both system performance and security posture. Dependency management plays a key role in preventing compatibility issues by validating library versions, API endpoints, and integration connectors on a regular basis. In addition, comprehensive documentation and standardized operating procedures (SOPs) provide guidance for onboarding, troubleshooting, and maintaining the system. Together, these lifecycle practices safeguard long-term operational continuity and support both development and production environments.

### Integration Patterns Across Ecosystem Tools

Applying consistent integration patterns across enterprise tools improves maintainability, scalability, and reliability. Event-driven architectures connect agents, monitoring systems, and CI/CD pipelines through events, triggers, or message queues, enabling decoupled and asynchronous workflows. Middleware abstraction centralizes logging, monitoring, and API communication, simplifying management while reducing duplication. Configuration-driven behavior ensures predictable and reproducible operations by defining deployment parameters, monitoring thresholds, and workflow rules in declarative files. Finally, modular plugin architectures make systems extensible by allowing new tools, connectors, or monitoring agents to be added without disrupting existing workflows. These patterns create a flexible and scalable foundation for enterprise-wide agentic AI deployments.

These patterns reduce complexity, support scalability, and facilitate future expansion of the agentic AI ecosystem.

Ecosystem tools provide the necessary infrastructure to develop, test, deploy, monitor, and maintain agentic AI systems in enterprise environments. Development tools and IDEs enable structured coding, testing, and dependency management. Simulation environments allow safe evaluation of multi-step workflows and agent interactions. Observability tools, dashboards, and alerting systems provide real-time insight into performance and operational reliability. Deployment and orchestration platforms ensure consistent, scalable, and reproducible production execution. Lifecycle management practices, security protocols, and integration patterns support maintainability, compliance, and continuous improvement. Collectively, these tools create a robust ecosystem that operates agentic AI frameworks and APIs effectively within enterprise environments.

# PART VI: DEPLOYMENT AND SCALING

Designing agentic AI systems is only the beginning; bringing them into production requires robust strategies for deployment and scaling. This part focuses on the infrastructure, orchestration, and monitoring practices that ensure agents perform reliably under real-world workloads. It covers integration into enterprise environments, continuous improvement processes, and approaches to scaling through distributed inference and load balancing. By combining architectural discipline with operational safeguards, these chapters provide a roadmap for transforming prototypes into production-grade systems that maintain accuracy, reliability, and resilience at scale.

# Chapter 21: Deployment Architectures and Infrastructure Strategies

## Section 1: Scalable Deployment Architectures for Agentic AI

Designing scalable deployment architectures is a critical step in operationalizing agentic AI systems. These systems, which rely on large language models (LLMs), multi-step reasoning pipelines, and multi-agent orchestration, require careful separation of concerns, fault-tolerant design, and optimized communication patterns. This section provides a detailed examination of architectural strategies, deployment patterns, and scalability considerations for enterprise-grade agentic AI.

### Layered Deployment Architecture

A layered architecture divides agentic AI systems into distinct functional layers. This separation simplifies development, testing, scaling, and maintenance. Typical layers include:

- **Perception Layer**: Responsible for ingesting inputs from users, APIs, or sensor data. This layer handles preprocessing, natural language understanding, and contextualization of incoming requests.

- **Reasoning Layer**: Manages knowledge representation, inference, and decision-making processes. It includes components for task decomposition, multi-step reasoning, and planning.

- **Planning Layer**: Coordinates task execution, tool invocation, and workflow orchestration. It schedules actions based on priority, dependencies, and system resource availability.

- **Action Layer**: Executes tasks, invokes APIs, triggers workflows, or produces outputs for end-users or downstream systems.

- **Memory and State Module**: Maintains short-term session memory and long-term persistent memory for context retention and continuity across tasks.

Layer separation enables independent scaling of each layer according to workload and resource demands. For example, the perception layer may scale horizontally to handle high input volumes, while the reasoning layer may require GPU acceleration to perform LLM inference efficiently.

### Microservices Architecture

Agentic AI systems benefit from microservices-based deployment for modularity and operational flexibility. Key characteristics include:

- **Service Isolation**: Each functional component, such as task planning, reasoning, or API integration, runs as an independent service.

- **Independent Scaling**: Services can be scaled based on resource requirements without affecting other system components. For instance, reasoning services may be scaled with GPU nodes, whereas API connectors scale with network capacity.

- **Resilience and Fault Tolerance**: Service isolation reduces cascading failures, enabling partial system functionality even under localized outages.

- **Inter-Service Communication**: Services communicate via standard interfaces such as REST, gRPC, or message queues (Kafka, RabbitMQ) to maintain decoupling and reliability.

Microservices patterns support maintainable, extensible, and highly available deployments suitable for enterprise workloads.

## Single-Agent vs Multi-Agent Deployment

Agentic AI can be deployed as single-agent systems or multi-agent networks depending on task complexity:

- **Single-Agent Deployment**: Appropriate for tasks with linear workflows, limited concurrency, or low interdependency. Simpler infrastructure and lower operational overhead are required.

- **Multi-Agent Deployment**: Supports parallel task execution, specialized agent roles, and distributed reasoning. Key considerations include:

    - **Inter-Agent Communication**: Standardized message passing, coordination protocols, and shared state management are essential.

    - **Load Distribution**: Task assignment algorithms balance workload across agents, avoiding bottlenecks.

    - **Fault Isolation**: Failures in one agent do not compromise the entire system; redundant agents can maintain task continuity.

The choice between single-agent and multi-agent architecture is informed by task complexity, concurrency requirements, and performance goals.

## Load Balancing and High Availability

Ensuring system responsiveness and continuous operation requires load balancing and high availability mechanisms:

- **Load Balancers**: Distribute requests across multiple service instances to prevent overloading and reduce response latency.

- **Redundancy**: Deploy multiple instances of critical services with failover strategies to maintain up time during hardware or network failures.

- **Health Checks**: Periodically monitor service status and automatically redirect traffic away from degraded or failed instances.

- **Scaling Policies**: Combine horizontal scaling (adding more instances) and vertical scaling (enhancing resource capacity per instance) to accommodate variable workloads.

These strategies ensure that agentic AI deployments remain responsive and resilient under variable load conditions.

## Integration with Enterprise Systems

For agentic AI to operate effectively at scale, it must integrate seamlessly with existing enterprise infrastructure. API gateways provide a centralized control layer for authentication, rate limiting, and request routing, ensuring secure and efficient communication between agents and internal services. Data pipelines connect agents to enterprise resources, enabling ingestion from databases, message queues, or file storage systems. Security controls-such as access policies, encryption, and auditing-must be applied consistently across all integrated components to safeguard sensitive data. In addition, compliance requirements like GDPR, HIPAA, or other industry-specific frameworks must be met, aligning agentic AI with organizational governance. Standardized integration patterns ensure that interactions remain maintainable, auditable, and scalable across enterprise environments.

## Communication and Coordination Patterns

Robust communication and coordination are essential in agentic AI systems, particularly when multiple agents operate concurrently. Synchronous communication supports direct request–response interactions, making it suitable for low-latency operations that require immediate completion. Asynchronous communication, on the other hand, leverages message queues or event streams, allowing agents to process tasks independently while improving fault tolerance and throughput. Shared state management-using distributed memory systems, databases, or cache layers-provides agents with a consistent context for collaborative reasoning. Coordination protocols further structure multi-agent operations by managing task assignments, resolving conflicts, and tracking dependencies. The choice of communication pattern depends on latency sensitivity, task complexity, and reliability requirements within enterprise workflows.

**Best Practices for Deployment Architecture**

- **Service Decoupling**: Maintain independence of functional components to simplify updates, debugging, and scaling.

- **Resource-Aware Placement**: Deploy resource-intensive components such as LLM inference on optimized GPU or CPU clusters.

- **Redundancy and Failover**: Implement redundant instances and automatic failover to reduce downtime.

- **Monitoring and Observability Hooks**: Integrate monitoring early in the architecture to enable proactive detection of bottlenecks and failures.

- **Security by Design**: Enforce access control, encryption, and audit logging at architectural boundaries.

Adherence to these practices ensures scalable, maintainable, and secure deployments suitable for enterprise-scale agentic AI applications.

Scalable deployment architectures for agentic AI require layered separation of perception, reasoning, planning, and action components. Microservices patterns enable modularity, independent scaling, and fault isolation. Decisions regarding single agent versus multi-agent deployment are based on workflow complexity, concurrency, and reliability requirements. Load balancing, redundancy, and health monitoring ensure high availability and consistent performance. Integration with enterprise systems necessitates standardized APIs, secure connectors, and compliance with regulatory requirements. Communication and coordination patterns, whether synchronous or asynchronous, maintain task consistency and optimize throughput. Following architectural best practices supports robust, maintainable, and scalable deployments capable of sustaining enterprise-grade agentic AI operations.

## Section 2: Infrastructure Strategies for Reliability, Scalability, and Cost Efficiency

Designing deployment architectures for agentic AI systems requires infrastructure strategies that balance performance, reliability, and cost. Unlike conventional applications, LLM-powered agents must handle highly variable workloads, large-scale inference demands, and strict latency requirements. This section focuses on the infrastructure considerations that allow these systems to scale, remain resilient under failure, and operate within predictable cost boundaries. The discussion is organized around three pillars: scalability mechanisms, reliability engineering, and cost optimization practices.

### Scalability Mechanisms

Scalability is the ability of a system to increase or decrease its capacity in response to demand. For agentic AI deployments, scalability must address both inference workloads and auxiliary tasks such as retrieval, memory management, and reasoning orchestration.

### Horizontal and Vertical Scaling

- **Horizontal scaling** adds more nodes or instances to the system. It is well-suited for stateless services such as inference workers or task routers.

- **Vertical scaling** adds resources such as CPU cores or GPU memory to a single node. It is often applied to workloads that cannot easily be distributed, for example, training tasks or specialized fine-tuning operations.

In production systems, horizontal scaling is preferred for inference services because it avoids single points of failure and enables better elasticity. However, vertical scaling may be required when handling very large model variants that demand high-memory GPUs.

## GPU and TPU Utilization

Inference for LLMs is heavily dependent on specialized accelerators. GPU and TPU strategies must consider:

1. **Batching policies** to maximize throughput without breaching latency requirements.

2. **Mixed precision execution** (e.g., FP16 or BF16) to improve efficiency.

3. **Memory-aware scheduling** to prevent over-allocation of models on a single device.

A typical design is to dedicate GPU pools to specific functions: one set for inference, another for fine-tuning, and a separate pool for retrieval or embedding computation. This avoids contention and simplifies autoscaling logic.

## Autoscaling Policies

Cloud providers and orchestration platforms such as Kubernetes enable autoscaling based on metrics. For agentic AI systems, autoscaling must be tuned carefully:

- **CPU/GPU utilization metrics** drive scaling for inference workloads.

- **Queue length metrics** indicate backlog in message brokers or request routers.

- **Latency metrics** ensure that end-user experience remains within defined SLAs.

To prevent cost overruns, autoscaling policies should include both scale-up thresholds and scale-down cooldowns. For example, scale up when GPU utilization exceeds 75 percent for five minutes, but scale down only after utilization remains below 40 percent for thirty minutes.

## Regional and Multi-Cluster Deployment

Workloads are increasingly deployed across multiple regions to reduce latency for end users and to improve redundancy. Agentic AI systems benefit from distributing inference clusters across geographic zones. Load balancers or traffic routers can direct users to the nearest cluster while ensuring fallback to secondary regions during outages.

## Reliability Engineering

Reliability is the property of a system to perform correctly and consistently, even under stress or partial failure. Agentic AI deployments cannot tolerate frequent downtime, especially in enterprise or regulated environments. Several strategies are applied to achieve high availability.

## High Availability (HA) Architectures

High Availability (HA) in agentic AI systems is achieved by introducing redundancy across compute, data, and service layers. Compute redundancy involves deploying multiple inference workers distributed across availability zones to ensure no single point of failure. Data redundancy is implemented through replicated databases and vector stores, maintaining consistency and resilience against data loss. Service redundancy includes duplicating critical components such as message brokers, gateways, and APIs to maintain uninterrupted communication. For example, inference clusters can be deployed across three availability zones, with requests routed through a global load balancer. If one zone suffers performance degradation or failure, traffic is automatically redirected to healthy zones, ensuring continuous service delivery.

## Disaster Recovery (DR) Planning

Disaster Recovery (DR) ensures that agentic AI systems can recover quickly and effectively from catastrophic failures. Key planning metrics include the Recovery Time Objective (RTO), which defines the maximum allowable downtime before service restoration, and the Recovery Point Objective (RPO), which specifies the maximum acceptable data loss measured in time. Backup strategies play a crucial role, with frequent snapshots of vector databases, model weights, and orchestration configurations enabling rapid restoration. Enterprises often adopt a warm standby model, where secondary clusters are kept running at reduced capacity and can be scaled up rapidly if the primary cluster fails. This approach balances resilience with cost efficiency, providing robust protection against large-scale disruptions.

## Load Balancing and Traffic Shaping

Load balancers distribute requests across inference workers. Several strategies can be applied:

- **Round-robin distribution** for uniform balancing.
- **Least connection strategy** for adaptive load management.
- **Latency-aware routing** to minimize user response times.

Traffic shaping mechanisms such as rate limiting and circuit breakers protect the system from overload. For example, requests may be queued or rejected when system utilization exceeds safe thresholds.

## Observability for Reliability

Reliability requires constant measurement. Observability frameworks should include:

- **Metrics:** GPU utilization, request throughput, queue lengths, and response times.
- **Logs:** detailed records of requests, errors, and agentic decisions.
- **Traces:** end-to-end visibility across service boundaries.

A common stack includes Prometheus for metrics, Grafana for visualization, ELK or OpenSearch for logs, and OpenTelemetry for distributed tracing. These tools allow engineers to detect anomalies early and trigger automated remediation actions.

## Cost Optimization Practices

Agentic AI systems can quickly generate unsustainable costs if infrastructure is not managed carefully. Cost optimization ensures that systems remain financially viable while maintaining performance.

## Resource Allocation and Right-Sizing

Workloads should be matched to appropriately sized compute nodes. Oversized nodes waste resources, while undersized nodes cause latency and instability. Techniques include:

- Profiling inference latency at different batch sizes.

- Mapping workloads to GPU tiers (e.g., A100 vs. T4).

- Using node pools with mixed instance types for flexibility.

## Spot Instances and Preemptible Nodes

Cloud providers offer discounted compute in the form of spot or preemptible instances. These can reduce costs significantly but may be terminated at short notice. Safe use cases for spot instances include:

- Embedding generation.

- Batch fine-tuning tasks.

- Non-critical memory indexing operations.

Inference clusters with strict latency SLAs should not rely solely on spot instances but may combine them with on-demand nodes for cost efficiency.

## Hybrid and Multi-Cloud Strategies

Organizations with sensitive data or cost constraints may adopt hybrid approaches. Options include:

- **Hybrid cloud:** deploying inference on cloud GPUs while hosting sensitive data stores on-premises.

- **Multi-cloud:** distributing workloads across providers to reduce vendor lock-in and take advantage of pricing differences.

Decision matrices can be used to compare strategies:

| Strategy | Advantages | Challenges | Best Fit Use Case |
|---|---|---|---|
| Cloud-native | Elastic scaling, managed services | High recurring cost | Startups, rapid prototyping |
| On-premises | Full control, predictable fixed costs | High upfront investment, limited elasticity | Regulated industries, predictable workloads |
| Hybrid | Balance of control and elasticity | Increased operational complexity | Enterprises with sensitive data |
| Multi-cloud | Redundancy, cost optimization | Cross-cloud management overhead | Global deployments, vendor hedging |

## FinOps and Cost Governance

Financial operations (FinOps) practices bring transparency to AI infrastructure costs. Effective measures include:

1. **Cost tagging:** labeling workloads by team, project, or environment.

2. **Budgets and alerts:** automated warnings when costs exceed thresholds.

3. **Reserved instances:** committing to predictable workloads for discounted pricing.

4. **Periodic audits:** reviewing idle resources, underutilized GPUs, or unoptimized storage.

Cost governance should be integrated with technical monitoring. For example, dashboards can display both performance metrics and cost per request, allowing engineering teams to weigh trade-offs explicitly.

**Putting It Together**

When combined, scalability, reliability, and cost strategies form a coherent infrastructure foundation. For example, a production-ready deployment might use:

- Regional GPU clusters with Kubernetes autoscaling.

- Load balancers configured for latency-aware routing.

- Hybrid cloud strategy for sensitive memory data stores.

- Spot instance pools for background embedding tasks.

- Observability stack integrated with both performance and cost dashboards.

A layered design ensures resilience: compute redundancy protects against node failures, regional redundancy guards against zone outages, and cost governance prevents uncontrolled expenditure.

## Section 3: Continuous Operations, Monitoring, and Reliability Strategies

Enterprise-grade agentic AI systems require continuous operational oversight to ensure reliability, maintainability, and scalability. Continuous operations encompass monitoring, logging, alerting, automated scaling, redundancy management, and lifecycle maintenance. This section details the strategies, tools, and best practices necessary for sustaining agentic AI performance in production environments.

**Observability and Monitoring**

Observability is the foundation of effective monitoring, providing insights into system behavior through the collection of metrics, logs, and traces. Metrics collection should include both system-level indicators-such as CPU, GPU, memory, and network usage-and application-level data like API latency, tool invocation success rates, task completion rates, and error frequencies. Distributed tracing across agent workflows helps pinpoint bottlenecks and provides visibility into multi-step task execution, with tools such as OpenTelemetry or Jaeger enabling end-to-end traceability. Regular health checks validate service responsiveness and availability, and when integrated with orchestration platforms, can trigger automated failover or scaling. Dashboards built with visualization tools like Grafana or Kibana present real-time and historical performance trends, allowing teams to detect anomalies early and maintain smooth operations.

**Logging and Auditability**

Structured logging is critical for both operational troubleshooting and regulatory compliance. Interaction logs record details of agent behaviors, including task sequences, tool calls, and decision points, ensuring traceability. Error logs capture failed task executions, system warnings, and API errors, supporting rapid diagnosis and resolution. Retention policies determine how long logs are stored, balancing storage limitations with compliance and analytical needs. Audit trails provide complete records of system activities, supporting reproducibility and accountability, while also demonstrating adherence to regulatory standards. Together, these practices ensure transparency, reliability, and compliance in agentic AI workflows.

Proper logging frameworks allow teams to correlate system performance with operational outcomes, supporting both maintenance and compliance audits. **Automated Scaling and Resource Management**

Dynamic workloads in agentic AI systems require automated scaling strategies:

- **Horizontal Scaling**: Increase or decrease the number of agent or service instances based on workload metrics. Kubernetes, Docker Swarm, or cloud-native auto-scaling can automate this process.

- **Vertical Scaling**: Adjust compute resources per instance, such as allocating additional GPU memory or CPU cores, to accommodate intensive reasoning tasks.

- **Load-Based Triggering**: Define threshold-based triggers for scaling, such as CPU/GPU utilization exceeding 70% or task queue length exceeding a specific limit.

- **Cost and Efficiency Optimization**: Scale resources to match workload demands, avoiding overprovisioning while maintaining performance.

Automated scaling ensures consistent performance and responsiveness under varying workloads while optimizing resource utilization and cost.

### Redundancy and Failover Strategies

Redundancy and failover mechanisms enhance reliability and minimize downtime:

- **Redundant Agents**: Deploy multiple instances of critical agents to ensure continued task execution if one instance fails.

- **Service Replication**: Maintain multiple service replicas for key infrastructure components, such as databases, inference services, or orchestration engines.

- **Failover Mechanisms**: Implement automatic routing to healthy instances when failures are detected, preventing disruption of user-facing services.

- **Geographic Redundancy**: Distribute agent and service instances across multiple data centers or cloud regions to maintain availability during regional outages.

These practices ensure that agentic AI systems remain operational under hardware failures, software errors, or network disruptions. **Maintenance Workflows and Version Control**

Maintaining agentic AI systems over time requires structured workflows for updates, patching, and versioning:

- **Model Updates**: Regularly retrain or fine-tune LLMs and other AI models to maintain performance, accuracy, and compliance with evolving datasets.

- **Code Versioning**: Track versions of code, APIs, and integration modules using Git or similar systems to enable rollback and reproducibility.

- **Dependency Management**: Monitor library and framework versions to prevent incompatibilities and maintain security.

- **Scheduled Maintenance**: Define maintenance windows for deploying updates, performing backups, and conducting system tests without disrupting production operations.

- **Change Management**: Document changes, approvals, and deployment steps to maintain accountability and operational transparency.

These practices reduce operational risk and ensure the continuous integrity of agentic AI systems.

### CI/CD Pipelines for Agentic AI

Continuous Integration and Continuous Deployment (CI/CD) pipelines play a key role in ensuring that agentic AI systems can be updated rapidly and reliably. Automated testing-spanning unit, integration, and simulation tests-validates agent behavior before release, minimizing the risk of production issues. Build automation handles container creation, service packaging, and preparation of deployment artifacts, while deployment automation streamlines rollout to staging and production environments using tools such as Kubernetes, Helm charts, or cloud-native platforms. Robust rollback mechanisms are also built into the pipeline, allowing teams to quickly revert to stable versions in case of errors or regressions. Collectively, CI/CD pipelines accelerate delivery cycles, reduce manual errors, and maintain consistency across environments.

## Incident Response and Recovery

A structured incident response framework is essential for managing disruptions in agentic AI workflows. Alerting systems trigger notifications when thresholds are exceeded, such as high-latency tasks, failed API calls, or outages. Root cause analysis uses logs, traces, and metrics to uncover underlying issues and prevent repeat failures. Recovery protocols define clear steps for restoring affected agents, services, or infrastructure, ensuring minimal downtime. Post-incident reviews document the disruption, resolution, and lessons learned, feeding improvements back into operational processes. Together, these practices reduce downtime, mitigate operational risks, and strengthen overall system resilience.

## Best Practices for Continuous Operations

- **Integrate Monitoring Early**: Embed observability hooks during initial deployment to capture metrics from all critical components.

- **Standardize Logging and Metrics**: Use consistent formats and units to enable cross-service analysis and correlation.

- **Automate Scaling and Failover**: Reduce human intervention in routine operational adjustments to maintain consistent performance.

- **Conduct Regular Stress Tests**: Simulate high-load scenarios to validate scaling, redundancy, and recovery procedures.

- **Document Operational Procedures**: Maintain clear SOPs for monitoring, incident response, maintenance, and CI/CD operations.

Following these best practices ensures that agentic AI systems remain performant, resilient, and maintainable in enterprise environments.

Continuous operations, monitoring, and reliability strategies are essential for enterprise-grade agentic AI. Observability, metrics collection, and distributed tracing provide visibility into system behavior, while structured logging and audit trails support troubleshooting and compliance. Automated scaling, load balancing, redundancy, and failover maintain performance and availability under dynamic workloads. Maintenance workflows, version control, and CI/CD pipelines ensure updates are applied safely and consistently. Structured incident response and post-incident analysis further strengthen operational resilience. Together, these practices create a robust operational framework, ensuring agentic AI systems can be deployed and maintained reliably in production environments.

# Chapter 22: Enterprise Integration and Workflow Orchestration

## Section 1: Architectural Strategies for Enterprise Integration

Integrating agentic AI systems into enterprise environments requires a deliberate architectural approach to ensure compatibility, security, scalability, and maintainability. Enterprises typically operate with complex infrastructure including multiple databases, legacy systems, authentication services, and API-driven applications. Agentic AI systems must interface seamlessly with these components while preserving performance, reliability, and compliance standards. This section presents architectural strategies, patterns, and best practices for enterprise integration.

### Service-Oriented Integration Patterns

Service-oriented architecture (SOA) principles provide a foundational approach for integrating agentic AI components with enterprise systems:

- **Loose Coupling**: Components communicate through well-defined interfaces or APIs rather than direct databases or function calls, reducing interdependence and simplifying maintenance.

- **Service Reusability**: Agentic AI services, such as task execution, reasoning, or document retrieval, can be exposed for multiple workflows and applications across the enterprise.

- **Encapsulation**: Internal agent logic is hidden behind APIs, ensuring that changes to model updates or internal workflows do not disrupt enterprise consumers.

- **Interoperability**: Standard protocols such as REST, gRPC, and SOAP allow diverse enterprise systems to interface with agentic AI services.

These patterns facilitate modular deployment, simplify testing, and provide flexibility for future integration with additional enterprise services.

### API Gateways and Middleware

API gateways and middleware act as the control and coordination layer for enterprise integration:

- **Routing and Load Management**: Gateways manage request distribution across multiple agent services, ensuring load balancing and optimal response times.

- **Authentication and Authorization**: Centralized enforcement of enterprise authentication protocols, such as OAuth2, SAML, or LDAP, ensures secure access.

- **Monitoring and Logging**: Middleware captures request metrics, latency, and error logs, providing observability across integrated systems.

- **Transformation and Aggregation**: Gateways can perform protocol transformation, input/output validation, or aggregation of multiple service responses for enterprise applications.

Middleware and gateways standardize interactions, enforce security policies, and provide a single integration point for multiple agentic AI components.

### Enterprise Data Flow Management

Agentic AI depends on structured and unstructured enterprise data to execute tasks and support reasoning. Managing this data flow requires secure and efficient integration across multiple systems. Data connectors link the agent to relational databases, NoSQL stores, document repositories, and cloud-based storage solutions. To ensure interoperability, data normalization processes standardize formats and encodings across platforms. In-memory caching is used for frequently accessed knowledge or embeddings, reducing latency and improving responsiveness. At the same time, data governance frameworks enforce compliance with organizational and regulatory policies, ensuring that storage, access, and processing remain secure and auditable.

## Identity and Access Management

Integrating agentic AI into enterprise workflows requires strict adherence to security and identity management practices. Role-Based Access Control (RBAC) defines permissions at the agent level, limiting access to sensitive data and operations based on assigned roles. Federated identity solutions, such as SAML, OpenID Connect, or LDAP, enable seamless authentication through enterprise identity providers. Token management ensures secure, session-based authentication between agents and enterprise services. Additionally, audit logging records all authentication events, API calls, and data interactions, providing transparency and accountability. By enforcing these controls, enterprises reduce security risks and align agentic AI systems with broader governance requirements.

## Maintaining Data Consistency and Transactional Integrity

Enterprise integration often involves transactions across multiple systems, which must maintain consistency and integrity:

- **Atomic Task Execution**: Agentic AI should support atomic or compensating transactions to ensure that workflow steps either complete successfully or revert changes.

- **Distributed Transactions**: Implement coordination protocols, such as two-phase commit or Saga patterns, to manage state across multiple systems.

- **Conflict Resolution**: Define rules for resolving conflicts when multiple agents or workflows access the same data concurrently.

- **Event-Driven Synchronization**: Use event streams or message queues to propagate state changes in near real-time while maintaining eventual consistency.

Ensuring data consistency prevents operational errors, maintains trust in agent outputs, and supports enterprise compliance.

## Integration with Enterprise Applications

Agentic AI systems frequently interact with enterprise applications such as ERPs, CRMs, and business intelligence tools:

- **ERP Integration**: Agents can access supply chain, finance, or HR modules to execute automated workflows.

- **CRM Interaction**: Integration enables automated customer support, lead processing, or workflow augmentation.

- **Business Intelligence Integration**: Agents can provide insights or generate reports by querying BI dashboards or data warehouses.

- **Standardized Connectors**: Using vendor-supported SDKs, APIs, or middleware ensures robust and maintainable integrations.

Integration strategies should prioritize maintainability, reducing the risk of breaking workflows as enterprise applications evolve.

## Best Practices for Enterprise Integration

- **Decouple Systems**: Maintain separation between agentic AI and enterprise systems to facilitate upgrades and reduce interdependency.

- **Standardize APIs**: Use consistent naming conventions, data formats, and error handling across services.

- **Secure by Design**: Enforce encryption, authentication, and audit logging from the start.

- **Monitor and Observe**: Implement logging, tracing, and dashboards to detect integration issues proactively.

- **Document Integration Points**: Maintain up-to-date documentation of APIs, connectors, and workflow interactions for maintenance and audits.

Following these practices ensures that agentic AI integrations are robust, secure, and maintainable in enterprise environments.

Enterprise integration of agentic AI requires a structured architectural approach that emphasizes service-oriented patterns, standardized APIs, and middleware coordination. Secure and efficient data flow is critical for reasoning and task execution, necessitating connectors, normalization, and caching strategies. Authentication, authorization, and identity management protect sensitive enterprise data while enabling seamless integration. Maintaining data consistency and transactional integrity ensures reliable workflow execution across distributed systems. Direct integration with enterprise applications like ERPs, CRMs, and BI tools supports automation and augmentation of business processes. Diagrams, standardized practices, and operational monitoring reinforce maintainable and auditable integrations. By following these architectural strategies, agentic AI systems can be effectively deployed within enterprise environments, providing reliable, secure, and scalable support for complex workflows.

## Section 2: Workflow Orchestration and Task Management

Workflow orchestration is a critical component of enterprise-grade agentic AI systems. Agents often perform multi-step reasoning, interact with external services, and handle concurrent tasks. Effective orchestration ensures that these processes execute reliably, efficiently, and in a maintainable manner. This section outlines strategies, tools, and best practices for designing, implementing, and monitoring workflows in integrated enterprise environments.

### Defining and Decomposing Workflows

Complex enterprise workflows should be broken down into discrete, manageable tasks that can be executed by individual agents or agent teams:

- **Task Decomposition**: Identify logical subtasks within a workflow and define inputs, outputs, dependencies, and success criteria.

- **Atomicity**: Each task should be executed independently, with well-defined boundaries to facilitate retries or failure handling.

- **Data Flow Definition**: Clearly specify the data required for each task and the expected output, ensuring that tasks can be chained efficiently.

- **Parallelism Opportunities**: Identify tasks that can be executed concurrently to optimize workflow throughput.

A clinical workflow analogy can help illustrate decomposition: a diagnostic process can be divided into patient data retrieval, symptom analysis, test ordering, and report generation, each performed by a separate agent while passing data sequentially.

### Task Scheduling and Prioritization

Orchestration platforms manage task execution by scheduling tasks according to priority, dependencies, and available resources:

- **Dependency Resolution**: Tasks that rely on the output of previous steps are executed in order, while independent tasks can run concurrently.

- **Prioritization**: Assign priority levels to tasks based on business importance, deadlines, or SLA requirements.

- **Resource Awareness**: Scheduling should account for resource availability, such as GPU or memory constraints, to prevent bottlenecks.

- **Retry Policies**: Define rules for automatically retrying failed tasks, with backoff strategies to reduce load spikes.

Effective scheduling maximizes throughput, maintains SLA compliance, and ensures predictable workflow execution.

## Orchestration Platforms

Several widely adopted platforms support enterprise-grade workflow orchestration:

- **Apache Airflow**: Provides DAG-based orchestration, task scheduling, monitoring, and dependency management. Suitable for ETL-like pipelines and batch workflows.

- **Prefect**: Offers workflow orchestration with dynamic dependency handling, retries, and real-time observability. Supports both batch and streaming tasks.

- **Kubernetes-Native Pipelines**: Platforms like Argo Workflows leverage Kubernetes to orchestrate containerized tasks, providing scalability, fault-tolerance, and resource isolation.

- **Message Queues and Event-Driven Architecture**: Systems such as RabbitMQ, Kafka, or AWS SQS can trigger agents or tasks based on events, enabling reactive orchestration.

Selection of orchestration tools depends on workload type, scalability requirements, and enterprise IT constraints.

## Monitoring Workflow Execution

Continuous monitoring of task execution ensures reliability, visibility, and rapid troubleshooting:

- **Execution Logs**: Record tasks start and completion times, input and output data, and errors for traceability.

- **Metrics Collection**: Track task duration, failure rates, retries, and resource utilization to identify bottlenecks.

- **Alerting**: Configure alerts for failed tasks, SLA breaches, or abnormal performance patterns.

- **Dashboards**: Visualization platforms provide at-a-glance operational status for enterprise stakeholders and technical teams.

Monitoring allows teams to detect performance degradation early and maintain predictable system behavior.

## Error Handling and Fault Tolerance

Agentic AI workflows must be designed to handle task failures and service disruptions gracefully. Retry mechanisms automatically re-execute tasks that fail due to transient issues, using exponential backoff or fixed intervals to balance recovery with system stability. For non-idempotent operations, compensating actions are defined to reverse partially completed workflows, preventing inconsistencies. Fallback agents or alternate workflows can take over when primary agents fail, ensuring continued execution. Circuit breakers provide an additional safeguard by temporarily disabling malfunctioning components to stop cascading failures. These error-handling strategies collectively preserve workflow reliability while reducing the need for manual intervention.

## Scaling Multi-Agent Workflows

Scaling agentic workflows is vital for managing large volumes of concurrent tasks in enterprise environments. Horizontal scaling allows multiple agents to operate in parallel by leveraging containerized deployments and cloud elasticity. Vertical scaling adds more compute power, memory, or GPU resources for tasks that require heavy processing. Dynamic load balancing distributes workloads across agents based on resource capacity, task complexity, and priority, while task queues act as buffers to manage high-volume backlogs and enforce orderly execution. Together, these scaling strategies ensure that workflows maintain throughput, minimize latency, and meet enterprise SLA requirements.

## Table: Comparison of Workflow Orchestration Approaches

| Approach | Latency | Scalability | Fault-Tolerance | Notes |
|----------|---------|-------------|-----------------|-------|
| Apache Airflow | Moderate | Medium | Medium | Batch-oriented, DAG-based, ideal for ETL |
| Prefect | Low to Moderate | High | High | Dynamic dependencies, cloud-friendly |
| Kubernetes + Argo Workflows | Low | High | High | Containerized, supports parallel execution |
| Event-Driven Messaging (Kafka) | Very Low | Very High | Medium to High | Reactive workflows, near real-time execution |

This table provides a reference for selecting the appropriate orchestration approach based on enterprise requirements.

## Logging and Traceability in Orchestration

Traceability ensures reproducibility, compliance, and operational insight:

- **Task Logs**: Capture inputs, outputs, execution duration, and intermediate results for each task.

- **Workflow Tracing**: Link task logs across a workflow to reconstruct the full execution path.

- **Correlation IDs**: Assign unique identifiers to workflows or tasks to facilitate cross-system tracing.

- **Audit Compliance**: Maintain records for regulatory requirements, ensuring transparency in automated processes.

Robust logging and tracing enable troubleshooting, post-mortem analysis, and continuous improvement.

## Integration of Orchestration with Enterprise Tools

Workflows often interact with multiple enterprise applications:

- **Data Retrieval**: Agents pull structured and unstructured data from databases, document stores, or APIs.

- **Task Output Delivery**: Results are delivered to business applications, dashboards, or BI tools.

- **External API Calls**: Agents invoke third-party services or internal microservices to complete tasks.

- **Notification Systems**: Orchestrated workflows can trigger alerts or notifications based on task outcomes.

Integration points should be standardized and documented to maintain operational reliability and simplify future extensions.

**Best Practices for Workflow Orchestration**

- **Design Modular Tasks**: Keep workflows composed of discrete, reusable tasks to facilitate maintenance and scalability.

- **Define Clear Dependencies**: Explicitly specify input/output relationships between tasks to avoid execution ambiguity.

- **Monitor and Automate**: Use observability and automated recovery mechanisms to maintain operational reliability.

- **Implement Security Controls**: Ensure that workflow execution complies with enterprise access, authentication, and authorization policies.

- **Continuous Evaluation**: Periodically review task performance, orchestration latency, and resource utilization to optimize workflows.

Applying these practices ensures that enterprise agentic AI workflows remain reliable, auditable, and maintainable.

Workflow orchestration and task management are essential for integrating agentic AI into enterprise operations. Task decomposition, scheduling, and prioritization define how workflows execute efficiently and reliably. Orchestration platforms, including Apache Airflow, Prefect, and Kubernetes-native pipelines, provide robust tools for managing dependencies, retries, and parallel execution. Monitoring, logging, and traceability ensure operational visibility, while error handling and fault-tolerance mechanisms maintain workflow reliability. Scalable orchestration supports dynamic workloads, and standardized integration with enterprise applications ensures seamless task execution across the organization. By adhering to best practices, enterprises can achieve predictable, maintainable, and secure orchestration of agentic AI workflows.

## Section 3: Operational Governance, Security, and Reliability in Orchestration

Deploying agentic AI at the enterprise scale requires strict governance practices to safeguard compliance, security, and operational stability. Complex workflows, multi-agent coordination, and integration with sensitive enterprise systems introduce risks that must be carefully controlled. This section highlights strategies, frameworks, and best practices for observability, security enforcement, reliability, and incident management.

**Observability and Monitoring for Orchestrated Workflows**

Operational transparency is critical to managing enterprise-level AI workflows effectively:
• **Metrics Collection:** Track execution times, success/failure ratios, queue depths, and resource usage.
• **Distributed Tracing:** Monitor workflows across agents and services with tools like Jaeger or OpenTelemetry to identify delays and errors.
• **Health Checks:** Continuously assess agent and service availability, with orchestration platforms configured for automated recovery.
• **Dashboards:** Provide real-time visualization of workflow health, performance, and error patterns for engineering and operations teams.

Strong observability allows proactive detection and resolution of issues, reducing downtime and ensuring consistent enterprise performance.

**Logging, Auditability, and Compliance**

Structured logging and traceability are fundamental for ensuring compliance and reproducibility in enterprise agentic AI workflows. Task-level logs capture inputs, outputs, durations, and intermediate results, providing a granular view of each operation. Workflow traceability aggregates these logs, allowing complete reconstruction of execution paths to aid in debugging and analysis. Access and event logging further strengthen governance by recording authentication attempts, API calls, and modifications to enterprise systems. Finally, retention policies define how long logs are stored and who can access them, ensuring alignment with regulations such as GDPR, HIPAA, or SOX. Together, these practices enable accountability, transparency, and adherence to compliance requirements.

## Security and Access Control in Orchestration

When AI workflows interact with sensitive enterprise data, robust security and access control are indispensable. Role-Based Access Control (RBAC) ensures that permissions are scoped appropriately, limiting access by agent or workflow role. Federated identity management integrates with enterprise identity providers through standards like SAML or OpenID Connect, streamlining centralized authentication. Secrets management safeguards tokens, API keys, and credentials by storing them in secure vaults, reducing the risk of unauthorized access. In addition, data encryption-applied both in transit and at rest-protects information throughout the workflow lifecycle. These measures collectively maintain confidentiality, integrity, and controlled access across enterprise AI operations.

## Reliability Mechanisms for Enterprise Workflows

Ensuring continuous operation requires resilient workflow design:
- **Retry and Backoff:** Retry transient errors with exponential or interval backoff strategies.
- **Compensation Transactions:** Define corrective steps for non-idempotent tasks when workflows partially fail.
- **Redundancy:** Run critical agents and services in multiple instances to remove single points of failure.
- **Failover and Load Balancing:** Automatically reroute requests to healthy services and balance workload.
- **Event-Driven Recovery:** Trigger restoration workflows from event streams when disruptions occur.

These reliability techniques protect SLAs and minimize business risk.

## Incident Response and Root Cause Analysis

A formal response plan enhances resilience during failures:
- **Alerting:** Configure alerts for abnormal metrics, SLA violations, or workflow breakdowns.
- **Response Protocols:** Define clear remediation steps, rollback actions, and communication channels.
- **Root Cause Analysis:** Use metrics, logs, and traces to identify the underlying problem.
- **Post-Incident Review:** Document lessons learned and adjust workflows, pipelines, or governance processes accordingly.

Structured response and analysis reduce downtime and strengthen organizational confidence.

## Continuous Improvement and CI/CD Integration

Operational oversight must evolve alongside enterprise workflows:
- **CI/CD Pipelines:** Automate testing, validation, and deployment of agent logic and workflows. Include unit, integration, and simulation tests.
- **Version Control:** Maintain revisions of workflows, orchestration configs, and agent code for rollback and reproducibility.
- **Performance Reviews:** Periodically evaluate latency, throughput, and error metrics to target optimization.
- **Feedback Loops:** Feed monitoring data and incident outcomes back into workflow redesign and tuning.

This ensures workflows remain safe, efficient, and responsive to enterprise needs.

Governance, security, and reliability are non-negotiable for enterprise adoption of agentic AI. Observability delivers visibility into workflows, logging supports compliance, and strong security prevents unauthorized access. Reliability patterns-such as retries, compensation, redundancy, and failover-maintain operational continuity. Incident response and CI/CD pipelines ensure resilience and ongoing improvement. Together, these practices establish a comprehensive governance framework that secures the performance, integrity, and trustworthiness of enterprise-scale agentic AI deployments.

# PART VII: PRACTICAL PROJECTS AND HANDS-ON IMPLEMENTATION

The final part of this book bridges theory and practice through guided projects that demonstrate how agentic AI systems can be built step by step. Each project provides a structured blueprint with objectives, prerequisites, system architecture, and implementation phases, allowing readers to translate concepts into working solutions. Covering domains such as customer support, healthcare, finance, robotics, and multi-agent coordination, these projects highlight how perception, reasoning, memory, and action loops operate in real applications. By completing them, readers will gain practical experience, reinforce core principles, and develop the confidence to design and deploy their own agentic AI systems.

# Project 1: Customer Support Agent with External Tool Integration

This project focuses on building an LLM-powered agent designed to manage multi-turn customer support conversations. The agent will accurately interpret customer queries, retrieve the right information from a knowledge base, interact with CRM systems to handle tickets, and provide clear, context-aware responses. The aim is to demonstrate how perception, reasoning, memory, and action loops can be combined to deliver a reliable, enterprise-ready assistant.

Customer service is one of the most common applications of agentic systems. It requires strong perception to interpret diverse queries, reasoning to identify user intent, memory to sustain coherent multi-turn dialogues, and action to interact with external systems via APIs. This project highlights how these loops cooperate to build dependable business solutions.

## Objectives

By completing this project, readers will:
- Develop a conversational agent that supports multi-turn customer dialogues.
- Integrate the system with external resources such as a knowledge base (FAQ repository) and CRM systems (e.g., ticket management APIs).
- Implement memory loops to maintain session context across extended conversations.
- Embed validation and safety mechanisms into the action loop for reliable execution.
- Assess the system using metrics such as accuracy, latency, and robustness in support workflows.

## Prerequisites

### Skills:
- Intermediate programming knowledge (Python or similar).
- Experience with REST APIs and structured data formats (JSON).
- Understanding of LLM reasoning and prompt engineering.

### Tools and Frameworks:
- LLM service (e.g., OpenAI GPT-4 or equivalent).
- Agent orchestration framework (e.g., LangChain, Semantic Kernel, or custom solution).
- Vector database for memory management (e.g., Pinecone, Weaviate, FAISS).
- CRM platform with API integration (e.g., Zendesk, Freshdesk, Salesforce Service Cloud).

### Datasets:
- Structured FAQ or knowledge base (CSV, JSON, or DB format).
- Sample customer conversation transcripts for testing.

## System Architecture

### Perception Loop
- Parses customer inputs with intent detection and entity recognition.
- Validates schema and determines whether the request is informational (FAQ) or operational (CRM).

### Reasoning Loop
- Builds an execution plan: fetch FAQ entry, escalate to knowledge base, or create/update a ticket.
- Enforces constraint checks (e.g., ticket cannot be opened without a valid customer ID).

**Memory Loop**
- Tracks short-term session data for ongoing multi-turn conversations.
- Uses a vector store for retrieving relevant FAQs and long-term references.

**Action Loop**
- Executes API calls to the knowledge base or CRM systems.
- Validates outcomes (e.g., ticket successfully created with confirmation).
- Delivers structured responses back to customers in a consistent manner.

**Central Loops**
Perception and memory drive contextual understanding, while action provides seamless integration with enterprise systems.

**Implementation Steps**

**Phase 1: Setup**

1. Install libraries for LLM access, API handling, and vector database operations.

2. Configure CRM and knowledge base credentials.

3. Load FAQ dataset into the vector database using embeddings.

**Phase 2: Loop Design**

1. Perception: Build an input parser with intent classification (FAQ query, ticket creation, ticket update).

2. Reasoning: Implement a decision layer mapping intents to actions with structured prompts and rules.

3. Memory: Create two layers:
   o Short-term (session context).
   o Long-term (semantic retrieval via vector DB).

4. Action: Build API connectors for FAQs and CRM ticket management, ensuring schema validation.

**Phase 3: Integration**

1. Orchestrate perception, reasoning, memory, and action within a workflow engine.

2. Ensure perception outputs flow into reasoning, reasoning leverages memory, and validated actions trigger system calls.

3. Add monitoring and logging for metrics such as latency, accuracy, and errors.

**Phase 4: Testing**

1. Simulate interactions (e.g., password reset, billing escalation).

2. Evaluate accuracy of FAQ retrieval and correctness of ticket handling.

3. Test resilience with malformed queries and API/network errors.

4. Measure system responsiveness to confirm real-time usability.

# Project 2: Healthcare Workflow Assistant

The aim of this project is to create an LLM-powered agent that simplifies healthcare workflows. The agent can handle tasks such as booking patient appointments, retrieving diagnostic recommendations, and validating medical records against established clinical protocols. The purpose is to demonstrate how agentic loops can be applied in highly regulated, safety-critical environments where precision and compliance are essential.

In healthcare, agents must operate under strict regulatory and ethical frameworks. This project shows how perception loops interpret clinical language, reasoning loops enforce compliance and safety rules, memory loops preserve patient data for continuity of care, and action loops carry out verified operations-such as scheduling or retrieving guidelines.

## Objectives

By completing this project, readers will:
- Design an agent for healthcare workflows like scheduling and information retrieval.
- Implement perception modules that process clinical queries and patient identifiers.
- Use reasoning loops to validate requests against safety rules and clinical protocols.
- Apply memory loops to maintain continuity across patient sessions and longitudinal care.
- Integrate action loops with healthcare IT systems (e.g., EHR scheduling APIs) safely.
- Assess performance with metrics focused on accuracy, compliance, and safety.

## Prerequisites

### Skills:
- Understanding of healthcare data standards (HL7, FHIR, etc.).
- Intermediate programming skills (Python preferred).
- Familiarity with REST APIs and structured formats (JSON, XML).

### Tools and Frameworks:
- LLM service adapted for clinical contexts.
- Orchestration framework (e.g., LangChain, Semantic Kernel).
- Vector database or compliant knowledge base for medical guidelines.
- EHR or scheduling platform with sandbox API access (FHIR recommended).

### Datasets:
- Clinical guideline datasets (e.g., NIH, WHO protocols).
- Synthetic or de-identified patient records.
- Sample scheduling data (clinician availability, appointment slots).

## System Architecture

### Perception Loop
- Parses clinician and patient requests, recognizing medical terms, IDs, and scheduling needs.
- Validates structured inputs such as appointment dates and patient record formats.

### Reasoning Loop
- Determines request type: informational (guidelines), operational (scheduling), or verification (record checks).
- Applies compliance checks so scheduling respects availability, guideline retrieval matches conditions, and sensitive actions are validated.

### Memory Loop
- Stores short-term session data for ongoing interactions.

- Uses long-term memory for continuity of care, accessing prior treatments and interactions.
- Applies retention and access policies that meet compliance standards.

**Action Loop**
- Executes validated scheduling actions via EHR APIs.
- Retrieves guideline documents from trusted knowledge sources.
- Confirms and reports back execution results to the user.

**Central Loops**

Reasoning and memory are the most critical components, since clinical safety depends on precise interpretation and consistent record-keeping.

**Implementation Steps**

**Phase 1: Setup**

1. Configure LLM and orchestration environment.

2. Set up sandbox access to EHR APIs or synthetic healthcare datasets.

3. Load de-identified patient records and guidelines into a secure database.

**Phase 2: Loop Design**

1. Perception: Build input parsing for patient identifiers, appointment requests, and medical terminology.

2. Reasoning: Develop a module to apply clinical and compliance rules before producing outputs.

3. Memory:
   o Short-term: manage session histories.
   o Long-term: store and retrieve patient context and prior records.

4. Action: Create API clients for scheduling, guideline access, and record validation with schema checks and safety controls.

**Phase 3: Integration**

1. Connect perception, reasoning, memory, and action into a unified loop.

2. Require reasoning validation before any action is executed.

3. Add secure logging and anonymization for compliance tracking.

**Phase 4: Testing**

1. Test workflows such as:
   o Booking a follow-up visit.
   o Retrieving treatment guidelines.
   o Checking patient records for contraindications.

2. Run edge cases (e.g., missing IDs, conflicting appointments).

3. Evaluate system resilience under malformed or ambiguous inputs.

4. Measure accuracy, compliance adherence, and safety outcomes.

# Project 3: Financial Compliance Monitor

This project aims to develop an intelligent agent that monitors financial activities to detect compliance breaches such as money laundering, irregular transfers, or violations of regulatory thresholds. The system ingests transaction data, cross-checks it against compliance requirements, highlights potential violations, and produces structured reports for auditors or compliance officers.

Financial compliance is a domain where deterministic logic and verifiable action cycles are paramount. Perception loops validate incoming transaction data. Reasoning loops enforce compliance rules while identifying unusual activity. Memory loops maintain transaction histories and reference libraries of regulations. Action loops issue alerts, prepare compliance reports, or escalate serious violations. This project demonstrates how agentic AI can function effectively in high-stakes, rule-heavy contexts.

## Objectives

By completing this project, readers will:
- Develop an agent capable of analyzing structured financial transaction records.
- Design reasoning loops that combine strict rule-based compliance checks with anomaly detection methods.
- Apply memory loops to manage regulatory frameworks, historical data, and audit logs.
- Build action loops that deliver alerts, structured reports, or escalate issues for human oversight.
- Assess system performance across accuracy, precision/recall, robustness, and latency metrics.

## Prerequisites

### Skills:
- Knowledge of financial compliance regulations (AML, KYC, FATF).
- Intermediate programming ability (Python recommended).
- Familiarity with databases, anomaly detection models, and rule-based systems.

### Tools and Frameworks:
- LLM or hybrid reasoning engine.
- Agent orchestration framework (LangChain or a custom workflow engine).
- Transaction storage (SQL/NoSQL databases).
- Compliance regulation store (vector DB or rules engine).
- Visualization/reporting tools (Grafana, Tableau, or PDF libraries).

### Datasets:
- Synthetic or anonymized financial transaction datasets.
- Structured compliance rule sets (AML thresholds, suspicious activity indicators).
- Example audit/compliance reports for benchmarking.

## System Architecture

### Perception Loop
- Reads structured transaction inputs (amount, sender, receiver, timestamp, location).
- Validates schema consistency and field correctness.

### Reasoning Loop
- Applies strict rules (e.g., transactions > $10,000 automatically flagged).
- Uses anomaly detection to identify hidden risks (e.g., structuring via repeated small transfers).
- Determines outcomes: compliant, flagged, or escalate.

**Memory Loop**

- Stores transaction histories by entity.
- Manages compliance rules with versioning.
- Logs flagged incidents for future auditing.

**Action Loop**

- Generates alerts with structured details.
- Produces formatted compliance reports.
- Escalates severe violations to supervisors or human compliance teams.

**Central Loops**

Reasoning is the foundation, ensuring reliable enforcement of rules and anomaly detection. Memory is equally vital, maintaining histories and ensuring regulatory consistency.

**Implementation Steps**

**Phase 1: Setup**

1. Install required libraries for ingestion, anomaly detection, and reporting.

2. Load synthetic or anonymized transaction datasets.

3. Import compliance rule sets (e.g., AML thresholds, blacklists, sanctions lists).

**Phase 2: Loop Design**

1. Perception: Implement schema validation and normalize inputs (e.g., currency conversions, time zones).

2. Reasoning:
    - Rule-based enforcement for deterministic compliance.
    - Anomaly detection via clustering or statistical baselines.

3. Memory: Store transaction histories, anomalies, and rule sets with version control.

4. Action: Create modules to:
    - Generate structured alerts.
    - Produce auditor-ready reports.
    - Escalate serious violations via APIs or messaging systems.

**Phase 3: Integration**

1. Connect perception, reasoning, memory, and action modules into a unified workflow.

2. Add monitoring and logging for full traceability.

3. Implement security measures (encryption, access control) to comply with data protection laws.

**Phase 4: Testing**

1. Run test scenarios with mixed transaction batches (normal, borderline, and anomalous).

2. Evaluate precision/recall for anomaly detection and accuracy for rule checks.

3. Validate reports against audit compliance standards.

4. Stress-test with high transaction volumes to measure latency and scalability.

# Project 4: Code Review and Refactoring Agent

This project focuses on developing an LLM-powered agent that assists software engineers by automatically reviewing source code, suggesting improvements, and performing safe refactoring. The system inspects pull requests or code snippets, checks for adherence to style guides, detects flaws, and recommends optimized structures. The larger aim is to demonstrate how agentic AI can enhance developer productivity by combining contextual reasoning with iterative feedback loops.

The project highlights the need for perception, reasoning, memory, and action cycles within agentic AI. Perception enables the system to interpret code structure and semantics. Reasoning ensures compliance with coding standards and identifies risks or inefficiencies. Memory preserves organizational guidelines and past feedback for consistent application. Action delivers meaningful outputs such as structured comments or safe refactoring suggestions. This blend of deterministic rules and probabilistic reasoning demonstrates how AI can make software engineering both rigorous and flexible.

## Objectives

By completing this project, readers will:
- Develop an agent that can parse and evaluate source code.
- Implement reasoning loops that check against style guides, flag anti-patterns, and recommend improvements.
- Integrate memory loops that store coding norms, historical reviews, and team-specific practices.
- Build action loops that generate review comments or propose refactored code snippets.
- Benchmark performance using accuracy of detection, value of suggestions, and developer adoption rates.

## Prerequisites

### Skills:
- Proficiency in at least one language such as Python, Java, or JavaScript.
- Knowledge of static analysis and general software engineering practices.
- Intermediate understanding of REST APIs and common development workflows (GitHub/GitLab).

### Tools and Frameworks:
- LLM service optimized for code reasoning tasks.
- Agent orchestration tools (e.g., LangChain, Semantic Kernel).
- Parsing libraries such as Tree-sitter or AST-based frameworks.
- GitHub/GitLab API for integration with pull request processes.

### Datasets:
- Open-source repositories for training and evaluation.
- Standard style guides (e.g., PEP 8, Google Java Style).
- Annotated pull requests and review histories for benchmarking.

## System Architecture

### Perception Loop
- Transforms raw code into abstract syntax trees (ASTs).
- Identifies key structures such as functions, variables, and control flow.
- Normalizes representation for cross-language consistency.

### Reasoning Loop
- Applies style rules and linting checks.

- Detects anti-patterns, code smells, and potential security issues.
- Generates structured recommendations for refactoring or optimization.

**Memory Loop**
- Stores style guides and organizational standards.
- Remembers historical review data to provide context-aware feedback.
- Maintains consistency across multiple contributions in the same project.

**Action Loop**
- Produces structured review feedback suitable for pull request workflows.
- Suggests validated refactored code snippets.
- Integrates directly with developer tools to provide actionable insights.

**Central Loops**
Perception and reasoning are the backbone of this system: perception ensures correct parsing, while reasoning guarantees reliable analysis. Memory enforces consistency, and action ensures seamless developer integration.

**Implementation Steps**

**Phase 1: Setup**

1. Prepare the environment with LLM, orchestration, and parsing tools.

2. Connect to GitHub/GitLab APIs with appropriate permissions.

3. Convert coding standards into a structured and retrievable format.

**Phase 2: Loop Design**

1. Perception: Implement multi-language parsers to convert code into ASTs.

2. Reasoning:
   - Rule-based enforcement of style guides and syntax checks.
   - Pattern recognition for anti-patterns and vulnerabilities.
   - LLM-based suggestions for clarity and maintainability.

3. Memory: Store coding rules and historical reviews, enabling reuse across sessions.

4. Action: Deliver structured outputs such as review comments, diffs, or refactored code snippets with validation tests.

**Phase 3: Integration**

1. Connect loops so perception produces ASTs, reasoning applies rules, memory provides context, and action outputs developer-facing feedback.

2. Implement logging for traceability of flagged issues and suggested fixes.

3. Integrate into CI/CD pipelines for automated reviews during pull requests.

**Phase 4: Testing**

1. Test on synthetic repositories with intentional violations and bugs.

2. Measure parsing accuracy and reasoning quality.

3. Validate refactoring outputs by running regression tests.

4. Evaluate developer acceptance and trust in the agent's suggestions.

# Project 5: Robotics Task Planner

The objective of this project is to design an intelligent agent capable of understanding high-level verbal instructions, generating structured task plans, and executing them through robotic control interfaces or simulators. The system should transform spoken commands into optimized action sequences, rearrange tasks for efficiency, and adapt dynamically when the robot's surroundings change.

Robotics highlights the importance of integrating perception, reasoning, memory, and action cycles within agentic AI systems. Perception interprets sensory streams or natural language inputs. Reasoning formulates safe, step-by-step task plans. Memory preserves task progress and contextual history. Action translates validated plans into robotic execution. Unlike digital-only domains, robotics pushes agents into physical environments where adaptability, reliability, and safety are critical.

## Objectives

By completing this project, readers will be able to:
- Build a planning agent that converts human-level goals into executable robot actions.
- Implement reasoning loops that propose, check, and refine task strategies.
- Develop perception loops that parse language or sensor feedback.
- Employ memory loops to track progress, past states, and environment changes.
- Integrate action loops that safely deliver commands to simulators or real robots.
- Test the agent's robustness under noisy sensors, failed actions, or unexpected events.

## Prerequisites

### Skills:
- Knowledge of robotics (motion control, planning, safety principles).
- Intermediate programming (Python recommended).
- Experience with APIs and structured task representations.

### Tools and Frameworks:
- LLM platform for reasoning and task planning.
- Agent orchestration layer (LangChain, Semantic Kernel, or custom).
- Robotics simulator such as Gazebo, PyBullet, or Webots.
- Robotic SDK or API (e.g., ROS – Robot Operating System).

### Datasets:
- Synthetic or simulation-derived sensor data.
- Reusable task libraries (e.g., navigation, pick-and-place).
- Example sets of natural language task instructions.

### System Architecture

### Perception Loop
- Converts high-level user requests (e.g., "place the box on the shelf") into structured actions.
- Analyzes sensor data to verify task execution or detect obstacles.

### Reasoning Loop
- Breaks complex tasks into smaller executable steps.
- Optimizes order of operations while respecting robot constraints.
- Checks safety and feasibility before dispatching actions.

**Memory Loop**
- Tracks task states such as ongoing, finished, or failed.
- Stores contextual details like object positions and obstacle history.
- Provides continuity across multi-step or interrupted missions.

**Action Loop**
- Communicates validated instructions to robots via API or simulator.
- Processes execution feedback to identify success, failure, or anomalies.
- Adjusts, retries, or escalates based on outcomes.

**Central Loops**
Reasoning and action form the core: reasoning generates executable, safe plans; action ensures reliable execution. Memory supports continuity, while perception enables accurate interpretation of both inputs and outcomes.

**Implementation Steps**

**Phase 1: Setup**

1. Prepare a robotics simulator or connect to a physical testing robot.
2. Install orchestration framework, LLM integration, and middleware (e.g., ROS).
3. Create a starter task library and synthetic sensor dataset.

**Phase 2: Loop Design**

1. Perception: Implement parsers for natural language and sensor streams.
2. Reasoning: Build planners that decompose and validate tasks.
3. Memory: Develop modules to record task progress and environment context.
4. Action: Build API connectors to simulators or robots with schema validation and safety controls.

**Phase 3: Integration**

1. Link loops so perception triggers reasoning, reasoning consults memory, and verified plans flow into action.
2. Ensure action feedback updates memory and reasoning for adaptive planning.
3. Implement monitoring tools for logging progress, results, and recovery steps.

**Phase 4: Testing**

1. Run scenarios such as navigation, pick-and-place, and obstacle avoidance.
2. Measure parsing accuracy and plan execution reliability.
3. Test resilience with missing objects, blocked paths, or noisy sensors.
4. Evaluate responsiveness and latency in both simulated and physical settings.

# CONCLUSION

Agentic AI is a big step forward for artificial intelligence. It goes from static models that answer queries to systems that can see, think, remember, and act on their own. We make these systems more resilient, adaptable, and scalable by arranging them around iterative cycles. These are all important properties for real-world use.

We have talked a lot about how important it is to base design choices on engineering discipline throughout this book. To make agents that work well when things are uncertain, you need modular designs, strict evaluation metrics, and thorough trade-off analysis. The fields of robotics, enterprise automation, healthcare, and finance are all different, but the basic ideas are the same.

There are problems that are not just technical, but also organizational, ethical, and regulatory. Engineers need to work with compliance frameworks, product leaders need to plan for large-scale integration, and researchers need to keep improving evaluation criteria. To be successful, you need to combine good system design with responsible governance.

The goal of this book is to give people a complete foundation for understanding, using, and growing LLM-powered agentic systems. The guided projects show how theory can be put into reality, and the thorough reference materials give professionals the skills they need to design for safety, accuracy, and durability.

In the future, the path of AI development will depend not just on bigger models, but also on how well they are turned into agents who can deal with complicated surroundings. By following the rules laid out below, people who work with AI may make sure that agentic AI systems are developed with clarity, reliability, and purpose. These systems should be able to help with real-world activities while still being trustworthy and accountable.

# Exclusive Bonuses

Enhance your learning experience with these exclusive resources included with the book.

Simply scan the QR codes to access them instantly.

## Video Lessons

Learn the key concepts and see practical demos explained step by step.

⊞ Scan the QR code below to watch the playlist

## Printable Cheat Sheets (PDF)

Quick-reference guides for commands, libraries, pipelines, and ready-to-use code snippets.

⊞ Scan the QR code below to download

## Exclusive Resources Page Access
Always-updated tools, repositories, and additional downloads curated for you.

⊞ Scan the QR code below to explore

www.ingramcontent.com/pod-product-compliance
Lightning Source LLC
Chambersburg PA
CBHW061408210326
41598CB00035B/6144